Transformative Teachers

Transformative Teachers

*Teacher Leadership and Learning
in a Connected World*

Kira J. Baker-Doyle

HARVARD EDUCATION PRESS
CAMBRIDGE, MASSACHUSETTS

Paperback ISBN 978-1-68253-032-0
Library Edition ISBN 978-1-68253-033-7

Library of Congress Cataloging-in-Publication Data

Names: Baker-Doyle, Kira J., author.
Title: Transformative teachers : teacher leadership and learning in a
   connected world / Kira J. Baker-Doyle.
Description: Cambridge, Massachusetts : Harvard Education Press, [2017] |
   Includes bibliographical references and index.
Identifiers: LCCN 2016052868| ISBN 9781682530320 (pbk.) | ISBN 9781682530337
   (library edition)
Subjects: LCSH: Educational leadership. | Professional learning communities.
   | Teachers—Effect of technological innovations on. | Educational
   technology. | Information technology. | Effective teaching. | Educational
   change.
Classification: LCC LB1025.3 .B335 2017 | DDC 371.102—dc23 LC record available
   at https://lccn.loc.gov/2016052868

Published by Harvard Education Press,
an imprint of the Harvard Education Publishing Group

Harvard Education Press
8 Story Street
Cambridge, MA 02138

Cover Design: Endpaper Studio
Cover Photo: Dan Callahan
The typefaces used in this book are Adobe Garamond Pro and Helvetica Neue.

This book is dedicated to my teachers,
who shaped my mind,
and to my husband and son,
who shaped my heart.

Contents

Foreword

The hackerspace housed in the Atlas Institute at the University of Colorado Boulder, where I currently work, is called the Blow Things Up (BTU) Lab. Its name—which apparently is not widely embraced by the university administration—reflects several facets of the space, including the playful qualities of both the physical space and its participants and the ways in which conventional notions of learning, inventing, and investigating scientific ideas are taken apart and reconfigured. According to its website: "The BTU Lab is a place for experimentation and hacking. We make science fiction science fact and vice versa."[1]

The BTU lab is open to the public during its monthly hack nights and provides a space for a broad range of participants to engage in transformative practices. On the day that I visited, a graduate student was patiently constructing high heel shoes from a 3D printer (a thirty-six-hour process that she had to restart when the printer was accidentally unplugged), while other people were engaged in ostensibly more serious experiments with the wide range of materials available to them in the lab.

The spirit and commitments of the BTU Lab are at the heart of Kira Baker-Doyle's timely book, *Transformative Teachers: Teacher Leadership and Learning in a Connected World*. The affordances of our digital age have meant that teaching and teachers have been transformed through new technologies and the new types of interaction with other teachers available to them, in much the same way that Atlas's hackerspace is transforming teaching and learning on the CU Boulder campus. Like the hacking practices Baker-Doyle describes in her portraits of teachers and teacher communities, the Blow Things Up

Lab is focused more on creating new ideas and products than the disruptive connotations generally associated with its name.

As a new, young teacher in the late 1970s, I benefitted from the teachers' center movement in Philadelphia that has many connections to the current work described in this book, where I met new colleagues as we constructed innovative materials for our classrooms, including number boards from cardboard, and pegs and weaving looms from abandoned large heavy cardboard tubes and thin nails. Like the teachers Baker-Doyle describes in her book, I learned from other teachers as we shared ideas and constructed materials that helped us teach in new ways. A group of teachers that profoundly shaped my understanding of teaching as a new teacher and continues to influence me today, the Philadelphia Teachers Learning Cooperative (PTLC), began in one of these teacher centers funded by the School District of Philadelphia. After the school board discontinued funding for teachers' centers, a group of about fifteen teachers decided to continue to meet every Thursday afternoon after school in one another's homes to examine their teaching practices and learn with and from each other. The group uses a set of structured oral inquiry processes developed with Patricia Carini, founder of the Prospect Center for Education and Research, to describe children, children's work, classroom practices, and educational issues that grow out of the daily work of teaching.[2] The group's approach to learning is captured in this description by Carini:[3]

> Slowness: to pause. Slowness: to linger. Slowness: to practice acts of attention. Attending, to learn to see in the child's dancing, the child's storytelling, the child's painting, the child's construction—in the child's play—how this child particularizes and selects the world, learning it actively and in the process of that making, making her own self as well.

The opportunity to focus on the strengths and interests of children—and their teachers—provides an important counterpoint to the current movement to evaluate teachers based on their students' scores on standardized tests through what are called value-added measures and the focus on deficit language that is so prevalent in our discourse about students, teachers, and schools today. The PTLC continues to meet regularly, though most of its founding members are now retired, alongside the plethora of teacher activist networks and online communities described in this book. As Baker-Doyle explicates, these varied opportunities to learn together have transformed the work of teaching for those lucky enough to join a network or find an electronic or physical space for teachers. Although the slowness that Carini describes is much more rare in our increasingly technological and social network, the emphasis on making (along with hacking, connecting, and designing) as a centerpiece for learning and knowing has remained constant. Neither the teacher leaders described in this book, nor the members of the PTLC, advocate for blowing things up, yet their work provides a radical vision of teaching that is an important counternarrative to the dominant discourse of teaching as preparation for high-stakes tests that is so prevalent in the United States and much of the world today.

In contrast to so many of the portraits and reports in the mainstream media, Kira Baker-Doyle provides an optimistic view of the teaching profession and the possibilities for its transformation through the leadership of teachers themselves. While there has been much needed attention to the problem of teacher retention along with the dire consequences of teacher shortages, this book provides compelling portraits of teachers who choose to stay in the field along with detailed descriptions of the actions and networks that support this decision. Through technologies that support collaboration, leadership, and participatory practices that reinforce democratic forms of schooling, teachers have found ways to share their understandings, collectively organize for equitable and inclusive practices, and form new alliances that make their lives and work better and more satisfying. Although the media has primarily focused on why teachers leave, Baker-Doyle focuses instead on why teachers stay and the technological affordances that support them to continue to do so, while making their knowledge and choices public.

In the early days of 2011, as Baker-Doyle mentions, the Arab Spring began in Tunisia when a produce seller set himself on fire. Word of his actions spread rapidly through social networks across Tunisia, throughout the Arab world, and around the globe. Within hours of the event, the texts, tweets, and videos spawned protests across Tunisia. The protesters demanded political freedom and freedom of the press, wielding social media as a weapon, despite the censorship that had previously silenced their voices. They metaphorically blew things up through the power of words and actions. In the United States, when an Oakland, California, labor organizer wrote a response on Facebook about the acquittal of George Zimmerman in the wake of the shooting of Trayvon Martin, the hashtag #BLACKLIVESMATTER was born and came to symbolize a growing movement in which activists have seized social media to organize and make their voices heard. Baker-Doyle explains how the hashtag has been used to identify a range of teacher communities, often signaling the transformative and equity-focused potential of collective action and social media for the teaching profession.

In recent years, activists have deployed social media to engage in political activity and register their outrage for the conditions of their lives. This same use of social media has been taken up by teachers as individuals, and perhaps even more powerfully, by groups of teachers organized in a wide variety of social networks. The power of this book is that it provides an explanatory framework for this phenomenon engaged in by teachers, as well as a call to action for new and veteran teachers, teacher educators, and activists to understand, participate in, and extend the use of new technologies and social media. As such, it reflects one of the most optimistic views of the future of teachers and schools that I have read in a very long time.

Katherine Schultz
Dean of the School of Education
University of Colorado Boulder

PART I

What Is a Transformative Teacher?

ONE

Transformative Teaching
in a Connected World

We never know how our small activities will affect others through the invisible fabric of our connectedness . . . In this exquisitely connected world, it's never a question of "critical mass"; dramatic and systematic change always begins with "critical connections."

—Grace Lee Boggs, educational and civil rights activist[1]

IN 2010, I MET A TEACHER who helped to initiate a change in my understanding of transformative teacher learning and leadership in the digital age. That teacher is Samuel Reed III. Allow me to introduce him to you. Reed is a middle school teacher at the U School, a public school in Philadelphia. He maintains a regular blog column with the *Public School Notebook*, an independent education news publication. In his blog, he writes frequently about his work in the field and the classroom, often advocating the idea of "flipping the script," challenging others to see the strengths of his students and school community rather than focusing on deficits.

Reed has leadership roles in at least three or four different teacher-led professional development networks in Philadelphia. He hosts poetry slams for his students and community members and has received grant funding for his summer program, BoysWriteNow, in which boys in grades seven through twelve write together and produce essays or poetry for competitions. He has partnered with other teacher-network leaders to develop proposals for policies and activities that promote teacher-led professional development. His school district has adopted the policies and practices.

Reed is an avid fan of Twitter. If you follow him, you'll see him tweeting frequently, engaging with news reporters and scholars about work that he or other teachers are doing. Reed is difficult to miss, as he is a very active presence both online, in person, and in professional networks. He is, as Grace Lee Boggs says, "critically connected" with members of his personal and professional networks. Reed and the communities in which he has played a leadership role have made a profound impact on education in Philadelphia.

Reed epitomizes the contemporary transformative teacher. He is a passionate public intellectual committed to pursuing social justice and equity for all students through his craft. He is using digital-era cultural tools such as "making," "hacking," and "connecting" to design, organize, and lead collective efforts to grow teacher knowledge and agency. Reed is part of a new wave of teacher-led, networked social movements in education that are transforming the concept of the teacher from that of an isolated, passive, technical worker to a connected, sociopolitically active, knowledge-building agent of change, and, in turn, taking the lead in shaping the cultures and practices of contemporary teaching and learning.

The term "transformative teacher" has been used in education literature since the 1990s to describe an educator who seeks to foster positive social change through his or her work.[2] Yet, since then, there have been significant changes in the ways in which teachers connect, organize, and lead in their profession. This book describes the actions and the qualities of transformative teachers in the connected era and introduces a new developmental framework for educators—and those who want to help them—change the face of teaching. You will read about how transformative teachers are leveraging twenty-first-century connected technologies and participatory practices to take leadership roles in improving education from the ground up. The book describes the future of grassroots teacher leadership and professional development, and how individuals, organizations, and institutions can join in supporting teacher-led, networked social movements.

Who Is This Book for? What Will I Learn?

I wrote this book for teachers, teacher educators, education advocates, and scholars who want to understand how social justice–oriented teacher leadership lives and thrives in a connected world. It is, in part, a guide to the norms, discourses, and practices of educators that straddle digital cultures and justice-oriented teaching, as well as a documentation of the leadership and transformation that has emerged as a result of transformative teachers' work. What sets this book apart from many other texts that examine teachers' use of technology or teacher leadership is that the focus here is on technologically savvy teacher leaders who are working toward a larger purpose: one of organizing for equity and social justice for students, whether it is to bring more resources into under-resourced schools or provide rigorous, enriching learning experiences for students who otherwise would not have them or to equip young people with the information and tools necessary for advocating on their own.

In 2012, the US Department of Education began to urge educators to use connected technologies through its "Connected Educator Month" campaign, which included a website (www.connectededucators.org), a social network site, hundreds of webinars and online events, and heavy use of social media. Since then, the connected educator campaign has become a continuous program, focused on supporting educators to use connected technologies in their classrooms and professional lives. While this campaign, and the subsequent establishment of a new national program, serves to support a connected educator identity for many teachers, it does not attend to the underlying principles or beliefs that drive connected educator practices.

Yet research has shown that the connected "education influencers" in the areas of innovation and curriculum reform are the civically and politically engaged educators.[3] Furthermore, numerous studies have shown that teachers' beliefs, particularly beliefs centered on student equity and social justice, are far more important in affecting the outcomes of student learning than any other measure of teacher quality.[4] Today's transformative teachers are connected education influencers with principles centered on a commitment to social justice in education. Three cultural movements influence their principles: participatory (digital era) culture, grassroots community organizing, and teacher inquiry. Thus, in order to understand the making of a transformative teacher, I examine not only the technology side of the work, but also the ways in which transformative teachers think about, organize, collaborate, and inquire about their work.

This book is not a surface exploration of teachers using technology; it is a cultural guide to the ways of the transformative teacher. Readers will learn about the historical roots of transformative teachers' practice and the emerging cultural tools that they use to design, organize, and lead educational change. These cultural tools (making, hacking, and connecting) are the heart of the book. I focus on these actions because they demonstrate the principles of transformative teachers and give concrete examples for readers to learn about and perhaps engage in with others. These examples and additional data demonstrate the impact of transformative teachers' work on educational policies, practices, and curricula.

How *Transformative Teachers* Came to Be: A Brief History

There is no one way to trace how the idea for this book came about: an amalgam of life experiences, meeting people at just the right time, reading just the right book, and a bit of meditation created the stew in which the book was born. Yet, I suppose the first tangible thread, the first time I used the term "transformative teacher," was in my professional blog. When I began my blog in 2013, I was relatively new to the digitally connected world.

However, I was by no means new to the idea of connectedness. My research over the previous ten years had focused on teacher networks, and I am one of only a few scholars in the field of social network analysis in teaching. Yet, my focus had been primarily on face-to-face networking. Shortly after my first book, *The Networked Teacher*, was published in 2011, I started to receive queries about how teachers network online. While I was familiar with network theory, I was still learning about teachers' online interactions.

At this point, I decided there was only one way to learn: jump in. I began actively using my Twitter account (dormant after a failed start several years earlier), started a professional blog, and downloaded nearly every social media app available on my iPhone. As I followed the online chatter, several voices began to emerge and I connected with them. They were teachers advocating for their students, for educational equity, and for community engagement. Then I noticed they were not just advocating; they were organizing.

When I started the blog, I quickly realized that these teachers needed a platform and I had one to offer. I started a series of posts called "Transformative Teacher Profiles," in which I interviewed the teachers about their work and posted their responses verbatim. As I met more teachers through the blog, I developed my own transformative teacher network and became immersed in the community conversations.

Concurrently, I was working face-to-face with a group of English teachers who were trying to rewrite their curriculum in a transgressive teaching style amid a high-stakes testing environment. I noticed that these teachers were using some of the same practices and strategies as the transformative teachers I had profiled. They were so successful in challenging the deeply engrained traditional practices that their school had retained for decades that, after two years of collective inquiry work and organizing, the entire district adopted their approach. Several were invited to be formal teacher leaders to usher in the new curriculum.

These experiences convinced me there was something to study. Yet, they were only the beginning of my deep involvement with educators that embraced connected practices to foster social justice for students. I began to meet nationally and internationally with scholars and teachers involved in the Connected Learning Alliance, which focused on the pedagogical end of equity and technology. All this networking led to my development of a graduate certificate program in connected learning at my school, Arcadia University.

Suddenly, I was enmeshed in the connected educator community, and it seemed to take over almost every aspect of my life. So I decided to embrace the inevitable—to write a book. I embarked on a study of transformative teacher narratives, reaching out to those teachers and allies that I had worked with to hear their whole stories. I sought out additional stories of transformative teaching by taking road trips around the United States to visit teachers and organizations that were improving education from the ground up. I learned about the constant challenges and the collective joys of working for social justice in this connected era. I witnessed the energy of the growing, overlapping, and intertwined educational movements led by communities of transformative teachers. Here, I tell hopeful and authentic stories of real teachers taking the lead in transforming education. I do not mythologize hero teachers through this book; rather, I share the stories and voices of everyday teachers who take a social justice stance and act on it.

This book was not developed from just one story or research project. It began with my small inquiries into a trend and eventually became a grand inquiry into the lives and work of transformative teachers, drawn from interviews, documentation, case studies, and teacher writings. In addition to my research for this book, I draw on findings from several empirical studies on teacher networking and collaboration I have conducted over the last several years. The framework of transformative teacher beliefs and practices is what ties all the stories together. This framework serves as both a lens for understanding the practices and a guide for teachers and educators inspired to engage in transformative teaching.

Overview of the Book

Transformative Teachers is organized in three parts. The first part defines the concept of the transformative teacher by describing the ideologies, cultures, and social movements that have shaped current practices and offering profiles of fifteen transformative teachers. The second part examines how transformative teachers design, organize, and lead through the use of three key cultural tools: making, hacking, and connecting. The final section provides an overview of the collective impact of transformative teaching on education and gives information for individuals, groups, and institutions to engage in or support transformative teaching. This section includes case studies of three organizations and institutions that support transformative teachers.

Part I: What Is a Transformative Teacher?

Chapters 2 and 3 describe the beliefs and norms guiding the transformative teacher movement and offer real examples of those engaged in connected, transformative work. Chapter 2 discusses the principles that inform transformative teachers' work. These principles draw from three cultural movements: participatory culture, the culture of community organizing (and social movement practices), and teacher inquiry frameworks. Participatory cultures (shaped and nurtured by digital connectivity) are centered on creating expressive work, sharing, and membership in communities, and are nurtured by connected technologies and social media.[5] Community-organizing practices are rooted in shared understandings of social mobilization and collective agency, critical analysis of power, and public accountability.[6] Teacher inquiry frameworks are guided by beliefs in student-centered teaching, teacher knowledge built through collective inquiry, teaching as an iterative process driven through inquiry, and a phenomenological stance on gathering and interpreting information about students and their educational contexts.[7] The chapter describes how transformative teachers' perspectives reflect elements of these cultures and provides a set of principles that frame transformative teacher practices.

Chapter 3 moves from foundational history and theory to practice. It identifies eight domains of thinking and learning that reflect the principles of transformative teachers and illustrates these domains through fifteen profiles of transformative teachers. The domains are not rigid but, rather, defined from a developmental perspective of adult learning. The resulting framework incorporates these domains and illustrates how teachers can progress along a spectrum from "technical" to "leader." Thus, the developmental framework described offers a tool for thinking about the diversity, growth, and professional development of transformative teachers.

Part II: Designing, Organizing, and Leading in a Connected World

Chapters 4 through 7 introduce the cultural practices of transformative teachers. Chapter 4 provides a road map for understanding the networked world of the transformative teacher. It describes the new lexicon of collaboration that has been informed and mediated by participatory culture and identifies different kinds of spaces (e.g., online, hybrid, face-to-face) in which transformative teachers connect. This chapter sets the context for chapters 5 through 7, which describe how transformative teachers design, organize, and lead change. At the end of each chapter are profiles of prominent voices in the fields of education and connected technology to give further history and context of the concepts.

Chapter 5 describes how transformative teachers incorporate a maker mind-set into the process of designing inquiries and learning experiences. Making is rooted in the exploratory and creative constructive play that has become the hallmark of the maker movement.[8] The maker movement has grown in popularity through Maker Faires, makerspaces, and Maker Ed resource networks. This chapter offers a history of the maker movement in education and describes how transformative teachers have adopted the concepts and mind-sets. The chapter concludes with profiles of two prominent voices in maker and connected education: writer-artist Howard Rheingold and photographer-educator Jonathan Worth.

Chapter 6 discusses how transformative teachers adopt a hacker ethos to organize for change. Far from the devious connotations that the term "hacking" raises for some, in participatory culture, hacking means transforming ideas or things to meet current needs, fit specific contexts, or change a message. Hacking is remaking, remixing, and innovating.[9] In this chapter, readers will learn about teacher hacks such as mash-ups or adaptations of curriculum or practices, a redesign of objects and spaces to improve educational experiences, and disruption or rewriting of negative narratives about teachers or students through the use of online social media. Educational thought leaders Audrey Watters and Antero Garcia are profiled at the end of this chapter to provide further insight into the hacker ethos in education.

Leadership through connecting communities is the focus of chapter 7, which describes how transformative teachers build authentic connections to foster collective teacher agency. It explains how transformative teachers go public with their work, build power through their networks, and create shifts in educational policies and practices. Scholar Mimi Ito and teacher-coach Sarah Langer are profiled to illustrate the ways in which connecting influences teacher learning and leadership.

Part III: Transformative Teachers and Educational Change

Chapters 8 and 9 broaden the view of transformative teaching from a focus on individuals to a perspective on how the collective work of those teachers is changing education, and how to support the development of future transformative teachers. Chapter 8 begins with a big-picture look at the influence of transformative teacher movements and communities on student learning, institutional cultures, policies, discourse, and teacher agency. It traces examples of several transformative teacher–led, networked social movements that have directed change in their schools, school district, and beyond.

Chapter 9 examines how to support the growth and development of transformative teachers. It returns to the developmental framework introduced in chapter 3 as a tool for identifying the focus in supporting teacher growth and highlights the work of three organizations to demonstrate how groups and institutions can create contexts and structures that cultivate fertile ground for transformative teaching.

The first organization spotlighted is the EdCamp Foundation, a national organization that links together teacher-led professional development "unconferences." The network has grown rapidly since its first EdCamp in 2010 to hosting over six hundred EdCamps worldwide by 2014. The second organization highlighted in chapter 9 is the Philadelphia Education Fund, a longtime foundation whose mission focuses on the Philadelphia Public Schools. I describe the development of their Teacher Network project, which linked over thirty active teacher-led networks in Philadelphia to foster communication, joint events, and a policy-level change in the school district for teacher professional development.[10] The final example focuses on the Connected Learning Alliance, a collective of educational organizations that promote connected learning, an approach that supports educational equity and opportunity for twenty-first-century learners.

Through an analysis of these case studies, I identify a range of specific strategies for organizations, teacher educators, and educational advocates to support the work and development of transformative teaching. The book concludes with a call to action for all who support the development of teachers in the institutional changes required to prepare them for the connected era.

TWO

The Roots of Transformative Teaching

DIGITAL-ERA TRANSFORMATIVE TEACHERS are more than connected educators; they are principled agents of change, engaged in cultural practices that foster teacher agency and voice. To understand these cultural practices, it is important to begin by uncovering the roots of the principles that guide them. This chapter reviews the historical shifts and cultural movements that influence transformative teachers' principles and cultural practices. This review identifies some of the key principles that drive their work and provides a backdrop for understanding the cultural tools and tactics that transformative teachers use to develop agency and leadership in education. It also introduces some of the signals and signs of the emergence of transformative teacher movements to provide some guideposts for the stories presented in later chapters.

Historical Shifts: From Smart People to Smart Rooms

Historical shifts in the nature of knowledge, professionalism, and connectedness have had an important role in setting the stage for transformative teacher practices. Many of these shifts have emerged from the increased accessibility to connect with others and our more explicit and visible understanding of how social networks influence our lives. What is key here are not so much the tools that have allowed us to connect, but the ways in which these tools have reshaped our ways of thinking about the world.

By example, I share the story of a colleague, Michael Wesch, an anthropologist who worked for several years with an isolated society of people in Papua New Guinea.[1] Before he arrived to do his research, the people established their houses—buildings on stilts constructed by the villagers out of local timber—in what initially seemed to him a random order across the land. Yet, as he came to know the people, he began to understand their organizing principles, which centered mainly on how they related to each other. One year, the government began to conduct a census, gathering names and kin relations and numbering each house in its ledgers. Afterward, Wesch noticed that people began to arrange the location of the houses across the land in a different way—in linear rows, arranged according to the census data. The government's introduction of this tool for understanding and seeing relationships also influenced the way the people began to understand themselves.

In a similar way, the rise of connected technologies has allowed us to see how we connect and communicate in a different way, and we begin to reorganize how we understand knowledge, relationships, and ourselves differently. As Wesch would put it, new forms of media *mediate* our relationships. Here I identify three key historical shifts that have mediated our ways of thinking about knowledge and relationships as we have entered the era of the "Network Society."[2]

The first major contextual shift in this era is the increased democratization of knowledge and information.[3] As David Weinberger notes in his book *Too Big to Know: Rethinking Knowledge Now That the Facts Aren't the Facts, Experts Are Everywhere, and the Smartest Person in the Room Is the Room*, the rise of the open web has caused our notions of expertise to shift radically, since anyone can publish for broad audiences and groups ("crowds") and can collectively work together to solve problems or answer questions. In the past, we had a small group of experts who published books or articles that held great authority.[4] Now we have multiple voices telling us multiple things, and the notion of expertise is fractured. For example, one of the most widely cited sources of information on teachers' Internet activities is the Cybraryman.com website, run by retired middle school teacher Jerry Blumengarten. Although he does not have the traditional credentialing of a PhD, his expertise on the

subject of teaching and the Internet has been recognized by his avid followers due to his skills in curating meaningful information.

The democratization of knowledge challenges our fundamental assumptions
about it. Knowledge was once popularly understood to be static information
that could be passed on to the next generation, like a package. Now, knowledge is understood to be a more dynamic, fluid, and changeable concept. For
example, in studying digital media and consumerism, media scholar Henry
Jenkins identified a trend as a rise in "convergence culture," in which the producer or consumer role of individuals and groups has blurred due to increased
access to digital connectivity and creative tools.[5] We have more access and voice
to contribute to and reshape bodies of knowledge. This context contributes to
teachers' power to create and innovate in their profession.

Another major shift relates more directly to how teachers' professional development occurs. Teacher education scholars Ann Lieberman and Lynne Miller
identify this shift clearly in their book *Teachers, Transforming Their World and
Their Work*.[6] They note that, before the 1990s, professional development was
generally a top-down, one-shot workshop in which teachers were expected to
replicate what they learned directly in their classrooms. Since the 1990s, the
emphasis has increasingly been centered on encouraging teachers to work collaboratively over time to develop practices that meet the needs of their students
and particular contexts.[7] An alternative view on teachers' roles has emerged: a
perspective in which teachers are seen less as individual technical agents, and
more as collaborative professional inquirers and developers. While the more
traditional approach to professional development persists in many areas, the
alternative notion of professionalism has significantly reshaped discourse and
practices in the field, and offers a stark contrast to the previous norm. The newer
perspective offers teachers greater agency in their work.[8]

Finally, along with the shifts in notions of expertise and professionalism, a
more tangible shift has taken place in recent years: the intergenerational use
of connected technologies. From cellphones to tablets, wearable technologies
to laptops, connectedness is ubiquitous. A Pew Research Center international
survey on emerging nations found that, even in countries where individuals have difficulty accessing clean water, a majority of people have access to

cellphones.[9] There are many more ways to collaborate, build networks, share ideas, and broadcast information on a global dimension. Also, trends in the generational use of connected technologies shifted dramatically between 2001 and 2015. In 2001, teachers were labeled "digital immigrants" and youth were called "digital natives." However, as of 2015, the original digital natives are middle-aged adults who use the Internet and social networking sites at the same rate (or higher) as youth.[10] The Pew Research Center found that, in 2014, 95 percent of teens (ages twelve to seventeen) reportedly used the Internet daily, compared to reports of 97 percent daily Internet use for eighteen- to twenty-nine-year-olds, 93 percent for ages thirty to forty-nine, and 88 percent for fifty- to sixty-four-year-olds.[11]

These shifts in notions of expertise, professionalism, and the broader access people have to connect quickly with many others offer several important affordances. First, individuals or groups can challenge experts and claim their own expertise. Second, teachers can be recognized as professionals when they work to transform or develop new practices. Finally, educators can connect easily and quickly with each other, other stakeholders, and the public to collaborate and share their work.

I contend that transformative teachers use the affordances of this era to transform education when many feel constrained by increasing standardization, high-stakes testing, and their demoralization by media, politicians, and school leaders. Their new approaches to fostering educational change are rooted in three key cultural movements that have shaped their practices: participatory culture, community organizing, and teacher inquiry. Next, I describe these cultural movements and how they have influenced transformative teachers' work.

Influential Cultural Movements

Participatory culture, grassroots community organizing, and teacher inquiry are three cultural movements that center on collaboration and have thus benefited from the historical shifts toward greater connectedness and networking. The understandings and beliefs about learning, knowledge, and power embodied in these cultural movements are reflected in the principles, cultural tools, and tactics in which transformative teachers engage. Transformative teachers are not a demographic, but a "psychographic."[12] They are characterized not by location, race, or gender, but by shared practices and principles. Thus, it is important to uncover the histories, influential thinkers, and core beliefs of these movements in order to understand transformative teacher principles.

Participatory Culture: Fandom, Makers, Gamers, and Geeks

Of the three cultural movements discussed here, participatory culture is the most recent cultural wave. Participatory culture developed in part due to our increased ability to connect and share on a broad scale; it is heavily mediated by digital, connected technologies. At its core, participatory culture celebrates collective efforts to exchange work and ideas for inquiry and mastery of a subject or practice. Jenkins lists the following characteristics as the foundational elements of participatory culture:

1. Relatively low barriers to artistic expression and civic engagement.
2. Strong support for creating and sharing one's creations with others.
3. Some type of informal mentorship whereby what is known by the most experienced is passed along to novices.
4. Members believe that their contributions matter.
5. Members feel some degree of social connection with one another (at the least they care what other people think about what they have created).[13]

Good examples of participatory culture can be witnessed in three subrealms: fandom, making/do-it-yourself (DIY), and gaming. Fandom is the community of practice that exists among fans of a particular artistic work or style. Media theorist John Fiske explains that fandom goes beyond typical media consumerism to produce a unique culture:

All popular audiences participate in varying degrees of semiotic productivity . . . but fans often turn this semiotic productivity into some form of textual production that can circulate among—and thus help define—the fan community. Fans create a fan culture with its own systems of production and distribution that forms what I call a "shadow cultural economy" that lies outside of the cultural industries yet shares features with them.[14]

Since the rise of the Internet, fans have had even greater opportunity to produce and distribute textual productions, and develop complex fan cultures.[15] For example, there is a large fandom community for the Harry Potter book series.[16] These fans are not only readers, but also contributors to a broader creative movement related to the books. Fans of Harry Potter write, read, and share "fan fiction" based on the texts; discuss books and concepts in online forums; attend meetings, sometimes even dressed as characters (called "cosplay"); and engage in fan activism.[17] The Harry Potter fan group is by no means small; there are over seventy-one thousand manuscripts of Harry Potter fan fiction published on fanfiction.net, just one of several repositories.[18] While the Harry Potter fan community is a good example of a large-scale group, similar fan groups exist for a multitude of authors, artists, texts, films, and other media. Fandom invites fans to contribute their voices to the larger narrative of an artistic work or style. Often, fans' contributions result in a disruption or hacking of the main narrative. By inserting their ideas into the narrative as coauthors and thinkers, they empower their voices and perspectives.

Another strong participatory culture realm supported by connected technologies is making and crafting (do-it-yourself or DIY). Maker culture focuses on the production of handmade tools, crafts, and art, as opposed to mass production.[19] Maker culture is not new; however, connected technologies have allowed makers more access to share and discuss their work and build a community around the practice.[20] For example, before the rise of connected technologies, there were three primary ways to learn to knit: from a family member or friend, from a book, or perhaps from an organized community of knitters. Thus, opportunities to learn to knit and to share knitting were somewhat limited. Now, knitters can learn new techniques and share their work with others more easily online. Knitters who do so are considered "makers" in participatory culture. In general, makers are individuals who work toward mastering one or more crafts by taking ownership of problems, connecting with others, tinkering, experimenting, playing, sharing, problem solving, and developing new tools.[21]

Finally, another realm of participatory culture is gaming, or participation in communities of practice engaged in mastering one or more video games.

Video games can generally be divided into two types of games: narrative games, in which a player must work through a series of challenges to move toward an end point; or "sandbox" games, in which players are encouraged to create worlds or contexts with a few rules or constraints that guide their practice. In each case, gamers must solve problems in order to be successful.[22] In gaming culture, sharing strategies or tips (called "cheating") is encouraged as a collaborative practice.[23] The notion of cheating here is different from the concept of cheating in the classroom. In this case, cheating is a collaborative problem-solving effort. Yasmin Kafai and Kylie Peppler argue that DIY (or maker) cultural practices and gaming are essentially the same, since they are both a form of participatory culture.[24] They identify four main practices:

- Technical (including coding, debugging, and repurposing).
- Critical (including observing, evaluating, referencing, and remixing).
- Creative (artistic choices, and making multimodal connections).
- Ethical (crediting ownership and providing information).

Thus, as with fans and makers, gamers exchange ideas, strategies, and questions with each other, mainly through connected technologies.

Although participatory culture is fostered by collective problem solving and engagement in a creative work or idea, for any of these creative works or ideas, there are typically individuals who are particularly passionate about the topic and provide guidance, modeling, and sustained commitment to the cause. In participatory culture, those in this small, but critical leadership force often call themselves "geeks."[25] Traditionally, this word elicits memories of unpopular or antisocial individuals who have difficulty engaging with others. Yet, in participatory culture, a geek is someone who is passionate about his or her work; "geeking-out" is thought of as becoming deeply enmeshed in a practice or topic.[26]

In addition to geeks, participatory communities can also include activists who engage in "participatory politics."[27] While there is little current literature on educators engaged in participatory politics, some research has been published on youth participatory political actions. Emily Weinstein, an education scholar in the youth participatory politics research network, conducted a study of youth's participatory political behavior.[28] She found that their behavior fell into three categories: blended, bounded, and differentiated. Blended youth, who shared their political views openly in socially networked spaces, made up over 50 percent of those studied. She suggested that the "personal is political" for youth online. Joseph Kahne et al.'s 2014 report on youth participatory politics suggested that new media and connected technologies helped to mediate youths' work to influence issues of public concern through practices such as collective investigation, dialogue and feedback, production, and mobilization.[29]

In summary, collective problem solving, changing or remixing mainstream narratives, creative making, openly networked (public) sharing and inquiry, and deep engagement in a question or topic are core elements of participatory culture and are also reflected in many transformative teacher practices. These principles are visible in the ways that transformative teachers think about their work, communicate with others, and teach their students.

Grassroots Community Organizing: Critical Perspectives and Public or Private Organizing Practices

Some principles of grassroots community organizing are also reflected in transformative teaching practices. While community organizing is not a cultural movement per se, there is a rich history of social movements that have engaged in such organizing to empower marginalized and oppressed communities to work collectively toward social justice, equity, and human rights. Community-organizing perspectives influence transformative teachers' understandings of power, relationships, equity, and social justice. Furthermore, Jennifer Earl and Katrina Kimport suggest there are a number of "ubiquitous movement practices" that exist across social movements and are adopted by a range of movements and groups as tactics for mobilization: "[Social] movement practices—including tactical forms—and the scripts and schemas that underlie social movement practices diffuse beyond the boundaries of social movements, and even political life. When these schemas and practices diffuse far enough and are institutionalized, we argue that they can become disconnected from political causes and instead serve as more general heuristics for how to make public claims."[30]

This tactical adoption behavior is enabled by easy access to how-to information on the Internet and collaborative technologies.[31] Community-organizing movements influence transformative teachers' tactical moves as well as critical perspectives, because individuals and groups can easily adopt organizing tools and tactics for issues of concern.

Scholars such as Dennis Shirley and Mark Warren have studied how grassroots community organizers understand issues of power and social change and how they engage in organizing, specifically in educational issues and school reform.[32] Their research reveals complex stories of how school reform organizers learned principles, tactics, and strategies for their work through knowledge and experience passed down from a long history of community organizing on a broad spectrum of issues. The Cross-City Campaign for Urban School Reform—Research for Action, and New York University's Institute for Education and Social Policy and its research partners were led by Eva Gold in a research project that identified the following criteria to distinguish school reform community-organizing groups:[33]

- They work to change public schools to make them more equitable and effective for all students.
- They build a large base of members who take collective action to further their agenda.
- They build relationships and collective responsibility by identifying shared concerns among neighborhood residents and creating alliances and coalitions that cross neighborhood and institutional boundaries.
- They develop leadership among community residents to carry out agendas that the membership determines through a democratic governance structure.
- They use the strategies of adult education, civic participation, public action, and negotiation to build power for residents of low- to moderate-income.[34]

Furthermore, Gold et al. identified four key facets of the "theory of change" for community organizing in school: leadership development, community power, social capital, and public accountability.

This theory of change and many aspects of the criteria for community organizing are reflected in the work that transformative teachers do in their efforts to improve schools and their profession. Yet, this organizing work is primarily focused on the Alinsky model of engaging in the *public sphere* to organize for power. Susan Stall and Randy Stoeker suggest that this approach to organizing is male-centered, whereas focusing on the *private sphere*—building caring relationships, collectivism, self-transformation, and mutual respect—is more female-centered (and feminist).[35] The organizing perspectives adopted by transformative teachers also reflect private sphere–organizing characteristics. This may in part be due to the fact that the majority of teachers are female. While the public sphere is valued as a space in which power can be developed, the private sphere is valued as a space in which relationships, identity, and reciprocity are nurtured. Additionally, participatory culture promotes the blurring of public and private lives online.[36] The personal *is* political for transformative teachers.

Another aspect of a more feminist or private-sphere perspective of organizing is the emphasis on the collective rather than top-down leaders and figures. For example, EdCamp, a teacher-led "unconference" movement began in Philadelphia through a small collective of teachers in 2010. Within five years, over six hundred teacher-initiated EdCamps occurred worldwide. The foundational philosophy of this movement is that there are no top-down experts or presenters at EdCamp. Rather, teachers together propose topics on innovations, questions, and issues in their practice. Teachers are encouraged to share their work as a form of caring for others and the profession. (See chapter 9 for an in-depth case study of the EdCamp movement.)

Therefore, transformative teachers' principles are influenced by the history of public- and private-sphere approaches to community organizing. The commitment to equity, social justice, and democratic practices, the mobilization of social capital and collective agency, the use of public spaces to push for accountability, the embrace of the personal, and the emphasis on reciprocity and caring are all reflected in transformative teachers' work.

Teacher Inquiry: From Technician to Professional

The teacher inquiry movement is somewhat easier to trace and define than that of participatory culture and community organizing. Teacher inquiry practices began to emerge informally in the United States in the late 1960s, when teachers were invited to take a more active role in designing curricula as a result of post-Sputnik fears that science and technology innovation was not being fostered by traditional curriculum approaches. In a series of professional waves, teachers' roles began to transition from isolated, technical positions (with the job of implementing a given curriculum), to collaborative, professional positions in which teachers were considered knowledgeable enough to make informed decisions about curriculum and work together as professionals to create a knowledge base.[37] Teacher inquiry emerged as a core practice of such professionals; it is essentially an approach to researching one's own teaching and learning in order to make pedagogical decisions and contribute to the professional community.

The term "transformative teacher" first appeared in literature that described teachers engaged in inquiry and professional leadership. While I redefine the term to some extent in this book by framing it within the context of the digital era, there is a strong relationship between the history of the term and the transformative teacher concept described here. In particular, Henry Giroux's description of the teacher as a "transformative intellectual" captures the essence of the challenge to the traditional notion of the teacher as a technician.[38] In an essay, Giroux wrote that the perspective of teachers as transformative intellectuals promotes:

> A strong intellectual critique about the technocratic and instrumental ideologies underlying an educational theory that separates the conceptualization, planning, and design of curriculum from the processes of implementation and execution. It is important to stress that teachers should take active responsibility for raising serious questions about what they teach . . . [T]his means they should take a responsible role in shaping the purposes and conditions of schooling.[39]

Elsewhere, the term has been used in similar ways to describe teachers as individuals who play an active, inquiry-oriented role in educational change because of their perspective on the nature of the profession and their commitment to social justice. James Banks described transformative teaching in the context of how teachers can address issues of racism and marginalization in their classrooms by critically challenging dominant narratives about race.[40] He wrote, "Transformative teaching and learning is characterized by a curriculum organized around powerful ideas, highly interactive teaching strategies, active student involvement, and activities that require students to participate in personal, social, and civic action to make their classrooms, schools, and communities more democratic and just."[41] Banks and others thereby established a strong connection between inquiry and social justice in defining the nature of the transformative teacher.

Furthermore, while some might interpret the term "transformative" to mean "transforming student learning outcomes" in past literature and the present text, this term primarily refers to the agency of teachers to transform the discourse and practices of their *profession*. Lieberman and Miller provide a clear example of this conceptualization. The authors focused on the ways in which teachers are "transformative" in the sense that they are building greater agency within their profession.[42] This difference is crucial, in that measuring teacher knowledge and leadership on the basis of student outcomes alone shifts the focus away from teachers' contributions to the knowledge base, discourses, and practices of their profession. As an example, Nicole Mockler highlighted many scholars critiques of "classical professionalism," which supports a teacher-as-tool for implementing a curriculum paradigm for advocacy of "transformative professionalism," a concept that encourages a teachers-as-tool-*developers* paradigm, in which teachers work to "act with autonomy, to openly acknowledge their learning needs and to work collaboratively with other teachers to constantly develop their understanding and expertise."[43]

Despite the historical movement toward greater transformative professionalism, the traditional positioning of teachers as tools or technicians has not disappeared, especially in the contexts of high-stakes testing environments, where teachers are often pressured to follow prescribed curricula that align with tests.[44] Teacher inquiry challenges such scenarios; teachers who engage in inquiry practices believe that good teaching emerges from the deep, reflective study of practice and cannot be prescribed.[45] In addition to this value, those engaged in teacher inquiry have a different understanding of expertise and professional knowledge than the traditional views of teaching. In teacher inquiry, the most powerful forms of professional knowledge emerge from a teacher-led phenomenological study of practice, which leads to situated, grounded approaches to teaching.[46] In contrast, professional knowledge is primarily considered to be a form of human capital in more traditional perspectives, gained by outsider experts leading workshops or courses on a topic.[47] Furthermore, teacher inquiry commonly occurs within a community of practice, in which members share and exchange questions and findings. Traditional practices value individualized professional development and ranking.

Teacher inquiry can range from personal journaling and reflection to involvement in collective thinking about student work and educational issues.[48] Within the category of collective teacher inquiry, many groups have developed their own processes. For example, one type of collective teacher inquiry can be witnessed at the Philadelphia Teacher Action Group (TAG)'s annual Education for Liberation Conference. At the conference, various Inquiry into Action Groups (iTAGS) share their findings on questions and issues they worked together to investigate over the course of several months. In 2015, the iTAG groups included topics such as "Queer Issues in Education," "Revolutionizing Education with Youth Participatory Action Research," "Hip-Hop: The Good, the Bad, and the Ugly," and "Teaching Ferguson and Beyond."[49] The iTAGs are designed so that the participants begin with shared questions and work toward developing actionable steps in their classrooms or professional lives based on their investigations.

Another example of teacher inquiry is the descriptive review process developed by Patricia Carini and colleagues at the Prospect Center in Vermont in the early 1970s.[50] Members of the Philadelphia Teachers' Learning Cooperative use this process weekly to uncover questions about their students and their practice.[51] In a typical descriptive review, an individual shares a description of a student or his or her work for a long, uninterrupted time. The individual identifies a focusing question for which the group can provide insights and recommendations based on what they heard during the description. The group is facilitated by a chairperson who helps guide the process and allows all voices to be heard. Presenters can choose how to use members' recommendations in their classrooms.

As the examples of these two groups show, while approaches and processes to inquiry can differ, the common elements include positioning teachers as intellectual thinkers and transformative professionals, questioning, collecting information, focusing on the present or particular, presenting work in public, and committing to using inquiry to improve teaching and learning.

The Principles of Transformative Teachers in the Digital Era

Participatory culture, grassroots community organizing, and teacher inquiry share some common principles, namely a focus on collective problem solving, a strategic use of public space for feedback, accountability, change, and a grounded sense of expertise (that valued knowledge comes from people working and living in the field). These overlapping principles are also present in the work of transformative teachers. Table 2.1 lists these principles organized by "transforming knowledge" and "transforming relationships." The table highlights a focus on the development and exchange of expertise and knowledge through collective and creative means toward teacher agency and leadership.

As we shall see in the profiles in chapter 3, these principles are reflected in the practices that transformative teachers engage in and the perspectives they share through their work. The principles, and the contextual history from which they emerged, are the roots of the transformative teacher phenomenon. The following chapters further define the characteristics of transformative teachers, show how they are innovating, organizing, and leading educational

TABLE 2.1 Transformative teacher principles

TRANSFORMING KNOWLEDGE	TRANSFORMING RELATIONSHIPS
• Teacher as intellectual	• Democratic processes
• Grounded expertise	• Social justice and equity
• Focus on particular and pragmatic	• Public work
• Use of research and data	• Private sphere/blurred lines
• Inquiry	• Collective problem solving
• Changing/hacking dominant narratives	• Reciprocity/caring
• Creative making and crafting	• Contribution to the whole

change, and offer examples and suggestions for how to support transformative teacher development.

Signals of the Emergence and Influence of Transformative Teachers

The contextual history and key principles described here lay the groundwork for identifying the trends, impacts, and practices of transformative teaching, which at times feel like a nebulous or ubiquitous shift in teacher practice and leadership. This shift is akin to similar societal changes in pedagogical thinking, such as the postmodern curriculum movement, which scholar Handel Kashope Wright once described as about as easy to define as "nailing Jell-O to a wall."[52] Yet there *are* signals and evidence that point to not only the emergence of the transformative teacher phenomenon, but also to the impacts of this phenomenon in education. While the majority of this text serves to create a full picture of this phenomenon in detail, here I point out a few of the signals or guideposts for recognizing transformative teacher practices and impacts.

Several measurable changes in the ways in which teachers are innovating, organizing, and leading reflect transformative teacher principles. One signal is in the development of new forms of teacher-led professional development, communities, and movements, including "unconference"-style professional development events, hashtag communities, teacher-led schools, and teacher-led networks. These new, more connected forms of professional development reflect the principles and traits of transformative teaching in that they: (1) are teacher-led and informed by practice on the ground, (2) foster democratic participation and leadership, (3) leverage connected technologies to amplify teacher voice and presence, and (4) are oriented toward equity, social justice, and innovation. The growth of these trends is evident both on the ground and through recent scholarly work on the phenomenon. For example, Scott Richie identified over twenty studies on the rising trend of what he calls a "countermovement" of social justice–oriented teacher networks in his 2012 study of one such network.[53] Also, the professional development unconferences have also demonstrated growing influence and involvement through sheer numbers. An estimated three hundred thousand teachers globally have participated in such events since 2010, based on an analysis of the number of events advertised online in three of the most popular unconference groups (EdCamp, TeachMeet, and MeetUp).

Another signal of the emergence of transformative teaching is the new pedagogical tools and practices, developed and adopted by teachers, that are rooted in the principles and practices of transformative teaching, such as maker education, project-based learning, mindfulness practices, sustainable "green" teaching, game-based learning, and youth-led participatory action research. As with the new forms of connected professional development, these trends are apparent in the growth of new literature on the subject, as well as increased use of the tools in the classroom.[54] For example, the number of published books and journal articles on maker education has increased from fewer than five in 2012 to more than two hundred between 2012 and 2016.[55] The practices reflect the transformative teacher paradigm in that they foster an ethos of critical, participatory, peer-to-peer, and multimodal learning. They are out of the norm for most schools, so teachers may require networks of support to develop skill in their practice and garner the collective agency to try them in their classrooms. Thus, the emergence of such practices also suggests that teachers are finding support outside the traditional professional development offered by their schools and districts.

Finally, a third measurable signal of change is the rise in the number of teachers publishing professionally related work on social media and in academic journals. A recent survey of more than one thousand educators in two teacher-led networks (the National Writing Project and a network of advanced placement class teachers) found that 39 percent of the teachers maintained a blog (compared to 14 percent of adult users overall), and 26 percent used Twitter (compared to 16 percent of all adult users).[56] Formal organizations and news media also provide hints about the presence and impact of teacher-bloggers. For example, the educational news organizations Education Week and Edutopia host over twenty teacher-written blogs combined on their sites. The National Blogging Collaborative, a network of teacher-bloggers, supports hundreds of teachers as they learn to write about their work. In their 2009 review of the trend, Marilyn Cochran-Smith and Susan Lytle, two scholars who have studied the emergence and development of practitioner research over the last two decades, argued that teacher inquiry and research is flourishing worldwide.[57] As some proof of their contention, the first journal solely dedicated to publishing practitioner research was established in 2016 by Diane Yendol-Hoppey and a team of scholars at the University of South Florida.[58]

Other intangible signals of influence and change have more to do with mind-set and discourse than online publishing. One shift is in the way that teacher leadership is described and acknowledged in discourse about educators. Teachers are increasingly positioned as leaders and voices for their profession. For example, prompted by increased discourse about teacher leadership, the US Department of Education initiated its "Teach to Lead" program in 2016, which worked to "catalyze fundamental changes in the culture of schools and the culture of teaching so that teachers play a more central role in transforming teaching and learning and in developing policies that affect their work."[59] While this was a top-down initiative, it demonstrates a turn in the ways that the role of a teacher is conceptualized.

Another signal relates to the ways in which issues of equity and social justice are interrogated in dialogue about teaching and education. This is especially visible on social media through networked social movements such as #EduColor, #OptOut, and #Techquity. Dialogue has increased in these spaces and in teacher networks about how to address marginalization and inequities that have been created by institutional practices, social contexts, and behaviors. This is related to a third intangible shift: the way that transformative teachers are organizing for change in the connected era. Scholars of networked social movements argue that such movements now share certain traits: they are "flat" (have an inclusive, non- or semihierarchical structure), they leverage connected technology to influence media discourse and connect with each other, they share and make through multiple forms of media, and they connect both face-to-face and online.[60] Transformative teachers' leadership practices also embody these organizing trends.

In part II of this text, you will read specific examples of the signals in action, learn more about how their practices came about, and learn of their impact on transformative teachers and their collaborative work. Part III provides voices of writers, scholars, activists, and advocates who support transformative teachers to return to this issue and address the question of "what is the impact of transformative teachers on education?"

THREE

Transformative Teachers: Practices and Profiles

T HE PREVIOUS CHAPTERS provided an overview of the changes in education and society that have cultivated the development of new forms of teacher leadership and learning. I've described the history and contexts that have positioned teachers to have greater agency in transforming their profession and pedagogical practices. Yet, without specific stories and examples, these changes can feel more theoretical than real and make the picture of a "transformative teacher" blurry at best. In this chapter, I aim to address this opacity through the stories of real, transformative teachers. I also introduce a developmental framework for transformative teaching based on these stories and other research that identifies key dispositions and characteristics of transformative teachers.

The stories I share here are drawn from my research on teachers and their networks in Philadelphia, New York, Chicago, and Boston. While, elsewhere in this book, I share brief stories and examples of transformative teachers from other cities around the United States (and globally), the stories in this chapter offer a deeper and more nuanced illustration of the beliefs and practices of transformative teachers in my studies. Furthermore, a unique aspect of these stories is that all the teachers profiled here have graciously agreed to allow me to share their real names in their profiles. I asked these teachers for permission to use their names because, in many cases, they have a public presence online.

As a reader, you can learn more about them by following them on social media or connecting with the professional networks in which they are involved.

While these profiles can stand alone as exemplars of transformative teacher practice, here they also illustrate concepts in a framework I have created that identifies the core characteristics of transformative teachers. I constructed this framework from my analysis of key characteristics of teachers in the case studies, documentation of transformative teacher practices (particularly in social media), and existing scholarship on teacher leadership and professional learning, and I based it on a developmental understanding of adult learning. I suggest that learning to become a transformative teacher is developmental and can be described on a spectrum from traditional, "technical" approaches to teaching to those of a transformative teacher "leader," a stance that reflects current research showing that learning to teach occurs through a developmental progression of adult learning.[1] As with other developmental paradigms, individuals may shift between and enter into stages depending on the contexts, scaffolding or support, and their previous learning experiences. Furthermore, a teacher's position along the spectrum is unique; some may reflect characteristics of several stages, depending on domain.

Table 3.1 shows the framework of learning for transformative teacher leaders that is related to the transformative teacher principles described in chapter 2. In that analysis, I listed the key principles from three driving cultural forces that influence transformative teachers in two categories: *transforming knowledge* and *transforming relationships*. These two categories are represented as the main organizing themes in the developmental framework. Each organizing theme includes four domains of transformative teacher characteristics. The scale ranges from technical teaching (not transformative), to emerging (exploring and learning), participatory (active participation), to leadership (leading and sustaining transformation). The framework does not attend to content knowledge or pedagogical practices, such as the pedagogical developmental framework presented by Allan Black and Paul Ammon or Punya Mishra and Matthew Kohler's TPACK (technology, pedagogy, and content knowledge) framework.[2] This is not because they are unimportant to good teaching, but rather because I want to highlight domains of knowledge and skill that relate particularly to the principles of transformative teaching.

TABLE 3.1 Transformative teacher developmental framework

	TECHNICAL	EMERGING	PARTICIPATORY	LEADER
			Knowledge construction	
1. Learning	• Works in isolation. • Views professional development as a means to fulfill requirements.	• Seeks advice from peers when needed. • Can identify some topics/areas of professional interest.	• Regularly seeks and offers advice to members of the emerging professional learning network. • Views professional learning as an inquiry process.	• Collaborates with members of professional networks on common projects or issues. • Uses inquiry-based professional learning to enact change.
2. Techno-social development	• Uses technology primarily as a device to complete a task. • Perceives technology as nonsocial.	• Uses connected technologies as an information consumer and/or primarily in personal life. • Perceives technology as socially and politically neutral.	• Uses connected technologies to engage in discourse with other professionals. • Begins to understand the social complexity of technologies.	• Uses connected technologies as a producer to design, facilitate, and share social learning opportunities. • Understands the social contexts and issues that shape equity in the digital era.
3. Modalities of learning and production	• Views text as the most valid representation of knowledge and learning.	• Views digital media as supplemental knowledge and learning to text-based representations.	• Recognizes arts, crafts, and digital media productions as valid representations of knowledge and learning.	• Shifts from a focus on end-product to process when thinking about learning and knowledge development. • Values the processes of making and "hacking" art, crafts, hardware, software, text, and digital media in learning.

continued

TABLE 3.1 *continued*

	TECHNICAL	EMERGING	PARTICIPATORY	LEADER
4. Voice and storytelling	• Does not see a role for personal stories in teaching or learning.	• Has an awareness of the value of personal story/knowledge in teaching and learning.	• Is developing storytelling abilities. • Creates opportunities for student voice and storytelling.	• Demonstrates strong skills as a storyteller. • Uses storytelling as means to empower learners to address social issues and injustices.
Relationship development				
5. Sociopolitical development*	• Believes that individual faults are the causes of inequities and therefore the world is just.	• Notices discrimination, yet avoids difference or conflict.	• Questions systems of inequity. • Begins investigating ways to personally address inequities.	• Achieves a critical consciousness of systems of oppression in society. • Works as a change agent for social justice in education.
6. Social capital and agency	• Unaware of or inattentive to developing diverse social support networks.	• Aware that social networks can be used to locate information and resources. • Seeks assistance for professional work occasionally.	• Connects to learn with others. • Aware of the diversity of the network.	• Connects with others to organize for learning and change. • Seeks diverse perspectives. • Develops a sense of agency through professional communities.
7. Role of the teacher	• Relies on prescribed curricula. • Primarily perceives teaching as a scripted performance.	• Attempts to adapt prescripted curricula to address individual student needs. • Perceives the primary goal of teaching as meeting set standards.	• Creates culturally responsive curricula that engage learners and meet their needs. • Perceives teaching as a process of learning and developing mastery.	• Facilitates culturally responsive learning experiences that empower learners to be civically engaged. • Has a critical understanding of the political dimensions of teaching.

	TECHNICAL	EMERGING	PARTICIPATORY	LEADER
8. Hybridity/ third spaces	• Believes that teaching should be impersonal, i.e., "Don't smile until Christmas." • Distinct separation between home life and school life.	• Wrestles with the vulnerability of revealing authentic personality, personal interests, and hobbies to students. • Socializes with some colleagues outside of school time.	• Occasionally reveals aspects of authentic personality in school. • Integrates some personal interests into curricula. • Seeks professional communities in third spaces (beyond just school or home) for learning as a drop-in visitor.	• Consciously seeks to connect authentically with students. • Blends interests and passions of home, third space, and school life. • Participates in professional communities in third spaces as a regular member or leader.

*Roderick J. Watts, Nat Chioke Williams, and Robert J. Jagers, "Sociopolitical Development," *American Journal of Community Psychology* 31, no. 1–2 (2003): 185–94.

In the following sections, I review the characteristics and stages of the framework and use it as an organizing tool to share the profiles of transformative teachers. As you read the profiles, you will see a great deal of diversity in the type of work that teachers engage in, yet the similarities in terms of how their work is reflected in the domains of the development framework; all of the examples reflect the "leadership" end of the framework. Everyone grows at his or her own pace and has his or her own unique passions and interests. My intention in sharing this framework is *not* to provide a tool that can be used to evaluate or measure teachers, but rather to offer a focused way to learn about and explore the concept of transformative teaching.

The overall purpose of this chapter, then, is to create a clearer picture of transformative teachers' key characteristics and ways of knowing. The chapter does not explore the scholarly literature behind the framework, nor the ways it can help organizations and institutions to support teachers. I discuss these topics in the final chapter. The order is intentional; it is important for readers to develop a rich understanding of the characteristics, cultural tools, practices, and impacts of transformative teachers described here and in chapters 4 through 8 before returning to the question of teacher support. Transformative teacher work is ultimately led and owned by teachers, not the scholars who write about them (myself included); thus, by presenting their stories and actions first, I am trying to respect their agency and voice through the structure of this book.

Transforming Knowledge

The four domains of transformative teacher developmental characteristics within the theme of "transforming knowledge" are learning, techno-social development, modalities of learning and production, and voice and storytelling. These are categorized under the theme of transforming knowledge because each relates to the ways in which we understand, create, use, and develop knowledge.

Domain 1: Learning

Transformative teachers are rabid learners. They seek opportunities to challenge themselves, working their "teaching muscle" in sometimes uncomfortable ways in order to develop greater knowledge and skill as a teacher. They believe that learning is social and actively look for opportunities to collaborate and learn with others. Also, the inquiry process is central to how transformative teachers learn; the cycle of developing questions, gathering information, analyzing, experimenting, taking action, and reflecting is woven through many aspects of transformative teachers' work in and outside the school.

At the leader end of the developmental spectrum, the transformative teacher uses inquiry to bring about action and change, and intentionally places him- or herself in challenging contexts in order to model vulnerability to others and bring about growth and change. While some emerging and participatory transformative teachers understand how challenge and vulnerability lead to learning and the power of community to sustain themselves, it takes time to develop the capacity for coping with challenge to develop what Sandra Hollingsworth calls "relational knowledge," or the understanding of how to develop communities of learning support.[3]

TRANSFORMATIVE TEACHER PROFILES:
SAMUEL REED III AND MEENOO RAMI

Samuel Reed, introduced in chapter 1, is a teacher at the U School in Philadelphia. He is a public figure in the city's education community, with a regular blog column in the popular "Philadelphia Public School Notebook" and a leader in several local networks, including the Philadelphia Writing Project, Teacher Action Group, BMe Leaders, and the Caucus of Working Educators. He calls himself a "teacherpreneur," a term borrowed from the Center for Teaching Quality and Barnett Berry et al.'s book of the same name.[4] He looks for opportunities to build and connect others, and is committed to changing negative discourses that describe urban students and communities, and to see the value of the cultural knowledge and practices of students in his community. He is well known for the summer program he co-organizes with Scholastic Art & Writing and the Philadelphia Writing Project—BoysWriteNow, which engages boys in creative writing and poetry (he is also cofounder of Girls on Fire, a similar summer writing group for girls).

In addition to his participation in networks and initiation of community projects, Reed regularly presents his work at local and national education conferences and gatherings. He often invites several colleagues from different aspects of his network to speak together on a particular topic in order to facilitate dialogue and build stronger connections between teachers. In his role, he is somewhat like a teacher-ambassador of Philadelphia and is a hub in the network of transformative teachers. Much of his energy to engage in these networks and develop programming comes from his drive to learn the best ways to engage his students in learning.

Perhaps due to the respect he has garnered from his work and energy, Reed was invited to be a founding teacher for an "innovation school," the U School, in the fall of 2015. The school is founded on competency-based learning and individualized, asynchronous learning. The founding teachers and principal codesigned the school. Students design their goals and learning pathways and have individualized learning experiences. The central spokes of the school are learning labs, essentially different kinds of makerspaces called "innovation labs." There is an "Organize Lab" (action research space), a "Highlight Lab" (media-making space), and a "Build Lab" (construction space). Here, students explore, experiment, prototype, and build projects and tools related to their learning. This school design has been an important part of Reed's professional inquiry, and he hopes to learn how to help students become independent learners and makers.

Meenoo Rami is known by her colleagues as a nurturer of networks and connections. As a teacher, she cofounded #EngChat, one of the most well-known online chat communities for teachers on the Internet; co-organized EduCon, a popular educator-led annual conference; and wrote a book, *Thrive: Five Ways to (Re)Invigorate Your Teaching*. Yet, for Rami, her work as a connected educator did not come from an interest in using technology or in creating a large network. It came from a desire to learn about teaching. She said:

> I didn't set out to be a connected educator. Now this idea is big in the field. My need to learn from others is innate and my need to connect stemmed from my abilities that were lacking in my practice as a growing educator. I was very honest with myself about that and I wanted to be better. I didn't think I was incapable of improving, but I didn't have the tools. Instead of turning

to books or taking a class, I created a lifelong class for me that's still ongoing. Getting involved in organizations in networks like the National Writing Project, seeking mentors . . . I was building relationships in which we were updating each other, checking in, and being honest about our struggles. I modeled vulnerability (now looking back and connecting the dots I see this); I was open about the things I was struggling with and it allowed others to say, "Hey, I have some of the same struggles." Collectively we have found resources with each other, online, face-to-face. We've really created a lifelong class.

Rami now works to help support teachers in networking with each other. In this role, she has seen how the idea of "connecting" has emerged in teaching in ways that both excite her and worry her:

What excites me is—just like our students, learning never ends. I can carry with me the spirit of "always be learning, always be curious, always be kind" everywhere I go. I don't feel alone in this . . .

What worries me is—when a lot of this work began, like EdCamp, #Eng-Chat—there was this real openness to collaboration and share . . . But in some instances now I see that an unfortunate outcome is that we are not seen as people but rather we are a "brand," which is corroding the social fabric of our networks. It's losing sight of students, work, each other.

Hence, Rami believes that the work of building connections should be based on a desire to learn and an openness to share one's struggles. In her book, *Thrive*, she provided an honest account of the way she, as an educator, built networks, found mentors for her work, and thought deeply about how to connect the curriculum and her pedagogy with her students' interests and needs. Connected technologies and online social networks were important support tools for her; however, the center of gravity in her work is always on "thriving" through building meaningful connections with others.

I asked Rami to recall an example of the connections she developed through #EngChat or EduCon influencing her classroom teaching. She had a plethora of examples; however, one of the most important changes was a shift in her thinking about the boundaries of the classroom. She told me about a student who was writing a paper on teens and sleep. While doing research, the student found an article that was behind a paywall. She encouraged the student to reach out to the researcher via e-mail. An exchange began that resulted in the researcher connecting with the student and being available for other questions. The classroom walls were no longer the boundaries for learning in this case; the student was living and learning in the world, making authentic connections for his own learning.

Domain 2: Techno-Social Development

The term "techno-social" comes from Mary Chayko's writings on "Techno-Social Life," in which she discusses the inextricable links between digital technologies and our social worlds.[5] This domain concerns how teachers perceive, use, and understand technologies as related to the social world. In addition to having an ability to understand the ways in which our technologies (and the people who design or own them) mediate our social interactions, transformative teacher leaders are not just consumers of tools and information; they are producers. They contribute to the digital discourse. Furthermore, transformative teachers leverage connected technologies to organize and connect with others for positive social change and to reflect and grow as teachers. They have well-developed professional learning communities (PLCs) and are involved in learning communities online and face-to-face.

On the opposite end of this spectrum is the technical teacher, who lacks understanding of the tools and thus may live in fear of them, only using technologies when mandated and sometimes in ways that are detrimental to student learning (such as overly rote learning). In the middle of this spectrum are emerging and participatory transformative teachers. Emerging teachers are not as afraid of the connected technologies and occasionally use them instrumentally, perhaps, for example, for locating a fun activity on Pinterest. While emerging teachers are passive consumers, participatory teachers understand that connected technologies can support them in sustaining their PLCs, and they are interested in learning about new uses of technologies. Yet, participatory teachers may not have a critical understanding of the ways in which technology can be used by those in power and authority to control discourse, and how organizers can likewise use the same tools to shift power dynamics and narratives. This understanding emerges as transformative teachers become leaders and must develop a more complex understanding of both the positive and negative effects of technology on our social interactions.

TRANSFORMATIVE TEACHER PROFILES:
TARA LINNEY AND JOSHUA BLOCK

Tara Linney is a technology educator at the Singapore American School. Linney has worked in a variety of school contexts, from bilingual, urban schools to single-sex schools to rural schools. Across all these experiences, her focus has been to empower students to show their unique talents and knowledge by being creators, rather than passive consumers. She is aware of the ways in which students can be labeled or pigeonholed as one stereotype in school and seeks to break these patterns through her work with teachers and students.

One example of her effort to empower and reshape stereotypes through making is her work on coding. She was teaching students to use programs like MIT's Scratch. One year, she ran an afterschool club for coding and found that over twenty boys signed up, but only one girl. This imbalance concerned her; she worried that other girls would be dissuaded from joining the club in the future. So, the following year, she started an all-girls group for coding. She found that in this context, seven more girls were interested in participating. Just creating welcoming environments and contexts can make a major shift in who participates, which, Linney notes, mimics the situation in the adult world. As a biracial woman, Linney has encountered many challenges entering spaces in which technology is used and discussed. She noted, "[B]eing a double minority, you have to be a lot louder than you think you are. You may say something and think that people hear it, but they don't." It is important for her to attend to these issues early on and empower students who are typically marginalized in these spaces due to race or gender to break the patterns and participate.

From a pedagogical point of view, her work to teach coding also focuses on empowerment. Linney notes that learning how to make, from the ground up, rather than just using a technological tool, can give students a sense of agency and possibility:

Oftentimes, kids are put in front of an iPad. Like, "Oh, play this game." Kids, especially from a very young age, they have this whole inquiry mind-set where their number one question is, "Why?" . . . If we shut that down, then we're not encouraging them to think and to really consider why things are the way they are and how they work.

A couple of things that I really like about the maker movement and the coding movement is that it gets students thinking outside of the box and becoming those creators, because if students aren't creating things, we're just going to have a whole society of couch potatoes, right?

Linney noted that an essential part of her teaching (and her own professional learning) is connecting and sharing with others. One of the most important professional networks to her right now is #EduMatch through Voxer, which allows her to connect, through audio recordings, with educators worldwide. Linney told me how the community helped both her and her student learn to conduct a personal inquiry project on whales:

I remember a couple weeks ago, when I sent a Vox to the #EduMatch group, within just a few minutes . . . , I had three people responding. One saying, "Oh, talk to this person on Twitter." Another saying, "Talk to this organization on Twitter," and then someone whose daughter is a marine biologist. Then someone else came out whose sister is a marine biologist. [I thought], "Oh my goodness." . . . I contacted a statologist in San Diego who is going to connect with the student, who is searching about whales, to answer all of their questions.

Joshua Block is a humanities and history teacher at Science Leadership Academy, a public school in Philadelphia. He is a regular blogger for Edutopia.org and also publishes his own blog, "Mr. J. Block, Reimagining Education." Block is known regionally for the public art displays and digital publications that his students produce through their studies in his class. To Block, going public with his learning and giving his students opportunities to create and share their work publicly is central to teaching for social justice and critical inquiry.

He has developed his own social justice pedagogy that operates on three levels of teaching. The first level is the classroom community. When facilitating the classroom dynamic, he asks himself, "What's the community that's being created within the classroom and . . . are [students] being asked to create things and amplify their voices in different ways?" The second level is that of the curriculum. When planning, Block poses the question to himself, "In what ways do [the things we study] relate to people's lives?" and "Why do they matter with to his students?" The third level relates to the process of the students' learning and work. Block wants his students to produce work that influences the community by generating critical dialogue around an idea. Regarding this level, Block considers the question, "What's the action that we would like to take or what can we do or create?" Block usually creates websites, blogs, or wikis to share his students' creations and sometimes reaches out to reporters to inform them about the great work his students have done. This sense of making for a purpose and for the public engenders a sense of ownership and engagement in the curriculum for his students.

Block uses blogging and connected technologies as a means to be more conscious and open about his intentions as a social justice–oriented educator. By explaining the design choices he made on his blog, he must answer and reflect upon the questions about social justice that he poses for himself to a broad audience. Block described his rationale to me:

> [I]t's just kind of articulating one's process, but I think the main thing is to be able to almost have a meta experience of what's going on, because teaching is so all immersive and intense. There's not inherently reflection built into it anyway, but I do feel like it's a process of a reflection . . . Even if the process of reflection is reading what other people write, then just mentally connecting it to yourself. I think it sustains teachers and it makes the teaching career something that continues to progress.

Two of Block's recent projects are good examples of his pedagogy. The first was the "Social Justice Alphabet" project, a public art display of photographs of students holding up words that represent important terms in the history of community organizing and social justice movements. The students spent weeks researching the terms and designing their images. Block worked with other teachers, community businesses, and student photographers to do the project. The photos were displayed along several blocks in the heart of the city. Block reflected on the project: "It was just a great experience for students to see themselves or see their peers. The messages are quite profound."

Another project that Block has worked on regularly is community dance performances in collaboration with the Leah Stein Dance Company, in which his students participate alongside dancers to choreograph and perform site-based dances. The students research the location in which they are to do their dance and incorporate its history and stories into their performance. Block loves how students develop a deep sense of ownership and empowerment in their learning through this project, which often goes beyond their school years: "Many students that come back after they graduated talking about how they remember that project. I think it's about the autonomy and the independence and the process of creating and making."

Domain 3: Modalities of Learning and Production

The modalities of learning and production domain is related to the "social turn" in research on literacy, which recognizes that literacy—or the ability to decode and make sense of a message—occurs in multiple cultural, textual, and modal forms. Before this shift, literacy was generally understood to be the ability to read and write in the dominant cultural language. Now the concept of literacy has expanded to "literacies."[6] One can be fluent in multiple literacies, in which communication can occur in multiple modes. For example, digital literacy is the ability to navigate the digital sphere. Today, there is greater recognition of nontraditional (or marginalized) literacies and forms of expression. It means that teachers, and their students, can construct messages and stories in ways beyond the printed page, from coding video games to building simple robots, to choreographing a dance; this work may be recognized as a form of knowledge that is valuable to learn and develop.

Furthermore, this shift is aligned with the emergence of participatory culture and, in particular, maker culture, which values making and sharing crafts and creations of all genres and modalities. Transformative teachers engage in multiple modalities of learning and creating as a means to connect, inquire, and give back to the community. In contrast, technical teachers perceive multimodal forms of expression and literacies as unnecessary add-ons to learning. They have difficulty understanding that dominant knowledge modes and expressions replicate marginalizing structures of discourse and power, and because of this, they only replicate the norms. Emerging and participatory teachers begin to understand the connections between making, self-expression, and empowerment, and may start to explore alternative modes of expression in their lives or classroom. Transformative teachers intentionally use multimodal forms of expression to transform knowledge and cultivate agency for teacher learning and student empowerment.

TRANSFORMATIVE TEACHER PROFILES:
BEVAN WEISSMAN AND ALLISON FRICK

Bevan Weissman is a high school teacher and director of the Workshop Industries program at the Workshop School in Philadelphia. He has deep roots in the maker movement, as an early member of the Artisan's Asylum (a makerspace in Somerville, Massachusetts, which was established in 2010) and the cofounder of New American Public Art (NAPA), a company that creates interactive public art. Before the rise of the maker movement, Weissman often felt torn about his identity as an engineer, artist, tinkerer, and educator, but then, he explained, "with the advent of Makerism as a term, I felt like there was a word that finally described who I was, not just what I liked to do, but who I was." He feels that a core tenet that guides his work as a maker is to follow his passion and apply that intense work for the social good.

At his school, he runs a workshop space that is outfitted with many industry-grade tools for construction and mechanical work such as biodiesel cars, solar-powered street lamps, and hydroponic gardening systems. Through the workshop, students partner with local community organizations and build resources for them, make art installations on commission, and develop entrepreneurial projects in which they have a fifty-fifty profit share. Weissman notes that this aspect not only makes the school a more authentic and engaging experience for the students, but also changes the notion of school itself;

it is conceptualized as an important resource for the community. Members of the school community also build deep, intergenerational connections with the broader community through these projects.

An example of a community connection is the workshop's project with Bartram's Gardens, a historical botanical garden in Philadelphia. The students have constructed storage areas and worked on the boat house for the gardens. In our interview, Weissman suggested that this experience gave students an authentic experience and pride in their learning: "It was real. For a lot of school work if you don't finish you get an incomplete, you get a bad grade, and you move on. If you don't finish a product that's going out the door to a client, there's a lot more serious ramifications . . . They understood the gravity of that work. They rose to the challenge . . . That feeling of satisfaction of a job well done was huge."

His students also developed professional engineering skills in a real-world context through their work on the "Your Big Face" art installation. The project was an iteration of a public art display developed by NAPA as an interactive piece that could project the image of a person's face onto a giant, Wizard of Oz–like face. Thus, his work with NAPA extended into his work as a teacher, connecting his two communities of practice. Similarly, his ideologies about making in both realms intersect. Whereas NAPA was founded on a belief that art can be a social good when it helps bring diverse communities together in a public space to engage in thinking and problem solving, many of the projects Weissman introduces in the workshop classroom reflect the same principle.

There is also an opportunity for students to pursue their own interests and be entrepreneurial. One student became a local celebrity when he invented the "Jawnament," a wooden Christmas ornament that spelled "Jawn," a favorite Philadelphia word meaning "thing." The Jawnament was sold on a website the students created to sell their wares. It immediately became a top local news story and notable personalities such as the mayor and several city council members tweeted pictures of themselves with the ornaments. The ornaments sold out within a few days, bringing in $9,000 for the program and the students to share. Weissman described the multiple facets of knowledge and skill development students experienced through this kind of work: "[It's] such a great little micro example of the kinds of projects that involve this broad-based learning, real-world application. It's a way to earn money. It also teaches those business skills, management, soft skills, leadership, team work, all those kinds of things that are becoming more important and given more attention in education today."

I asked Weissman about connections between makerism and teaching. He suggested that teaching is a part of being a maker, noting, "[In makerism] you learn something and you immediately teach it to your peer or you're co-learning a new skill together. Education and teaching is an in-built part of being a maker because you have to [teach]. You just need to learn new skills all the time."

Allison Frick is a children's librarian in Glenside, Pennsylvania. She also teaches and directs children's programs at the Hacktory, a makerspace in Philadelphia. Frick found her way into teaching and making through her love of art and tools for making. She went to art school and focused on textile design. Then she attended school to become a librarian, focusing on youth services. While in school, a friend invited her to visit the Hacktory for a free event and she instantly fell in love:

> I was experienced with making some things, enough tech oriented to definitely make it [tech] oriented. I already had that within me. One of my friends from library school invited me to a free event that was run by the Hacktory . . . about how to make electronic fireflies that sync up with each other like real fireflies do, and then they learn how to blink in unison. That was a free event and I loved it. It was so cool. A lot of the pieces were cut out on the laser cutter and I was like, "Ahh, this is the tool for me. I want to learn how to do this stuff."

Frick described the Hacktory as a makerspace that stood out in contrast to some of the aspects of the maker movement that have opened it up to criticism by Frick and others that the field is dominated by white males. The Hacktory is a "friendly, inclusive, on-ramp for technology for a lot of people," according to Frick. There are several intentional design structures and social rules that make it so. For example, whereas Frick found that, in many makerspaces, worktables are often built at a height suitable for an average male, at the Hacktory, care has been taken to make worktables at a height that works for women and children as well. Similarly, supplies are stored at a level that most visitors can reach easily. Frick pointed out that there are social rules, too, such as not talking down to others or showing off. In addition, the Hacktory has scholarships for children of color and offers programming for youth and adults.

Frick runs maker projects for students at both the Hacktory and the library in which she works. Through the Hacktory, she has access to important maker tools such as laser cutters for wood and 3-D printers. Examples of projects include simple robots (made with a battery, wire, and small motor), electronic art and toys (Harry Potter wands made with light strips), and textile circuitry (such as weaving lights into a shirt or armband). She diligently works to get grants for supplies for the projects and keep them as free workshops and events.

Frick noted that there is a two-way relationship with the makerspace and K–12 teachers. Some members of the Hacktory became teachers because they enjoyed helping children make and design creations. Other teachers discover the makerspace through onetime events and take many of the tools and ideas back to their classrooms.

What keeps Frick returning to the community is not only her love for making but also the spirit of the maker community of which she is a part. She described it as "a very altruistic, giving, and connected culture," in which people share ideas and don't feel a sense of ownership over them; instead, they hope and expect that those ideas will contribute to each other's growth or work.

Domain 4: Voice and Storytelling

Transformative teachers place great value in stories. Stories are data; stories show the complexity and reality of our lives; stories connect us; stories transform us. Transformative teachers use their stories, and encourage others to share stories, as a means to reflect, reach out, and bring attention to inequities and injustices. Furthermore, it is in keeping with the current cultural movement toward teacher inquiry, which values attention to the observed and the particular as a way to investigate issues of pedagogy and practice. This type of inquiry centers on "thick description," or richly detailed narratives of observation, which can reveal important patterns or themes that are not apparent in everyday interactions. Telling stories allows transformative teachers to slow down and take a mindful look at their practice.

There is also a relationship between storytelling and voice. In literature on teacher voice and student voice, the word "voice" is often synonymous with the idea of being heard or recognized as important and, thus, is a form of empowerment. Transformative teachers seek opportunities to tell their stories as a means to transform or engage in discourses about education. However, storytelling is an art in itself and thus requires practice and development. Transformative teachers have had opportunities to hone their voice. Emerging and participatory teachers are in the process of developing their voice. Technical teachers do not see the value of more than the dominant narrative and avoid opportunities for speaking out publicly for fear of seeming out of the norm.

TRANSFORMATIVE TEACHER PROFILES: ANISSA WEINRAUB AND NOGA NEWBERG

Anissa Weinraub is a public high school teacher in Philadelphia, as well as an artist, actress, and community organizer. She is teacher leader in the Teacher Action Group (TAG) Philadelphia, the local node of a teacher-led grassroots professional development and activist group in the United States. She credits her work with TAG and similar organizations for helping to sustain her during difficult times in her teaching and helping her to understand the deeper systematic issues that shape education. In reflecting on her work with TAG to address the school district's sudden move to close over twenty schools in primarily poor, African American neighborhoods, she noted: "Without [TAG] people to help me develop new ideas and inspiration to push my own teaching practice, understand the level of coordinated attack against the communities in which we teach, and together build the skills and collective power we need to defend and transform public education, there's no way I could have weathered the storm of our dysfunctional district."

Weinraub believes that her students have valuable life experiences and knowledge that are often unrecognized or seen as deficits by standardized measures in schools and media narratives about urban youth. She uses storytelling as a way to help to "hack" the negative narratives to help students feel appreciated and valued in school. She describes how her beliefs shape her practice:

> I am a performer at heart, and I believe in the power of coming to voice through sharing stories about things that matter to me. So, at the core of my teaching philosophy is the understanding that education must ignite something within my students, help them put language to their lived experiences, and create an open space for self-growth and expression. In my teaching, this looks like creating a classroom environment in which students' own stories fuel forward the rest of our work. We write, share, listen, and give critical feedback (on each others' writing and lives in general). In drama, we are on our feet, creating original work, exploring our talents, and making space for people to feel proud, confident, and self-actualized.

Weinraub maintains a blog about her work in the classroom (*After The Return: Analysis from the Heart in These Transitional Times* at afterthereturn. blogspot.com), and the community has published several articles, including an academic publication with the University of Pennsylvania Graduate School of Education, *Perspectives on Urban Education Journal*.

Noga Newberg is a sixth-grade teacher at the Folk Arts–Cultural Treasures Charter School (FACTs) in Philadelphia. She seeks opportunities to learn with others and is sustained by the communities in which she is professionally involved. Before teaching, she had several experiences working with teachers and observing classrooms that led her to understand the importance of listening to and sharing stories from the community in teaching for social justice. Some of the communities in which she exchanges and tells stories include her school, the Philadelphia Teachers' Learning Cooperative (PTLC, a teacher-led professional network), Need in Deed (a nonprofit organization for service learning), and the Ethnography in Education Research Forum at the University of Pennsylvania Graduate School of Education.

PTLC meets weekly to discuss issues of classroom practice. PTLC is rooted in the Teacher Center movement of the 1960s and uses the descriptive review process for teacher inquiry work, which was developed by Patricia Carini. These are essentially detailed classroom stories; the group's belief is that everyone can gain insight about his or her own work by listening to each others' stories. At a typical meeting, a teacher presents a case from his classroom for which he would like feedback or help. Some of the inquiries that Newberg has presented to the group include questions on how to make a readers' workshop more appealing to boys who resist reading and how to structure peer revision activities.

Need in Deed enabled Newberg to connect with others outside her school for her unit on community activism and her writing unit on research-based essays. The stories of the community that the students uncovered through the project helped them gain new perspectives on their own roles and agency in the world. In our interview, she described the process of gathering stories and to understand the key issues in their community:

> We began the year by assessing our neighborhood and community. I asked the students to interview their family, friends, and neighbors about points of pride and disappointment in their community. We then read dozens of articles on social issues that the class deemed to be the most important. They then created PowerPoints and tried to persuade their class to vote on their issues. The top two issues that won were police brutality and poverty. Eventually the class debated between these two issues and chose poverty because they felt it related more to their lives. We then were able to use all of our writing time to research three topics within poverty: homelessness, hunger, and minimum wage. Need in Deed brought in community experts to teach the kids more on these topics.
>
> This project helped them become more outspoken and learn how activists can truly have an impact on the world . . . What I think [the students] get is understanding other people's stories, and being able to connect to that and relate to it, or compare.

Newberg also attends the Ethnography in Education Research Forum "Practitioner Research Day" to go public with her inquiries and connect with other teachers doing similar work.

Relationship Transformation

The four domains of development under the theme of relationship transformation include sociopolitical development, social capital and agency, role of the teacher, and hybridity and third spaces. These domains are grouped in this theme because they pertain primarily to understanding social systems and networks.

Domain 5: Sociopolitical Development

This domain is adapted directly from the sociopolitical development scale set forth by Roderick Watts et al.[7] They describe it as a framework that identifies a developmental progression toward Friere's concept of "critical consciousness."[8] They note: "Sociopolitical development (SDP) emphasizes an understanding of the cultural and political forces that shape one's status in society. We use it to describe a process of growth in a person's knowledge, analytical skills, emotional faculties, and capacity for action in political and social systems."[9]

The framework identifies five stages: acritical, adaptive, pre-critical, critical, and liberation. Individuals in the acritical stage perceive inequities in society as arising from real disabilities and incapabilities in groups of people and, thus, the world as it should be. In the adaptive stage, individuals acknowledge inequities, yet the order of society is seen as static and unchangeable. Individuals at this stage tend to self-segregate in order to maintain a sense of positive identity. In the pre-critical stage, individuals begin to develop some concerns about inequities. In the critical stage, these concerns begin to shape individuals' actions, spurring them to learn more about injustice, oppression, and liberation. At the liberation stage, individuals develop a critical analysis of social power and structures and become actively involved in anti-oppression and social justice work in their communities.

Transformative teachers embody the liberation stage of SDP because of their critical analysis of how schooling can play a role in replicating power imbalances and their commitment to organizing for social justice in and beyond their classrooms. Emerging and participatory teachers celebrate diversity and difference, yet are still learning how structures, systems, and society can reinforce racism, sexism, homophobia, and other forms of marginalization or oppression. They also may wonder how or if they can make a difference through their work. On the opposite end of the spectrum, technical teachers do not attend to issues of marginalization or oppression in their work because they do not see or understand its relationship to schooling and education.

TRANSFORMATIVE TEACHER PROFILES: SCOTT STORM AND KELLEY COLLINGS

Scott Storm fell in love with theories of critical pedagogy and the idea of social justice in education at an early age. One summer in high school, he traveled from his home in rural Pennsylvania to attend a five-week "Governor's Academy" on educational theory and practice. There, he realized his calling—to be a transformative teacher.

Fast forward to the present, Storm now teaches at a public school in New York City that he helped to design, Harvest Collegiate High School, frequently presents papers on his teacher inquiries and critical literacy practices at academic conferences, and collaborates with other teachers around the United States on important issues in teacher leadership and education. His understanding of his role as a transformative teacher goes beyond classroom practice: "I want to be a teacher that is socially just for our profession. What I mean by that is I want to work to be a teacher who makes our profession more intellectual, more political, more collaborative, to have the stance of a teacher leader. I do that through the inquiry projects that I do, through the writing that I do, even going to [conferences], and through talking to you, and all of these different things."

The classroom is where you can see Storm's theories and understandings in action. As a teacher, he asks students to delve into the complexities of identity and culture by examining and reflecting on literature from diverse contexts and voices. One example of this type of exploration is Storm's "Identity Quest" inquiry unit. Students begin the unit by reading about issues of identity from scholars such as Gloria Andalúza, Prudence Carter, bell hooks, and Audre Lorde, and reflect upon their own identity. Then, they use their understandings of identity to explore literature such as *The Hobbit* and *The Odyssey*. Students generate critical and complex understandings of the literature through this process.

Storm talks frequently about how he is not alone in his work. At his school, he collaborates with colleagues and participates in a critical friends group, a type of professional learning community in which members assist each other in addressing problems of practice. He is also a member of the Literacy Research Association and the National Council of Teachers of English, which have connected him with similar-minded teachers and fostered collaborations around teacher inquiries. He sees teacher inquiry as a way to "formalize, think through, and reflect upon the process" in front of peers who can give him feedback. It is also a form of organizing and action for him. For example, Storm conducted a teacher research project on student questioning with a team of teachers at his school when students were using a scripted curriculum from the district and contrasted it with constructivist lessons. The data from his inquiry showed that students taught according to the constructivist approach asked questions on a far higher level of Bloom's Taxonomy than those with the scripted curriculum. As a result, the principal agreed to allow them to use the constructivist approach instead of the scripted curriculum.

Collaboration and inquiry, for Storm, are inextricably tied to the idea of teacher leadership. While hierarchical leadership positions can be important, Storm argues that teacher leadership should be understood as a "stance" that includes three elements: elevating the profession, collaborating, and teaching for social justice. He described how this stance can play out in a teacher's life: "Those three things are one; you take it public, or collaborative in some way. That could be you're talking to your critical friends group about it a lot, and other people are maybe trying it in their classrooms because of that. Maybe you're presenting it at a conference, maybe you're working on it with people across schools. Maybe you're writing a paper about it for a journal. You're somehow going public with it."

This perspective represents how transformative teachers' generally talk about teacher leadership; it is relational, connected, political, and public.

Kelley Collings is a middle school math teacher in Philadelphia and a teacher leader for the Caucus of Working Educators (WE), which includes members of the teacher union, parents, education advocates, and community members.

Collings has a background in community organizing and started teaching later in her career after doing some organizing as a parent of children in public schools. She was aware early on when she began teaching that it would be important to become involved in support networks and organizations to sustain her work:

> [B]ecause of my organizing I knew the network was going to be the key to my survival. I got trained to be a critical friends coach and I started a critical friends group at my school. I just think that, in so many contexts, it's that network that allows you to give yourselves what you don't get from whatever institution you're embedded in, surrounded by, or part of . . . It's the relationships and the networks that you build. That gives you the critical framework to sift through what you're dealing with.

As a math teacher, Collings looks for what she calls the "cracks in the sidewalk," or openings in which students can make critical connections with the topics they study. She noted:

> I try to help kids develop a math literacy that's about understanding that there are choices being made [with math] that are about power. The easiest way to talk about that issue. You have a data set. You describe that data set. You have choices and those choices are politically charged. You usually have lots of dynamics, formulas, and choices that aren't apparent. The same way you have to read between a politician's words, you have to read between the numbers in a way that allows you to see the motivation of the people putting those numbers out.

Collings's work in the classroom is indicative of her work on a broader level to address issues of inequity and power in education. She works with organizations to build power and opportunity for change. In the city, she is a leader in the WE organization, known particularly for her work with the Opt-out campaign to resist high-stakes standardized testing practices. She and several teachers in WE reached out to parents and community members to build an information campaign around the drawbacks of high-stakes testing that resulted in the development of an Opt-out movement in the city. Some of the drawbacks the group highlighted were the narrowing of the curriculum, the lack of focus on the whole child, and the large amounts of funding for testing and testing preparation when schools did not have money for nurses, counselors, or extracurricular activities.

Collings does this work because she feels that educational change is connected at every level and that all teachers' work is political.

> You have to be engaged in that bigger-picture thinking in a way that positions you to address the forces that are shaping your work . . . Teaching is political now. There are so many political implications of our teaching. So many ways that the politics surrounding public education affect our teaching . . . I don't understand how you can show up and not be driven to try to change things that impact your ability to do your job. Don't you just want to be a better teacher? There are all these forces out there that are tying your hands behind your back. Fight against them. Fight for what is going to make your job easier.

Thus, Collings works to help her students, colleagues, and community members gain a critical understanding of the contexts in which they live, and the complex systems of power that position them.

Domain 6: Social Capital and Agency

The social capital and agency domain is primarily concerned with how teachers understand the value of social capital or networks in their work. Technical teachers view their social network and the development of social capital as irrelevant to their work in the classroom. Emerging teachers see the value of building relationships with others online and face-to-face primarily to gain information. For example, they might seek a colleague to get a copy of his or her lesson plan or go online to search for lesson plan ideas. Participatory teachers believe that there is professional learning value embedded in their social networks and seek to develop personal (or professional) learning networks and opportunities to connect and learn with others. Transformative teachers also believe that networks are valuable for professional learning, but they take it a step further and view networks as a source of agency and strength for the profession. They build networks to organize for change.

TRANSFORMATIVE TEACHER PROFILE:
JOSÉ LUIS VILSON

José Luis Vilson is a teacher, writer, and activist in New York City. When he is not teaching middle school math, he is organizing and speaking out on issues of race, education, and social justice online and in print. He has a popular blog, TheJoseVilson.com, and a book based on his teaching experiences published in May 2014, *This is Not a Test: A New Narrative on Race, Class, and Education.*[10] In addition, Vilson is an active organizer of #EduColor, an online movement to reshape discourse about race and education. Vilson is nationally recognized for his powerful ability to speak directly about issues in education that have been hushed or are taboo, yet do so in an inviting, poetic way, encouraging others to unite with him and speak up as well.

When I talked with Vilson about his approach to connecting with others in public ways, he noted the importance of thinking beyond oneself in these spaces: "If we're not willing to push the boundaries of education, and if [we] only push the boundaries for ourselves, instead of pushing it for everybody else, then we're repeating the same oppressive cycles, that we perhaps ought to vanish." He warned others against obsessing over numbers of followers on Twitter. This focus can derail people from speaking up about critical issues for fear of being shunned. Rather, he suggested that when networking online, educators should care about promoting good pedagogy and work to unite others around issues of social justice in education.

His tenacity in being a voice for unspoken topics and marginalized people has connected him with other like-minded educators. #EduColor is one such community that has connected as a result of public conversations and concerns about race in education (it was initiated at a conference, EduCon, and grew online from there). This core group of educators generates internal support for its members and is also a powerful network that can influence educational policies and practices. For example, Vilson noted that the #EduColor group has been able to connect with journalists, policy makers, and politicians around issues of race, especially during moments of intense public discourse on implicit racial bias, such as when the media highlight shootings of unarmed black males by police officers: "We've been able to have discussions with policy makers, with other educators, at schools all across the country, and internationally too, around these issues of cultural competence. Developing curriculum to talk about black boys and girls. Things that were really difficult, and we found spaces, and we were able to say, 'We can construct something out of this really terrible moment.'"

Vilson is fundamentally committed to building relationships and respect between people—his students, his colleagues, and the broader public. In his book, his stories of teaching highlight how he builds individual relationships with each of his students and also a critical understanding of how social and institutional systems shape those relationships. "Relationships are at the core," he noted, and argued that teachers have a responsibility to make schools and school systems work for all students through this lens: "We can say, 'We're not political, we're not political,' but just our being there [as a teacher in a classroom] is a political statement . . . Why not act upon it and say, 'Here are some recommendations we need to make in order to restore that student to learning'? We're in a prime position to do that."

Domain 7: Role of the Teacher

Is a teacher a technician, whose primary role is to deliver a prescripted curriculum that others developed? Or is a teacher a transformational professional, who not only combines his or her professional knowledge and learning experiences to develop curricula that meet the needs of particular students but also develops the profession as a whole by contributing new ideas and outcomes of teacher research to the education community? Beliefs about the role of the teacher in classroom curricula form another domain along the transformative teacher spectrum. Transformative teachers understand that they are part of a larger system of social order and are active agents in shaping it through attending to equity and social justice in their professional work at every level. Emerging and participatory teachers understand that, to be a *professional* teacher, one must have the agency to make decisions and judgments about their curriculum, yet they are still developing a complex understanding of how schooling, and their own work, can shape the social order.

TRANSFORMATIVE TEACHER PROFILES:
ANNIE HUYNH AND JOHN MCCRANN

Annie Huynh has had multiple leadership roles in her teaching career. As an elementary school teacher, she was a leader in teacher-led professional networks. More recently, she has assumed the role of director of curriculum and assessment in a New York City school, where she empowers other teachers to lead. Her story of becoming a formal leader began when she joined the Philadelphia Writing Project (PhilWP, a teacher-led network and local node of the National Writing Project) early in her teaching career. Through the network, Huynh connected with other teachers for support and collaboration, such as Kathleen Melville (profiled later). She saw Melville as her "writing mentor." Huynh recalled:

> I felt comfortable with her to share my work, my blog post, and reflection. She said, "Oh, this is great." She and a couple other teacher networks had compiled a list of places to publish for different kinds of work. They said, "This publication does mostly research. This publication does narrative. This publication does mostly how-tos," that type of thing . . .
>
> She gave me some feedback. We went back and forth about revisions . . . I submitted it in April and I heard back from somebody that said, "Yeah. I think it's good for our publication." . . . That was really powerful for me like, "Wow, I'm actually published in a book." That was really great, and then I became an ASCD Emerging Leader [a selective network of educational leaders run by the Association of Supervision and Curriculum Development].

PhilWP played a critical role when she began teaching. When she was ready to quit, PhilWP kept her going:

> It literally saved me and kept me teaching. It helped me reframe my thinking about my role as a teacher. It's not someone that's passive about making things happen, but it really helped me to find my teacher voice and empowered me to say, "I don't have to ask for permission to try different strategies to engage my students to talk about race or to write about what I'm going through" . . . [I]t made me realize that a lot of teachers went through the same difficult

challenges in teaching practice. It's a daily struggle, but you have to embrace the magic and the mess.

Yet her connections with this network did not simply keep her in teaching, they set off a series of experiences that led her to become an outspoken leader in the city. She joined Teachers Lead Philly, an organization initiated by her PhilWP mentor, Melville, because she wanted teachers to have a stronger voice in the community:

> I felt that teachers were not getting in as much air time as other leaders in education. The premise is that teachers are leaders; that is teacher leadership. They can add to the education reform conversation. They have something to say and they should be the ones talking because they're closest to the learning process. The mission of the organization is to be a double funnel where we share what's going on, the grassroots day-to-day grind as well as funneling what's happening in the greater education scene, whether it's state government or federal government.

Huynh began to write articles, blog posts, and white papers about issues in education and shared them publicly through social media.[11] She began to understand teacher leadership as "influence" and not necessarily as a hierarchical role. Huynh explained, "Some people frame teacher leadership as an actual position, teacher leader. That's not what we mean by teacher leadership. It's more like a state of mind. It's also a position . . . [W]e want more teacher influence on the education world."

Her new views on teacher leadership changed the way she thought of the work of teaching and how important connecting with others is to professional leadership and growth:

> When teachers are being more vocal of embracing the power that they have over themselves in their profession, in their classroom, in their practice, I think there's a trickle effect. There's a lighting of a candle, if you will, because when you bring so many teachers who are like-minded from different schools together, they share resources, give you help. Twitter has really helped spread the idea of teacher voice and teacher leadership because you can connect with people all over the world and discuss these issues . . .

I've seen definitely a lot of teacher networks popping up, supporting each other, sharing practice . . . I think the students can only benefit because they see their teachers who are leaders in the community. Teachers are trying and taking risks, and taking risks is important for learning. They're modeling taking risks for their students, which we rarely do. I think school leaders that allow teachers to take risks are also leaders in their own right, not just because of their title, but they help facilitate that and say, "That's okay. You're doing great things, adding to our school."

The shift in her professional identity had an impact on her teaching. She shared the story of how her new perspective on connecting greatly enhanced the learning experience of one student in her class. For one of her literature projects, students made puppets of characters in Lenore Look's book, *Alvin Ho*. She tweeted a picture of it to the author: "Lo and behold, she actually replied back, said, 'Wow! These are absolutely amazing! I can't believe it.' We start this Twitter exchange of sorts. I said, 'Wow. I have never connected with an author like this before' . . . We tweeted back and forth, I even sent her e-mails. She sent a letter to my students. We wrote back letters to her. It was a lot. She actually came and visited our school in the fall."

From identity to voice, to pedagogy, Huynh's story illustrates the patterns of a teacher becoming a transformative teacher leader in the classroom and beyond.

John McCrann is a math teacher at Harvest Collegiate High School in New York City. He and several teacher colleagues founded Harvest Collegiate partly to find a way to move away from the culture of testing and toward an inquiry-oriented model of teaching and learning. McCrann is focused on "making the world a better place" through his work in the classroom, school, district, and at the national level.

In the classroom, McCrann constructed his own curriculum to help students use "math as a lens to reading the world," but did so with a critical understanding of the current reality of standardization and high-stakes testing. He built a curriculum that did not position him as the sole purveyor of knowledge but rather invited a range of perspectives on problems and problem solving. This, he said, felt like a curriculum rooted in social justice and equity.

McCrann is a chapter leader in his union because he would like to influence change at the district level as well. In our interview, he noted, "The idea is that I'm helping to shape policy and shape this policy in a way that is sustained and humane towards all people involved. That's really what's going to make change in the lives of people I come into contact with everyday."

In addition to formal leadership in organizations, McCrann also takes on informal leadership roles through blogging, writing articles for *Education Week*, and reading and responding to education Twitter chats or work by resource organizations such as FairTest. Although someone may occasionally post a harsh comment about one of his articles, this does not stop him from engaging in the public sphere, because all the feedback helps him develop as a teacher and a leader:

> When I picture teacher leadership, I sort of imagine the recycling symbol or something. Those are a sequence of arrows that starts with human being in classroom with students experiencing something and then it goes to that person reflecting and thinking and trying to think about that experience and "How did that experience shape me and shape my classroom? What was good about it; what was bad about it?" And then going to talk to someone else and that might be by going on Twitter or that might be presenting at a faculty meeting. Doing some sort of connection and then moving back around to that same place where the person who's in the classroom with students and experiencing now that situation having been informed by the change or policy or implementation.

Problem solving and seeing failure as an opportunity to learn became perhaps most tangible to McCrann in his first year at Harvest Collegiate. He told me how, in his first year of teaching there, he led a group of his advisory students on a camping trip and got lost along the way. In that moment, when the group needed to come together and figure out the right way to go, they formed a deep bond that has led to continued powerful learning experiences for both McCrann and his students. Four years later, at their graduation, the bond was still there, and it emphasized even more to him how much trust and democratic collaboration matter in being a leader. "That was a special moment for me . . . I handed them their diplomas and gave them a hug on stage," McCrann fondly recalled.

Domain 8: Hybridity and Third Spaces

Finally, the last domain on the spectrum, hybridity and third spaces, relates to how we navigate and interweave (or not) our personal and professional identities and worlds. Technical teachers separate their personal interests, feelings, and needs from teaching. Teaching is akin to detached performance in this domain; there is a reluctance to connect with students on a personal level. In the emerging stage, teachers recognize the importance of learning more about students' interests and background, but might hesitant to share their own (it is a one-way street). At the participatory stage, teachers begin to experiment with sharing personal stories, opinions, and feelings with students in the classroom as a means to connect with them personally. Through this experimenting, they might notice how their identities and voices shift between different spaces. They begin to participate in professional activities in "third spaces" or social gathering events and opportunities outside of home and school, where diversity of thought and identity flourish such as unconferences or even book clubs. These types of third spaces can provide important opportunities for learning. While teachers at the participatory stage are beginning to recognize these third spaces, teachers at the leadership stage are learning to navigate and leverage them for change. Furthermore, third spaces offer a way to bridge home and school identities and passions.

TRANSFORMATIVE TEACHER PROFILES:
KATHLEEN MELVILLE AND CHRISTOPHER ROGERS

Kathleen Melville is a teacher at the Workshop School in Philadelphia and a lead organizer of Teachers Lead Philly (TLP), a teacher-led professional network. As mentioned in the previous profile of Annie Huynh, Melville not only takes leadership roles in her professional community, but mentors future teacher leaders. Melville carefully distinguishes what she means by "teacher leader" when she describes herself and her TLP colleagues, knowing that many are hesitant when they hear the term:

> They don't want to be seen as somebody who has authority or power over their colleagues in the way that a principal might . . . That's something that we really push against. We really stress that it doesn't have anything to do with

formal roles, or being promoted or sanctioned by higher-ups, but it's really all about sort of a stance they take, about the profession and about what we as teachers have a right to weigh in on and what we have to offer.

Melville's views of teacher leadership developed mainly through her involvement in a summer institute held for teachers from across the United States at Swarthmore College through the Consortium for Excellence in Teacher Education (CETE), now in its sixth year. She credits it with helping her and others to build collaborative partnerships and feel empowered as educators to make change.

One aspect of her leadership involves fostering connections between her classroom work and her work in professional networks beyond the school walls. She is a member of Teachers Write Now, a network that has supported her in publishing articles about her teaching methods and inquiries in *Education Week* and other educational news outlets. Her work as a writer and maker is very much tied to her identity as a leader because she believes that relationship building is central to leadership and relationships are built through making together. As a codesigner of her school (a teacher-led school), she articulated how this belief translates into the school pedagogy: "We want to put relationships at the center, and that's why it's focused on projects. All of them [are] about creating something that can have an impact on the world. Because we believe that's what meaningful learning looks like. And I see that we are a project-based school, with a maker space, as deeply connected to the fact that we are a teacher-founded and teacher-led school."

One example of how this stance has translated into her classroom practice is Melville's work with her students to redesign their classroom space. To Melville, the initially crowded, cramped setting was a social justice issue of access to education, and she wanted to empower her students to redesign the space. In one article, she wrote: "My students have a right to space. Personal space is essential to concentration and deep thinking, to civil relationships, to healthy and safe learning conditions. How can we expect our young people to function productively in an environment that most adults would certainly reject?"[12]

Students have used the design process to investigate, create prototypes, and redesign the room to make it easier for them to learn with each other. Further, students usually blog about the work they do in her classroom to connect with the community and articulate their learning experiences to the public. Melville's social justice–oriented approach to designing and organizing for change in her professional community, school, and classroom has thus fostered empowerment and transformations across all three realms.

Christopher Rogers is an educational technology teacher in Philadelphia and the founder of JustMaybeCo., an innovation engine for community-based learning. Rogers envisions a social justice–oriented makerspace as a place that would "bridge the experiences of grassroots activism and advocacy projects with classroom learning spaces." He thinks critically about how the maker movement can foster greater inclusivity and diversity, particularly for women and minorities.

Rogers is a member of several teacher networks in the area and often facilitates small-group meet-up opportunities for teachers in the network to discuss how to reimagine the ways in which they can connect with and develop the communities in which they teach. For example, he's hosted an Inquiry into Action Group (iTAG) on the topic of connected learning (see chapter 7). Through grant writing and educational awards, Rogers has been able to secure a space in which teachers make, learn, and build together. He is especially interested in the ways in which teachers can incorporate youth-led participatory action research (YPAR) to develop solutions and responses to community issues with their students.

From Framework to Action: Making, Hacking, and Connecting

The developmental framework here offers eight domains that characterize transformative teachers. The profiles of the teachers describe how the characteristics translate into their own practice. While my attention to these domains revealed the ways of knowing and beliefs that are characteristic of transformative teachers, it did not focus on the commonalities of their *actions*. Thus, the common methods and practices of transformative teachers is the next issue to explore. Since transformative teaching is rooted in cultural movements, it is necessary, then, to take a cultural view of transformative teachers' actions.

Therefore, in part II, I'll explore the question, What cultural tools enable transformative teachers to do their work?

In part II, I describe the three cultural tools commonly used by transformative teacher to design, organize, and lead activities their profession: making, hacking, and connecting. The descriptions of these tools move the discussion from characteristics to action and provide a broader sense of what transformative teachers do. I suggest that readers approach this developmental framework as one part of a larger picture. The framework can be used as a resource for learning, yet, without an understanding of the cultural tools and methods of action, the concept of the transformative teacher is not yet fully conceptualized.

PART II

Designing, Organizing, and Leading in a Connected World

FOUR

The Connected World
of Transformative Teachers

F OR ALMOST FORTY YEARS, the Ethnography in Education Research Forum has been held on the third weekend of February at the University of Pennsylvania Graduate School of Education. Friday has always been scheduled as "Practitioner Research Day," and teachers who conduct inquiry in their classrooms and schools arrive from all over the United States, braving the cold and wintry weather to share their work. It has become one of my favorite places to learn about new practices, meet old friends, and make new ones. In 2016, the conference theme was "Mobility, Multiplicity & Multimodality: Theoretical Innovation in Educational Ethnography." Many teachers and scholars made presentations on the ways in which participatory practices and connected technologies were shaping their teaching and learning. I decided to attend a presentation given by two of my longtime mentors. They talked about their latest book and discussed how they have used inquiry practices for over thirty years with their students and professional community. When the talk was over, I went to congratulate my mentor (and former teacher). She has always been modest in discussing her work and immediately refocused the conversation on my work on networks and technologies. She commented that many presenters at the conference that year seemed to be talking about using technology. Initially, I took this as just a generational shift. Then she said, "I try to follow all of this, Kira. I look at your Facebook posts, but *none of it makes sense to me.*"

I thought to myself, *Of course, it makes sense; it's all rooted in the work that you* do. Then I decided to return to my Facebook page to see what could have been so confusing for her. A few days earlier, I had posted the following: "Hive mind: Help me figure out which app to use for making podcasts #21stCenturyProblems." Below that post, I noticed a link to an article written by a teacher with the words "connecting" and "curating" in the title, which were obscure terms for individuals not familiar with digital culture. Then it hit me. This was a different language for my colleague, who had taught between the 1960s and the 1990s. The discourse about how we teach and learn has shifted since then, and much of it comes from digital, participatory culture. For my friend, who has been one of the most transformative educators I've ever met, to cross the boundary into participatory, connected conversations and spaces, she needed help to be able to translate the new discourses and social practices. So this chapter is dedicated to my mentor, and all those who seek a meaningful translation for the discourse of the connected era.

In this chapter, I describe popular forms of discourse employed by transformative teachers in variety of spaces and communities (online and face-to-face). I begin by examining the characteristics of virtual and face-to-face spaces to meet and offer examples of social spaces and communities in which transformative teachers collaborate. After a brief overview of three core transformative teacher practices (making, hacking, and connecting, detailed in chapters 5 to 7), I explain popular discourse and terms that are used by individuals involved in these practices and across the spaces in which they connect.

Finding Space for Transformation

When transformative teacher Kathleen Melville travels to school each day, she is focused on the minutia: where to get materials for the next lesson, which student to connect with about yesterday's homework, and which teacher to turn to for advice on her next project. She travels to her workspace and becomes embedded in the social context of her school space. After school, she travels home, picks up her child from daycare, focuses on planning dinner and changing diapers, talks with family members, and grades papers. At home, she is surrounded by the thoughts, sounds, and ways of her home space. Yet when

Melville checks in with her social media accounts (Twitter and Facebook) and shares the op-ed that she and members of her Teachers Lead Philly group have written, tagging local journalists on Twitter and hashtagging #phled, she is neither at school nor at home. At that moment, Melville is in a third space, one in which she can say and do things she may not be inclined to do at school or home and reach people beyond the boundaries of her local network. This third space facilitates Melville's participation as a transformative educator because it makes room outside of school and home spaces for her to develop her identity as an educator and to use her voice to organize for educational change.

Melville and other transformative teachers seek and build third spaces to learn together and develop professional networks, both online and offline, in a way that is different from in-school professional development.[1] Thus, the "third space" is a foundational concept to define and examine. The term was first coined by political scientist Homi Bhabha in his research on nationalism and political movements.[2] Bhabha defined third space as "in-between spaces" in which dominant narratives or conceptualizations about identities, roles, and culture can be resisted and transformed. Later, this concept was incorporated into research on education. Notable educational studies that use the third-space concept as a theoretical lens include Kenneth Zeichner's research on school-university partnerships, Kris Gutiérrez's research on teacher-student dialogue in classrooms, and Michael Muller's research on negotiated co-construction of digital designs.[3] In each of these cases, the third space served as an important site of learning, growth, and development for diverse participants. Similarly, Alison Cook-Sather and Bernadette Youens describe the ways in which preservice students transformed into more critical and connected educators when they had the opportunity to work in "liminal" spaces with students.[4] In these liminal spaces, the preservice teachers stepped out of their traditional "teacher" roles to have ongoing conversations with students about issues of teaching and learning.

Whether they are online professional communities or face-to-face events, the third spaces that transformative teachers seek exist outside of school walls and are generally open to anyone who wants to join, making them diverse sites of collaborative learning in which participants have more freedom to express personal interests and opinions. Online, these spaces lend themselves to what Cohen and Kahne call "participatory politics," or politically driven online participation or activism.[5] In the stories shared in this book, you will read about the ways in which transformative teachers' engagement in participatory politics in some online third spaces have had impacts on the national level. There is evidence elsewhere that social media and connected technologies are important in driving contemporary social moments.[6] In a special issue of *Information, Communication, and Society* on the role of social media platforms in participatory politics, the editors contended, "[W]ith the more widespread use of social media and internet technologies and their absorption into the mundane practices of lived experience their potential to shape social relations of power becomes all the greater."[7] Todd Wolfson, a researcher who has studied the use of social network platforms in community organizing, suggests that social movements and actions that use social media to organize people have a more open and participatory social structure than traditional face-to-face organization, and this difference may lend itself to a greater flexibility and impact in the long run.[8]

Online tools therefore can facilitate broader connectivity, access to information, and the opportunity for teachers to share their voices publicly. Yet engaging in third spaces and participatory politics is not an act that is exclusive to online spaces for transformative teachers. Third spaces exist when educators engage in gatherings outside of school that invite diverse voices and perspectives. This can be a teacher-led professional development event, such as an EdCamp, or a meet-up of teachers and other educational advocates to discuss issues in their district. However, even in these spaces, many of the digital or participatory discourses and practices that have emerged online have become analogized and part of our everyday conversations. Therefore, digital spaces and discourses are important to understand for anyone seeking to participate in such third spaces.

Networked Third Spaces and Communities

Third spaces are the arena for building diverse relationships, a critical aspect of transformative teaching. There are a variety of third spaces in which teachers participate in and build social networks, or what I call, "networked third spaces." Four popular types of networked third spaces include hashtag communities, online teacher spaces, hybrid (face-to-face and online) teacher networks, and teacher-made spaces (the appendix has a helpful list of specific communities and spaces to visit and explore).

Hashtag communities are moderated networks brought together around a shared interest or cause. In hashtag communities, the hashtag is used functionally to engage in conversations about the topic and as a collective identity marker. Hashtag communities are different than the simple use of a hashtag to discuss a topic because they are led by a core group of moderators and operate as a community of practice with certain shared norms and principles. The moderators maintain and facilitate a regular (usually weekly) scheduled chat. Most chats are archived on a website so that visitors can, at any time, locate resources that were shared during the chat. Some hashtag communities also exist as an outgrowth or extension of a hybrid network, community, or class (in this case, they may not be directly moderated after a period of time). Conversely, some hashtag communities also evolve into hybrid networks or lead to face-to-face events. Hashtags are not exclusive to Twitter; they are now used across a majority of social media and network platforms.

Online teacher spaces give community members an opportunity to access, share, and discuss education-related issues. They can act as dynamic, interactive repositories of information and spaces for learning. In online teacher spaces, teachers prove by the work they share that they are professional, public intellectuals and leaders. The spaces can exist on a multitude of online platforms, from blogs to wikis to chat forums. Many incorporate multiple platforms on a website. Some are gated or semi-gated and require registration or membership to join.

Another type of online teacher space is a guest blog or participation in a blog feed, which publishes posts from multiple blogs. In this format, educators can share their voice or writing. Online teacher spaces such as these not only help educators, but also serve to elevate the profession by providing a space in which teachers can document and promote pedagogical practices that have emerged from their lives and work. This represents a reversal of traditional teacher professional development in which teachers are treated as technicians and told the best way to teach by others.

A *hybrid teacher network* engages in face-to-face and online collaboration and outreach. The majority began as physical networks and expanded into online spaces. Many are primarily face-to-face networks that use online networks and tools to share news about their work and connect with others.

A *teacher-made space* is one that a teacher creates for the purposes of sharing views, providing information, or connecting with others. Teacher-made spaces are typically blogs, but can include wikis, Ning networks, podcasts, or even hashtag communities.

Literacies of Making, Hacking, and Connecting: Reading the World of Digital Discourse

Transformative teachers locate networked third spaces that allow for diverse perspectives to be shared and leverage technologies to produce and amplify ideas to improve education. Entering and working in these spaces requires an understanding of the widely shared discourses and practices that have evolved (and are still evolving) in such spaces. When encountering a new form of communication such as digital, participatory discourse, readers need not only to be able to read the words, but also, as Paolo Freire and Donaldo Macedo believed, to "read the world" in the text.[9] Reading the world, not just the word, requires critical literacy and an understanding of the social context in which individuals are engaging in the discourse. Here, I'll use the cultural practices *making, hacking,* and *connecting* as a contextual framework to describe some key terminology and practices in these spaces. These descriptions will help readers not only decode statements like the Facebook posts shared in my story at the beginning of this chapter, but also understand their broader meaning in the world. This will be a primer of sorts for understanding participatory, digital discourse.

Making, hacking, and connecting are terms I use throughout this book to describe how transformative teachers design, organize, and lead educational change. I argue that transformative teachers use these practices as *cultural tools* to support teacher agency. This concept of cultural tools comes from sociocultural studies of agency.[10] From a sociocultural perspective, agency (or an individual's or group's ability to control or change its circumstances) is primarily influenced by social context and secondarily influenced by internal feelings or cognition. Thus, the tactics, social practices, and discourses that emerge through social contexts are considered meditational cultural tools that groups or individuals employ to enact change (i.e., develop agency). Looking at the cultural tools that teachers use to innovate, organize, and lead (in this case, making, hacking, and connecting) sheds light on how agency operates for teachers from a sociocultural perspective. Furthermore, this exploration of agency also reveals how transformative teachers work as collaborative leaders to change and develop their communities and schools.

Tools and Talk about Connecting (Online)

Photographer and educator Jonathan Worth, known for designing and facilitating #Phonar, a massive open online photography course (and online community), has a good metaphor for how connections are built on the open web. Worth poses the following scenario: *If you walked into a strange bar, would you expect everyone to immediately be friends with you? No, it is more likely that they would just ignore you.* The same is true for digital spaces, perhaps more so, because there we can create *avatars* (online personas) that may be different from our corporeal identity. Online connections are developed primarily through (1) reciprocity, (2) exchanges around shared interests, and (3) connections and recommendations by trusted people or sources. Reciprocity is fostered through sharing helpful information with others and recognizing their role or importance. In many platforms, including Twitter, Facebook, Google Plus, Tumblr, and blogs, this is done by *tagging* or linking particular people to something that you share. It is a way of both pulling someone into a conversation as well as recognizing them as important to the network or idea. Individuals join interest groups or follow particular topics because it helps them to weed through the crowd to connect with the people who can help them and understand them. This can be accomplished by *following* a person or group. Following also shows the person or group you are following that you are interested in their ideas, and it can foster reciprocity as well.

Through following, tagging, and sharing, individuals build a *personal (or professional) learning network (PLN)*, an egocentric (personalized) network of people and groups that an individual trusts and connects with online and offline. To use Worth's metaphor once again, building a PLN is akin to slowly developing relationships at a bar over time so you are no longer a complete stranger. Eventually, you develop a network of people with whom you can regularly connect.

Sometimes, all you need is advice or help from particular people in a PLN. However, the power of the open web allows you to call upon the *crowd* when you require major help. The crowd represents everyone to whom you can project your voice in an open online space. Typically, reaching out to the crowd involves calling out to your PLN and requesting that its members also request help from their PLNs for you. Also, terms such as *crowdfunding* (raising money through the crowd) and *crowdsourcing* (using the crowd to accomplish tasks) relate to this idea. When the crowd is involved in thinking or working collaboratively, it is sometimes referred to as the *hive*, indicating the collective power of a widespread network of individuals.

These terms can help to decipher the Twitter message from the Badass Teachers Association (known as BATs) in figure 4.1. On January 5, 2016, the BATs, a national teacher network that has worked to limit high-stakes testing and the hyper-standardization of curriculum, issued a message that rallied the crowd of its followers to participate in the Network for Public Education Conference. By tagging @NetworkPublicEd, BATs let the conference organizers know that they were putting the word out and supporting them. This act helped to build reciprocity between the groups. BATs also tagged some

FIGURE 4.1 Sample tweet from the Badass Teachers Association, 1/5/2016

Badass Teachers Association @BadassTeachersA
BATs will be flocking to @NetworkPublicEd in April! Sign up NOW https://events.bizzabo.com/NPEConference/home …
@carolburris @DianeRavitch @AnthonyCody

notable people in the education world at the end of the message. This tagging served several purposes: it was a subtle request for these individuals to retweet (share) the information with their PLN, it recognized their interest in the matter, and it showed others who was reading and involved in the issue. If Diane Ravitch, one of the people tagged in the tweet, chose to retweet it to her PLN, members of her PLN and her followers would likely trust the source of the message because they trust her.

While the terms can help to decipher cryptic Twitter messages, they can also help us to conceptualize how these tools and spaces shape discourses and interactions. There are unwritten rules for how connections are made, word is spread, and causes are supported in the digital realm, and these rules stem from the fragility of trust and the deep work it takes to build such trust online. Learning to build trust and develop a PLN is critical for engaging in these digital spaces, as well as in any third space in which diverse groups of people join together for a cause.

Tools and Talk about Hacking

The term "hacking," while rooted in coding culture, has evolved to mean transforming any problematic structures, in both the digital and the physical worlds. Here I discuss digital discourse that relates to rewriting narratives that marginalize or misrepresent people or ideas, innovating on existing tools to meet specific needs, and expanding capabilities amid limiting structures or systems. The *hashtag* is a hack term that represents many of these actions. It was created by Twitter users who wanted to find a way to convene around a certain topic or issue, because the Twitter platform originally lacked the functionality to do so. Eventually it became a central aspect of Twitter and several other platforms and is used not only to connect with others, but also to raise awareness about issues, challenge media narratives, and build movements. An example of the use of the hashtag to spur awareness and challenge media narratives could be witnessed in the use of the #whatif hashtag beginning in the winter of 2014, when Arne Duncan, then US secretary of education, tweeted, *"What if every district committed both to identifying what made their 5 best schools successful & providing those opps to all their students?"*[11] Many teachers and teacher networks used this question as a way to both critique the nature of the question and raise awareness about their own schools by creating the #whatif hashtag and posing questions such as the following:

> #whatif the DOE committed both to identifying what made their 5 worst reform initiatives failures & removing them from schools? (@kayringe, 2014)

> #whatif Every family & student boycotted @arneduncan's high-stakes testing & we moved to a well-rounded education w/ authentic assessment (@stop testing15, 2014)

> #whatif my ESL classroom wasn't a converted office with a dry erase sticker instead of a board? (@japaspanglish, 2014)

The #whatif hashtag became both a tool of questioning and critique, and a method for letting others know the reality on the ground for educators. Yet, while this hashtag was used to garner counternarrative stories, other hashtags are used to build community and action around an issue. The mantra of the #EduColor community is "a movement, not a moment," which borrows from the #BlackLivesMatter movement-speak. Conversations related to the #EduColor hashtag tend to be about issues of race and education. The hashtag is used as a central space for open conversation, yet the community is supported and reinforced by core members who maintain and facilitate a blog and frequently moderated *chats* (scheduled use of the hashtag for discussion on particular issues). The community leaders are very conscious of the ways in which hashtag conversations can be derailed and disrupted. They write that "even though hashtags are open to the public, those of us who started it reserve the right to push back and challenge tweets we see as leading the discussion astray."[12] The primary purpose of this statement is to create a safe space for participants to share their ideas and experiences.

The hashtag is one of several so-called "movement technologies," or tools that many organizers use to rally, speak out, and disrupt mainstream discourse.[13] Another common practice is to critique through parody and imagery primarily by creating *remixes* of popular images, videos, or statements. A remix is essentially a combination of several existing media to make a new statement; it is a critical *transmediation* (translation of a story or idea from one media format to another). The concept is related to hip-hop culture in which a DJ remixes or combines several beats or songs to make a new song. Perhaps the most popular form of a remix is a *meme*, in which an image of a typecast character or scene is overlaid with text that recontextualizes the messages. Memes and remixes have powerful effects because they begin with popular images with which many people can identify and then introduce new ideas or arguments. Web tools such as Canva.com and memegenerator.com, as well as photo-editing apps and software, provide easy access for many people to construct and share new remixes and memes quickly. Social media platforms often highlight images prominently, and they are more likely to be viewed. For example, a post with an image on Twitter is 35 percent more likely to be viewed and retweeted than one without an image.[14]

Figure 4.2 shows a tweet from a member of the #EduColor community, Sabrina Stevens. The tweet includes another, original tweet from EduShyster and comments on it—a way to both remix and keep the conversation going. Stevens also remixes the popular song by rap artist Drake, "Started From the Bottom," which repeats the line "started from the bottom now we here," in her line "started from the hashtag, now we here," effectively giving a subtle nod to the hip-hop community while outwardly sharing her message. The topic of the tweet is about the success of the #EduColor hashtag as a thriving community in the past year, which worked to disrupt and challenge racist media and narratives about educational issues including negative stereotypes about

FIGURE 4.2 Sample tweet and retweet from #EduColor member Sabrina Stevens, 1/5/2016

Sabrina Stevens @TeacherSabrina
Started from the hashtag, now we here
#EduColor @TheJLV @mdawriter @xianb8 @jybuell @RafranzDavis @losangelista

EduShyster @EduShyster
Hard to believe that #EduColor isn't even a year old. What's next???
@thejlv looks back and ahead. http://eepurl.com/bA_M7T

the abilities and talents of youth of color and the ways in which parents of color are treated and involved in their children's education.

Hashtagging and creating remixes are acts that challenge existing discourses and introduce new ideas to a community online. Individuals also practice hacking offline and use online spaces to seek feedback or contribute new content to the crowd. An offline hack or *life hack* is an object or structure that has been reengineered to fix a persistent problem or meet a need. Life hacks are frequently shared on social media sites (a popular one is Pinterest), which offer teachers the ability to curate content and share with others. Another way that individuals can collaborate and share their hacks is at a *hackathon*. The original hackathons were one- or two-day events in which entrepreneurial coders competed to adapt or invent new technologies. The term has been adopted for a variety of purposes, from hackathons for solving social problems to hackathons for inventing new curricula.[15] For example, the University of Denver held a curriculum hack in 2013 in which teachers came together to rethink and revise their curricula (read more about hackathons in chapter 6).[16] Several popular books on *education hacks* currently exist, such as *Hacking Education*, and *Hacking Assessment*, and *Teach Like a Pirate*.[17] These books focus mainly on how to make work more cost productive, efficient, and enjoyable.

Tools and Talk about Making

The hacking and making practices involved in online participatory culture borrow from several features of the studio design model, which emphasizes the role of process in project development, and of having *gated* (private or semiprivate) spaces to create and design, collaboratively or alone, as well as *open* public gallery spaces in which finished work is shared and curated. The concept of a *sandbox* space, a platform or experience in which users have free rein to create, play, and make, is drawn from studio design. Sharing drafts or examples of work from the sandbox is a key aspect of the peer feedback and evolving design process. *Curation*, which helps to focus attention on critically important work within the sea of information, is another important part of participatory culture influenced by art and studio design culture.[18] Teachers and organizations curate important articles, websites, and resources for others to read through blogging and social media. Curation is also an example of how new content can come from remixes of other content. *Original content* or *user-generated content*, typically a blog entry, photos, or an infographic, is highly valued on the web, because most web content is recycled.

Many of these ideas are reflected in @thenerdyteacher's Twitter post, shown in figure 4.3. The post speaks to the MakerEd community via the #makered hashtag, and includes acknowledgment and recognition of the production work of students in his class and school through the @GPSouthHS and @GPSchools tags. The post leads the reader to an original blog post on a website that curates information about makerbot work. In the post, the author cites the @thenerdyteacher's website and describes the ways in which he connects with others as well as the social mission behind his work:

> He blogs regularly on his website nerdyteacher.com, hosts podcasts at #Nerdy Cast, consults with educators to integrate technology into their classrooms, and is one of the founders of Edcamp Detroit, among many other highlights. As he's written, enhancing education with tech is about giving students "access to the best tools to prepare them for a world that expects them to know how to use them once they leave school."[19]

Note also the moniker "thenerdyteacher" in the Twitter name. This name hails to an aspect of maker culture—*geeking out*, which simply means to become focused intensely on learning and developing a particular craft or knowledge area. This work often involves spending time "tinkering," "messing around," and playing with tools and technologies (see this chapter and

FIGURE 4.3 Tweet from Nicholas Provenzano

Nicholas Provenzano @thenerdyteacher
Teaching for the 21st Century and Beyond with MakerBot - Features work by @GPSouthHS students. #makered @GPSchools
http://www.makerbot.com/blog/2016/01/04/teaching-for-the-21st-century-and-beyond-with-makerbot

chapter 5 for more comprehensive histories and the educational theories related to these terms).[20]

Digital Discourse IRL (in Real Life): Blended Networks and Spaces of Learning

The digital domain has produced a discourse that grew from the need to establish trust and safety in an arena where identities can be misrepresented and messages can be distorted. The PLNs that individuals build are like buoys that keep us safe in the storm of unknown personas and questionable information. To build a PLN, one must understand how to build trust and reciprocity through the digital discourses and practices that have emerged in virtual spaces, and understand the differences between the various spaces and networks. Furthermore, the PLN is not an online phenomenon, but a social network that is strengthened, intensified, and sometimes created, in face-to-face interactions. There is no dichotomy between the social interactions of the digital domain and the physical world; these worlds are blended and interdependent. Thus, developing an understanding of the history and discourses of the digital domain is essential for teachers who seek continued professional learning, connections, and educational change within the spaces and technologies in which they choose to work.

The goal of this chapter is to help readers interpret the networked third spaces and digital lexicon of transformative teachers, thereby providing insight into the underlying purposes and meanings of terms and practices as they relate to issues of trust, power, and social issues. The following chapters of part II give further detail about the cultural tools and practices that transformative teachers employ.

FIVE

Designing with a Maker Mind-set

SCIENCE TEACHER CHELSEA MEYERS had a problem.[1] She wanted to build a makerspace in her classroom so that students could explore the dynamics of aerospace engineering. Meyers was already convinced that a makerspace, or a laboratory for hands-on experimental design, art, and construction, would offer the best environment for her students to freely explore multiple ways to design aerodynamic objects that could sustain flight for several minutes. However, she shared her classroom with several other teachers and could not keep the equipment she needed in the space for more than a day. Invoking the spirit of the 1980s cult TV scientist-hero MacGyver, Meyers reached out to colleagues and the Internet for solutions to her problem. Then, the idea struck—"pop-up" makerspaces! She would create transportable boxes of materials for her makerspace and then would be able to set up shop anywhere she wanted. A few months later, Meyers took the idea of a pop-up makerspace even further by creating kits for various other explorations and providing them to afterschool STEM programs in underserved communities. She created a website and shared her ideas and work on makerspaces with others. Meyers was committed to helping learners (her students and others) develop a sense of inquiry and agency in their learning. She stated that, for her, the most important thing about a makerspace was "how kids feel about this space, which is their own place to hang out, and talk about geeky things and make things together."

Meyers's story embodies many aspects of the maker movement, from the emphasis placed on learning through production, to the multiple ways in which Meyers shared her work with others, to the ways in which she used her pop-up makerspace as a transformative tool for community change. If you have some background in the history of education, you are likely aware that the activities in which Meyers's students engaged in the makerspace have a long history rooted in progressive education. While the maker/DIY (do-it-yourself) movement does have a strong relationship to this educational perspective, it has emerged more recently as a combination of grassroots social movements, shaped by specific ideas, historical circumstances, and technologies. In this chapter, you will read about the history and theories of the maker movement and how it has shaped education and, most specifically, how transformative teachers have incorporated aspects of the maker movement mind-set into designing inquiries and learning experiences.

The Maker Movement and Education: A Brief History

On June 18, 2014, President Barack Obama hosted a Maker Faire at the White House.[2] A Maker Faire is a gathering of makers who come together to share their "makes." In his remarks on the event, Obama told the crowd, "Your projects are examples of a revolution that's taking place."[3] Why is making being called a revolution? Why is it happening now, and how does it relate to education and teaching? Obama and others believe that the maker revolution, the movement toward more participatory, grassroots, and collaborative ways of designing and creating art, crafts, tools, and even commercial products, is changing our economic model, culture, and society.[4] It is what the former editor-in-chief of *Wired* magazine called "the next industrial revolution."[5] The movement has been simmering for almost fifty years, with deep roots in DIY and 1960s counterculture, yet the catalyst for its emergence now is the increasing use of digital tools to communicate, share, and create work. The maker movement has a complicated relationship with education, in that it has both been shaped by and is shaping theories and practices in education.

Several scholars have contended that the roots of the maker movement and mind-set can be traced to education theorist Seymour Papert. He has been called the "father of the maker movement" because his concept of "constructionism" forms the basis for the norms and practices of the movement.[6] Constructionism builds from the concept of constructivism that was promoted by Piaget and Dewey in the early twentieth century.[7] Yet Papert was interested in the ways in which learners developed agency through producing and sharing their work with others. He developed this concept during the early 1980s, when personal computers had just become popular and only an elite few understood how they operated at the coding level. For Papert, it was important that everyone understand the ways in which computers were coded, or functioned at a basic level, in order to have agency over them. He wanted children to learn to produce their own computer code and to share it with others. This drew from Ivan Illich's earlier concept of the "conviviality" of tools, which suggests that humans should control tools and technology, rather than becoming slaves to them because humans do not know how they work.[8]

Papert's work in computing translated easily into other cultural movements that were committed to giving individuals agency over the tools, products, and practices of their lives. The concept of constructionism aligned closely with ideologies driving the counterculture DIY movement, which became popular in the 1960s and 1970s with the publication of the *Whole Earth Catalog* (essentially, a how-to text for making anything). By the 1980s and 1990s, personal computers allowed individuals to easily create their own publications; DIY "zines," or small-scale local serial publications, kept the movement afloat, yet it was still relatively obscure. DIY enthusiasts ranged from garage tinkerers to political protest artists and designers.[9]

The development of Web 2.0, which allowed individuals to easily share and converse online, brought the very diverse DIY community into the mainstream. With Web 2.0, the tinkerers and artists and amateur engineers of the movement could share their techniques, work, and crafts with others and build broader communities around their work. In 2005, the burgeoning DIY movement was further mainstreamed when Dale Dougherty founded *MAKE: magazine*, which gave the maker movement its name. *MAKE: magazine* became the heart of a larger media empire, O'Reilly Media (a $200 million company), which ran Maker Faires, promoted the development of makerspaces, and supported Maker Ed.[10] At the 2014 White House Maker Faire, Dougherty was the honored guest and lauded as a "champion for change."

But that is only half the story. The other half is rooted in the history of progressive education and the waves of school reform experienced in the United States and abroad over the last sixty years. Around the same time that the *Whole Earth Catalog* was published, two progressive educational approaches grounded in hands-on making and real-world application—the Montessori method (developed by Maria Montessori in the early 1900s, but which fell out of favor for several decades after exclusionary critique by male scholars) and Reggio Emilia—began to grow in popularity.[11] The hands-on approach to education was nurtured in the areas of engineering and design due to the international competition in the 1960s to develop Space Age technologies and a strong, future generation of scientists. Teachers were encouraged not only to teach hands-on science experimentation, but also to create their own materials for their classrooms.

The pendulum began to swing against progressive and experiential learning after the release of *A Nation at Risk: The Imperative for Educational Reform* in 1980, an analysis of the state of education in the United States that predicted dire future consequences if schools did not spend more time on basic skills and standardized curricula. The educators who had been trained and developed in the post-Sputnik era began to retire in the 1990s, and by the 2000s, when the No Child Left Behind Act (NCLB) established tough policies tied to standardized tests primarily in reading, writing, and math, there was little institutional memory or political will to promote experiential learning. Most schools dropped classes that focused on life skills and making, such as shop and home economics, in order to spend more energy on raising test scores in the major subjects. The close attention to academic tests and ranking was not limited to the United States; many Western countries developed more standardized approaches to measure and rank students.

Yet the early 2000s was also when the Internet became an expansive space for educators to explore, share, and connect with each other. While constructivism and experiential learning seemed to have been formally edged out by test preparation, many teachers used the web as a space to find information on integrating inquiry and production into their practice. Outside schools, many inquiry-based and production-oriented learning spaces for youth, such as the Beam Center in Brooklyn, New York, were flourishing, in part to make up for the void of hands-on learning experiences that was created when shop classes disappeared. Foundations, such as the John D. and Catherine T. MacArthur Foundation, Mozilla Foundation, and the Bill & Melinda Gates Foundation, began to invest in nonprofits that were working to engage learners in using new technologies. Higher education institutions, faced with incoming STEM students who had little knowledge of how to apply what they learned due to their NCLB-era educational experience, and with access to new tools such as 3-D printers and laser cutters, began to create fabrication labs, such as Paulo Blikstein's FabLab at Stanford University.[12] When *MAKE: magazine* popularized the maker movement in the mid-2000s, the educators in all of these realms—K–12 teachers, out-of-school educators, and STEM educators in higher education—found a term (making), and a community, that they could use to describe themselves and legitimate their practices. Nine years after Dougherty launched the first officially named makerspace in 2005, there were over two thousand independently run makerspaces, fabrication labs, and tinkering studios in existence globally, many of them in libraries and schools.

While some makerspaces are sites of product incubation and "maker gyms" for which individuals can pay a monthly fee for access, a good proportion are educational spaces, such as libraries, museums (e.g., the Makeshop at the Children's Museum of Pittsburgh and the Draper Spark!Lab at the National Museum of American History), and nonprofit organizations. Further, as in Meyers's example, some schools have dedicated labs as makerspaces, and individual teachers have developed makerspaces within their classrooms. Thus, the maker movement reintroduced many elements of progressive education into classrooms and connected these classrooms with a broader, interdisciplinary network of community institutions and stakeholders that were committed to using technologies for fabrication and networking. The teachers who joined the maker movement and incorporated those practices into their classrooms are initiating a grassroots shift of the school reform pendulum to a more inquiry-based, participatory, and civically engaged pedagogy.

What Makes a Maker?

Dougherty of *MAKE: magazine* is known for declaring that "anyone can be a maker," and that making could be simply defined as the act of designing and building a creation.[13] However, certain distinguishing features of the maker *mind-set*, *tools*, and *spaces* suggest that the maker movement embodies a set of beliefs and practices to which individuals become enculturated. Thus, making, when described within the context of the maker or DIY movement, is not just an activity; it is a cultural practice.

The Mind-set

In the range of literature, magazines, and websites about making, there is often a strong emphasis on the idea of a "maker mind-set."[14] Mark Hatch, CEO and cofounder of TechShop, wrote a "Maker Movement Manifesto" about mind-set, organized around nine key traits: making, sharing, giving, learning, tooling up, playing, participating, supporting, and changing.[15] These traits effectively summarize many of the shared traits of mind-set across various maker communities and spaces. The first, "making," reflects the importance of the process of creative production in the maker mind-set; it is the anchor for the whole of maker culture. Making is oriented around a studio design or design-thinking framework: a process of exploring, experimenting, and testing prototypes that takes human experiences, interests, and needs into account for production decisions.[16]

The second trait, sharing, speaks to the value of sharing produced work with communities and the public. The third, giving, is related to sharing, yet is more specifically associated with the ways in which makers collectively produce work available for the public to use and build on. For example, giving can be witnessed in the plethora of open-source programs on the web. People design open-source programs and offer them to anyone who would like to build from them. This often results in the development of programs that have been collectively coded by thousands of people. One popular site for open-source technology is Github.com, in which one can find a range of software that has been designed by a community of volunteer developers. This concept might best be described as crowd-based entrepreneurship for the collective good.

The fourth and fifth traits, learning and tooling up, refer to the importance of developing mastery over a craft and the tools of the craft through making, studying, and collaborating with others. Michail Giannakos et al. suggest that makerspaces should be constructed with a "low floor and high ceiling," which allows novices to participate in making, but demonstrates the unwritten expectation that makers develop mastery over their craft(s).[17] Mastery over particular crafts and tools is a long process, and few makes are perfect the first time. The sixth trait, playing, reflects the maker value of tinkering, messing around, and learning through failure. Makers are known for celebrating failure as a step toward a new version or iteration of an idea.[18]

Makers do not view themselves as solo operators in their craft. They are part of a community of makers and are expected to share and support each other's work. These beliefs are linked to the seventh and eighth traits noted by Hatch— participating and supporting. One reason that makerspaces are important in maker culture is because of the skill-sharing and collaborative nature of the maker mind-set. In fact, there has been an ongoing debate on the use of the term "do-it-yourself" within the maker community; some argue that it should be called "do-it-ourselves," "do-it-together," or simply, "do-it-yours*elves*."[19]

Hatch identified "changing" as the ninth trait of maker culture. It is rooted in the transformative and democratizing nature of making. Jonathan Worth, known for his international, open, maker-oriented, online photography course Phonar (see profile at end of chapter) says his goal is to teach everyone to be a photographer so that everyone will have a chance to share a story with the world. As Worth's mission demonstrates, making not only empowers individuals who might normally be marginalized in society to have a voice through their work, but also facilitates dialogue between makers, building opportunities for deliberative democratic engagement.

Many makers describe the purpose of their making as not simply to produce a thing, but to make a difference in the world through the process of making and through the product itself. So this trait of changing highlights not only the importance of purpose (making for the public good), but also the importance of process in making. The process is where the learning, collaboration, and change occur. The reason that some makers bristle at the idea of "recipe-like" scripted steps in a process is because it does not provide space for emergent learning and collaboration.[20]

Finally, there is a tenth trait to making that Hatch does not mention, perhaps because it is both a source of criticism and an evolution in the maker movement: equity. As you read this chapter, you will notice tensions related to inclusivity and the maker movement. The "branded" maker movement, popularized by *MAKE: magazine* and websites, has been marketed toward white middle- or upper-class males. However, makers and scholars alike have pushed back on this exclusionary orientation. In 2016, the American Educational Research Association hosted a presentation of eight research studies about equity and inclusion in maker education.[21] Many of the studies showed how maker-educators were actively fostering racial, gender, age, and cultural equity and inclusiveness.[22] Furthermore, one study suggested a reframing of the key tenets of the maker movement around equity and inclusivity.[23] When I share stories of transformative teachers and allies in these chapters, they are primarily about those who promote equity and inclusivity throughout their work.

The Tools

With the advent of technologies that allow anyone to easily produce complex objects, such as 3-D printers, laser cutters, die-cut machines, and computer-controlled robots, many makers are engaged in learning how to use these new tools, a signature of maker production.[24] A subset of tools related to these digital production tools are software programs that assist in computer coding, such as MIT's Scratch program and Gamestar Mechanic. Learning to code allows individuals to design online apps or simple robots that can help meet community needs. Arduino is an example of a program that helps people code software that controls robots or other electronics. Some other important digital tools are collaborative digital platforms such as collaborative writing apps (e.g., Google docs), wiki forums, and collective annotation software that allow users to share their makes, develop how-to guides for others, and seek support and community for the particular craft or skill they are learning.

Beyond the digital, maker tools are often related to craft, textile fabrication, and construction. These can range from power tools and lumber to knitting needles and fabric. Such craft and construction tools are often integrated with the use of digital tools and materials. For example, e-textiles or the incorporation of electronics, such as lights and sensors, into clothing and fabric are popular in some maker communities.[25] Another example is e-texts, in which paper-based texts are enhanced with electronics.[26]

The Spaces

Makerspaces, fabrication labs, tinkering studios, exploration spaces—these are all terms for spaces in which makers come together to make things. Makerspaces typically provide tools and materials, as well as assistance from makers skilled in particular crafts and techniques. There are generally three types of makerspaces: community or entrepreneurial spaces (in which users pay a monthly or weekly fee to use or attend classes or gatherings); STEM-related labs, typically located at institutions of higher education; and educational spaces, such as museums, libraries, schools, and classrooms.[27]

Makerspaces serve a critical purpose in maker culture and, some would argue, for our democracy. Erica Rosenfeld Halverson and Kimberly Sheridan suggest that makerspaces are the physical embodiment of a community of practice (CoP).[28] In a CoP, individuals become enculturated to the norms of the community through apprenticeship, moving from legitimate peripheral participation as novices on the edges of the community into full members who are developing mastery and becoming mentors to others.[29] Makerspaces reflect these characteristics and are vital places for a person to develop an identity as a maker.

Makerspaces are also spaces in which a diverse group works together, outside home and work. They are a form of a third space, described in chapter 3, a public gathering place for collaborative work, play, and conversation. The role of public spaces as a key element in fostering democracy and transformation is discussed by a range of scholars, from Robert Putnam, who emphasized the role of civic groups in sustaining democracies, to Habermas, who wrote about the role of the "public sphere" as a place for dialogue, debate, and the discovery of different perspectives and opinions.[30] Matt Ratto and Megan Boler argue that making and makerspaces are uniquely suited to supporting democratic growth and development because individuals are negotiating the making of a physical object, which eventually serves to represent this work.[31] The authors argue that the processes and practices that go into making also allow room for "critically infused reflection" into the object itself, producing a tangible, transformative relationship between the makers and their communities.[32]

Modern makerspaces, however, have been criticized for their tendency to cater primarily to white middle-class men via their outreach efforts and architectural design (e.g., the height of the tables).[33] This is an aspect of a larger critique of the movement: that women, people of color, and poor people can feel marginalized in the spaces and in the community of makers. For example, *MAKE: magazine* was recently criticized for the fact that the 85 percent of its cover photos showed white males.[34] Furthermore, issues of access to materials in under-resourced communities and time to spend on making limits the involvement of those living in poverty. However, a range of efforts are under way to address these disparities. First, women technologists and makers have sought to focus on educating girls in coding and other aspects of making through organizations like Girls Who Code, ChickTech, and Black Girls Code (see Tara Linney's profile in chapter 3). Second, some private and nonprofit makerspaces have considered how to make their spaces more inclusive through both architectural design and outreach efforts such as community partnerships and scholarships. Third, several foundations have begun to invest in makerspaces in urban schools, increasing access to youth in under-resourced neighborhoods. Finally, academic scholars such as Yasmin Kafai and Kylie Peppler have conducted action research efforts to provide maker education opportunities for girls.[35]

Transformative Teachers Designing with the Maker Mind-set

In the span of about five years—since makerism has become a more mainstream phenomenon—a flood of new teacher-written or -coauthored books, articles, blog posts, and other social media posts has revealed the ways in which transformative teachers have adopted the maker mind-set to design inquiries and learning experiences for their classrooms and work. Take, for example, teacher A. J. Juliani, who coauthored *Launch: Using Design Thinking to Boost*

Creativity and Bring Out the Maker in Every Student with John Spencer in 2016. In 2015, Juliani was also part of a team of four teacher colleagues nicknamed the "#EdJusticeLeague," who ran a podcast on how to use podcasts in the classroom. In *Launch*, Juliani told a story about his teaching:

> A few years ago, I (A. J.) was frustrated by the fact that the only thing my 11th- grade students cared about was their grade. Because of this frustration, I decided to launch a 20% project . . . I told students to follow their interests and curiosity, research a specific topic, create a product out of that research, and share it with the world in TED-talk-style live-streamed presentations. Students were more motivated than I'd ever seen in all my years of teaching . . . They learned sign language, made computers, rebuilt car engines, and learned to play the guitar. One student even tried to clone a carnivorous plant! The project was successful because it empowered students to learn and create based on their interests and passions.[36]

The authors described how to use the maker approach of design thinking as the way to support creative teaching and learning. They argued that "design thinking provides a way to think about creative work. It starts with empathy, working to really understand the problems that people are facing before attempting to create solutions." Throughout, the authors echo much of the maker mind-set, such as an encouragement to take risks, embrace failure, be a producer, and share with others.

Launch offers a sampling of the emerging maker-oriented discourse that transformative teachers are using in their posts and publications. Other popular teacher-written books that reflect these ideas include Larissa Pahomov's *Authentic Learning in the Digital Age: Engaging Students Through Inquiry*; Dave Burgess's *Teach Like a Pirate: Increase Student Engagement, Boost Your Creativity, and Transform Your Life as an Educator* (and related to this, *Learn Like a Pirate*, and *Play Like a Pirate*); and Todd Nesloney and Adam Welcome's *The Kids Deserve It! Pushing Boundaries and Challenging Conventional Thinking.* Teachers use other forms of social media to curate and share information about design thinking and maker-based inquiries. For example, Diana Rendina, a library teacher in Tampa, Florida, maintains a blog called *Renovated*

Learning: Building a Culture of Creativity and Discovery in Education in which she chronicles the development of her school makerspace and offers resources and support to other teachers and schools that would like to do the same. In her blog, she suggests the value of the makerspace is not in the tools that it offers, but in the mind-set and design processes that are used.

These examples and descriptions are evidence of a shift not only in practices or discourse in education, but also in *who* is taking the lead in articulating the means and methods of the shift: teachers. While the maker movement and progressive education have a long history, in the connected era today, transformative teachers are being vocal and public about how they initiating these practices in their classrooms and, thus, becoming important contributors to the movement and its implementation in classrooms.

How Teachers Use the Maker Mind-set to Design Inquiries: Adapting the Studio Design Process

Many scholars have identified the studio design framework as a guiding philosophical basis for the process of making.[37] I have observed the use of this framework in several of the organizations profiled in this book, including Hive Chicago, the Hacktory, the U School, and the Workshop School. Central to the studio design framework is the design cycle, which starts with a question or idea; progresses to tinkering, playing, and ideation; and then moves to the creation of a prototype to test; analysis and refinement; and a new start to the cycle. In the first phase of the cycle, sometimes called ideation, makers consider what they want to explore or understand through a project and then gather information to help them develop a humanistic understanding of the issue (or how others experience the problem, issue, or activity). In the second phase, the student makers develop a series of possible solutions or pathways and then settle on one to try out or prototype. They then test and evaluate the prototype, and in the final phase, make adaptations to create a finished product.

The U School, a teacher-led school in Philadelphia, has a design-based approach to teaching that offers a good example of how teachers and schools adopt design thinking to facilitate making and learning. The mantra of the school, "Love, Dream, Do," exemplifies the design cycle, and the teachers articulate the process further in a series of stages that students are taught to progress through: prediscovery (what is my concern?), empathy (how does it matter to people?), define (define the problem and working constraints), dream (develop possible solutions), prototype (try out a solution and evaluate it), deliver (create final project).[38] The teachers ask students to begin by identifying a "wicked problem," or something that affects them and their community.[39] As a result, students create innovative projects that have a human-centered design element and address their interests and concerns.

One wicked problem the students observed was that some found it difficult to stay focused on their personal inquiries in school. This observation represented the prediscovery phase. Students then began the empathy phase of the work by surveying and interviewing other students in the school to learn about their experiences and challenges in personalized learning. They identified several issues; one that stood out was the role of technology in both helping and hindering student engagement. They defined their inquiry: in what ways is technology distracting to learning, and what can be done about it? Students presented their inquiry at a practitioner research forum with their teachers to share their work and gather (dream) possible solutions from workshop participants. Using this information, each student developed his or her own proposals to prototype and evaluate. The projects could range from the development of new apps that help students keep track of their work, physical structures or tools, or even proposals for new school policies. In this way, the students used the design process to create solutions that met their needs as learners alongside their teachers.

This example illustrates how the maker mind-set translates into practice through the implementation of the studio design process. The process is not a foreign idea to transformative teachers because of their history in engaging in inquiry. Teacher inquiry values the process of identifying a question or need, observing and gathering data, analyzing and reflecting on these data, and implementing changes to teaching or an environment on the basis of this work. Furthermore, teacher inquiry is not ephemeral; it values the observed—what is seen and heard—over assumptions. Phenomenology, or the detailed and literal description of phenomena, is a methodology that guides much of teacher inquiry.[40] Thus, teachers who engage in structured inquiry around their work are using the same type of studio design approach as are makers of any craft.

How Teachers Use the Maker Mind-set to Design Democratic Learning Experiences

Learning experiences that are designed with a maker mind-set place democratic participation and the process of production at the center of the work of learning. The maker movement can be considered an expression of participatory culture, another historical root of transformative teaching, due to the characteristics of the foundational theory of the maker movement, constructivism. Yasmin Kafai and Kylie Peppler write, "While constructionism places importance on the individual learner, it also places equal importance on the role of social participation. Here the individual, the artifact, and collaborative input of the community shape learning, participation, and sharing."[41] Both participatory culture and constructionist theory emphasize the value of production, sharing, and community.

Through collaborative and participatory construction of works that reflect the voices, lives, and ideas of everyday citizens and the use of digital technologies to connect diverse peoples, the maker movement encourages what Ratto and Boler call "distributed citizenship," or a collective project for social change.[42] Other scholars, such as Paulo Blikstein, Kylie Peppler, Erica Halverson, and Kimberly Sheridan, concur that making is an exercise in democratic discourse and transformation.[43] Transformative teacher Joshua Block's community dance project epitomizes this idea. The goal of the project was for students to learn about the history and stories of a neighborhood and express the stories through dance. Students chose a local neighborhood for study and proceeded to research it by interviewing community leaders and read local histories. They had to make sense of the complicated social histories of the place in order to construct a cohesive narrative that told a story. They then needed to transmediate (retell a story that is in one form of media in a different media) their written research into an embodied narrative expressed through choreographed dance.[44] Not only did this work cultivate a sense of community and shared experience among the students as they worked together, it also deepened their understanding of the experiences of the community members. Finally, the students performed their dances in the neighborhoods that they researched, and Block shared images and video of these performances in his blog and on social media. This prompted dialogue with a wider audience about the students' stories about the communities.

Learning activities that have been designed with a maker mind-set therefore aim to give voice and agency to learners in a tangible way through making and to help learners become producers instead of just consumers. The shift from consumer mentality to producer mentality is a critical component of making, and it has been related by some scholars to Freire's theories of empowerment through self-actualization and critical consciousness, which ultimately serve to support full democratic participation in society.[45]

Making is done with the community in mind and, in particular, with a goal of improving everyone, not just individuals. Thus, learning experiences are designed for the learners to work toward a common good; there is a "we" mentality in making, which emphasizes giving for the sake of the community as a whole. While there is certainly an entrepreneurial spirit in maker culture, the entrepreneurship serves innovation, discovery, and the development of collective society.

However, some caution should also be taken in adopting the maker mind-set for designing learning experiences. In addition to issues I mentioned previously about exclusive practices in makerspaces and communities, several scholars have noted that the institutionalization and/or corporatization of maker activities could destroy the democratizing power of the movement.[46] As the maker movement becomes more popular and is brought into schools by teachers and nonprofit programs, it will be important to preserve the grassroots nature of the culture and to stand by the foundational principles that guide it to be open, nonstandardized, and inclusive.

Making in Education: Fad or Future of Schooling? An Examination of Impacts

Making in education as a pedagogical practice is in its infancy. Many people, including maker-educators, raise critical questions about the impacts of maker practices in education; practices are still evolving, and the long-term effects have yet to be determined.[47] However, recent research on makerspaces and maker practices in education has provided a window into the ways in which they shape schools, student learning, and teacher practices. One large-scale study that has helped to uncover the impact of the maker movement on schools was conducted by Kylie Peppler and a team of colleagues.[48] Their study examined makerspaces designed for youth across the United States. The majority of the makerspaces were in schools. The researchers found that 94 percent of the makerspaces aligned with STEM learning goals, and that about half aligned directly with Next Generation Science Standards. While it was clear that the role of makerspaces in these schools was primarily focused on STEM, the study also found that over 90 percent of programs promoted interdisciplinary study and cultivated both "hard" (tacit, academic) skills and "soft" (communication and collaboration) skills (also see research by Kafai and Peppler[49]). Thus, in schools, the maker movement is building more interdisciplinary connections between the sciences and arts-based disciplines and nurturing people skills in addition to developing academic knowledge.

Looking more closely at student learning in maker-centered educational activities, Shirin Vossoughi and Bronwyn Bevan provide a comprehensive overview of what students learn in these contexts; in their review of a range of empirical research on the subject, they found that maker-based education has impacts on students that go well beyond developing academic skill.[50] Students' dispositions toward learning, their views of themselves as learners, and their broader understanding of the interconnectedness of their learning in school and their civic participation in society evolved into more critical and reflective stances through maker-based education. Vossoughi and Bevan cite a statement from one study in particular to highlight how maker-based educational experiences had an empowering effect on learners: "the process of transforming lived and imagined experiences into original expressive works for significant audiences can provide a resource for young people to rewrite the stories that are told about them, against them or supposedly on their behalf."[51]

The effects of the maker movement in education are not limited to student learning. The movement has also had an impact on teachers' approach to professional development and their pedagogy. One study on maker-based professional development showed that teachers became more collaborative and developed greater levels of social capital through maker activities.[52] Vossoughi and Bevan argue that the same skills that students develop through maker education are the skills that Linda Darling-Hammond promotes as signals of high teacher quality, including collaboration, strong content-knowledge, teacher inquiry, and a social justice orientation to teaching.[53] Teachers learn from being makers and also contribute to the broader professional community through sharing their "makes." Yet there is still limited research on the effects of maker practices and maker culture on teachers' professional identity and development. While this book is one attempt to address this void, more research is needed in this area.

Voices from the Field:
Making in a Connected World

The profiles below are of two lead voices in the fields of connected learning, making, and multimodal learning. They provide a fuller picture of the history and work of making in education in the networked era.

Howard Rheingold: Being a Co-Learner in the Connected Era

Howard Rheingold is a thought leader in peer learning and connected technologies. The author of several books, including *Smart Mobs: The Next Social Revolution*; *Net Smart: How to Thrive Online*; *The Virtual Community*; *The Millennium Whole Earth Catalog*; and *Virtual Reality*, he was the executive founder of *HotWired* magazine. Rheingold has also been involved with the Digital Media Lab Hub at MIT as a collaborator and writer. He teaches at several universities, including Stanford and the University of California, Berkeley, yet intentionally avoids working full-time at any particular institution in order to have the freedom to explore and build learning and connecting opportunities outside institutional constraints. Rheingold described his decision to position himself outside traditional schooling as a choice about focusing his attentions for making educational change: "I made a decision that I was not going to put my energies into trying to reform institutions, but wanted to push on the envelope of what could be done with social media and the student-centric, openly networked pedagogy . . . and to find others and learn from them and support them and provide resources for them in terms of a bottom-up transformation."

Creating educational experiences outside formal systems, or "flying under the radar," as Rheingold calls it, has allowed him to delve deeply into different ways of thinking about learning and connectedness. A central part of his pedagogy is in dismantling the idea of the "teacher" and instead positioning the teacher as just one co-learner in a community. In this democratized paradigm of learning, a teacher (co-learner) learns alongside other learners, and his or her main role is to facilitate inquiry and learning networks among and beyond the community. The concept of co-learner relates to Rheingold's larger body of inquiry on peer learning. Rheingold is interested in how we connect and learn from each other in the networked era:

> [G]o ask your fourteen-year-old: how would you make a bow and arrow, configure a server, or play a ukulele? I'm willing to bet that they're going to say, "I'm going to search on YouTube," because there's another fourteen-year-old who's going to show them how to do it. Maybe they're good at showing them how to do it, maybe they're not good at showing them how to do it, but it used to be you had to go to ukulele school or IT school.
>
> I've spent a lot of my career looking at the future, and what my future sense is telling me now is that what all of these young people who've grown up knowing they could ask any question anywhere at any time, and they could learn anything they wanted, that they're a super-saturated solution. What they really lack is a more sophisticated know-how about learning.

Thus, what teachers as co-learners need to know is "how to grow, tune, and participate" in networks of learning, and to understand that "their learning is not confined to their co-students or their classroom or their campus."

Rheingold has been involved with the Peeragogy project (http://peeragogy.org) to support individuals in peer learning. For this project, he and other scholars and educators worldwide came together to develop an ever-expanding online "Handbook for Peer Learning." Members of the group still meet bimonthly to discuss additions to the handbook and their experiences in peer learning.

Another aspect of Rheingold's praxis is his focus on making with others. He has a long history of involvement in the DIY movement. In the 1980s and 1990s, he worked with friends to make large floats for concert shows, which led to participation in Burning Man. In 1990, he was the editor of the *Whole Earth Catalog*. More recently, a core group became involved in a smaller project called the Pataphysi-cal Slot Machine (http://pataphysics.us), an interactive art project that includes a computer programmed through Arduino that responds to human questions. Rheingold's work in making with others ties back to developing collective agency and building shared understandings between his colleagues and others. Regarding the maker movement, he noted:

> At the heart of it is the constructivist idea that you don't receive your learning; you construct your learning, and you do it by trying things out . . . Increasingly, we live in a world in which we're using sophisticated technologies that you or your hometown or your state couldn't create . . . Being able to take technology into your hands and make it for your own purposes without being a consumer who is ignorant of how the technology works, I think that adds a very strong social justice [component].

This philosophy is woven through much of his writing and work: be mindful of how you collaborate and learn with each other, be true to your passions, and seek out new ways of connecting. To learn more about Rheingold's work, visit his web-site at http://www.rheingold.com/learning.

Jonathan Worth: Learning to Speak through Photography

Jonathan Worth is a British photographer known for his work in such publications as the *New York Times*, *New Scientist*, and *Vogue* magazine, and is the founder of Phonar, an online, undergraduate photography course that he ran from 2009 to 2014 and was freely available to anyone. Thousands of people participated in Phonar, and its offshoot, Phonar Nation, which has been recognized for its abil-ity to foster engagement in learning online. I interviewed Worth primarily about his work in teaching and developing Phonar. He shared insights on the ways in which digital connections and tools have reoriented the possibilities for photography as a means for social change. He explained how his pedagogy evolved as a result of digital era cultural shifts:

> As a teacher of photography, I used to teach people to speak for other people. That was the job; you were trained in camera operation, visual literacy, and abided by a code of ethics that assured the reader that what you were saying with your pictures was fair and accurate.
>
> Then the class changed. The postdigital walls came down, and suddenly we were all potentially connected. So I open-sourced the problem and asked how I should

teach what it means to be a twenty-first-century photographer? And that in itself was twofold. I was asking both what we should teach and how should we teach it? If you look at Phonar Nation, that was a product of this; it was a class explicitly about enabling or better enabling young people to participate in their own representation.

My job had been ostensibly to speak for the people, so when it came to education, it was to teach other people to speak for other people. I think that moment has passed. We are well and truly post-Gutenberg. Everyone is a potential witness and publisher, and we need to enable people to speak clearly for themselves, to get heard and to move people to action.

Thus, through Phonar, Worth and his colleagues taught individuals how to tell their own stories and be producers and participants in the world through their photos. They used the Twitter hashtag #phonar as a means to spark community conversations and share work. This raised the question for him, however, of what it means to "be heard" and why people need to be heard. He said that he had a second revelation in teaching the course in regard to this question: that the larger purpose of the sharing was to make the world a better place: "I no longer think of photography as an ends, making beautiful pictures to hang on the wall. It's photography to change the world. I'm not interested in the craft of creating beautiful artifacts; I'm interested in being visually and digitally fluent. If anything, its agency through artifice."

He also recognized a shift in his own position as a teacher when he began to encourage others to use their stories to change the world. He noted, "It moves the teacher and the photographer in this case to places where they're advocate and activists; that's a step change from the detached and objective journalist. But I think that's a reflection of the changing structures of both news and information." Further, because Phonar encouraged self-organized learning, he began to see himself as a co-learner with the students.

Yet, with all the positive advantages, there were also critical issues to contend with in the digital environment of Phonar, such as privacy and trust. Would a student taking the class who lived under a repressive government get in trouble because of a photo he or she shared? Worth found that he had an important responsibility in helping students develop a critical understanding of the ways in which the Internet and other technologies tracked and stored data. Understanding these issues became an important part of the curriculum as well.

Worth's story of personal and professional growth through teaching photography with connected technologies illustrates many of the shifts, possibilities, and challenges that come with teaching and making for social change with connected technologies. He continues to explore how to improve social contexts through his work. In his current project, he is working with teachers to develop adapted versions of the multimodal Phonar method in order to scale up the open classes across disciplines and connect them to nontraditional learning environments. By partnering with nongovernmental organizations and traditional learning institutions, he aims to access the vast majority of those participants who aren't able to get into a physical classroom.

SIX

Organizing with a Hacker Ethos

No one is coming to save us. We're it. Get loud, teachers, get loud.
—Diane Laufenberg, Inquiry Schools[1]

LATE IN 2009, a handful of members of the Teacher Action Group in Philadelphia met with their union leaders to strategize on how to communicate their concerns about the lack of attention to issues such as racial justice, hyperstandardized testing, and the privatization of public schools. The members found that the union turned them away and ignored them, or worse, simply gave them lip service through formal lines of communication. Over the next few years, their frustrations increased, and the group decided that since the system was not working for them, they'd hack it with a system of their own. They started the Caucus of Working Educators (WE) in 2014, a side group of the Philadelphia Federation of Teachers (PFT) union, which welcomed educators, parents, students, and education advocates into its ranks. WE argued for "social justice unionism," an ideology that has been gaining ground across the United States, used grassroots transmedia organizing to get their message out to the media, and built a base of support in the community through face-to-face networking and a strong social media presence.[2]

Within six months, WE was well known to local journalists, who regularly quoted members in stories that covered their successful campaigns on issues such as testing and racial justice. By 2015, union leaders who had held their positions for over thirty years were not just talking with WE members; they were fighting to stay in power. In 2016, WE organized its own slate of candidates for the next union election, vowing, "[W]e're bringing a new kind of unionism to the PFT: grassroots, bottom-up, member-driven, powerful. #WEarePFT"[3]

In this chapter, I explain how WE and other transformative teachers (groups and individuals) harness the hacker ethos of open, critical, passionate, collective, systemic problem solving to organize change in their schools, districts, and profession. While the concept of hacking has its roots in coding and technology, the ethos of hacking has transcended these roots to a broader cultural construction that values participatory, creative problem solving toward systemic change.[4] In addition to providing real-life examples, I offer a protocol for analyzing how transformative teachers can "hack" problematic educational discourses, physical structures, and institutional systems at the classroom, district, and national levels.

Many readers may be surprised by my use of the term "hack" in a positive or empowering context. As you read about the evolution of the term, you will discover that while the popular media have painted the concept in a negative light, the true and original concept, which certainly aims at changing systems, is not negative and, in most cases, is playful, creative, and empowering. If you feel a sense of anxiety about the word, you might reflect on the stories and narratives that you have experienced in relationship to the word and see if it truly aligns with the history and definitions I share here. I encourage you to suspend some of your preconceived notions and open up new possibilities for how you understand and define the word.

Another issue that will become apparent is the connections between making and hacking. These two terms overlap; in many cases, hacking occurs during the making process. Furthermore, the maker mind-set and the hacker ethos have many commonalities. However, what sets hacking apart from making is that making is primarily physical, while the concept of hacking has evolved to encompass the hacking of discourses, policies, and practices in addition to the physical and digital, and the collective assumes an important role in work that reflects the hacker ethos. As such, hacking is strategy for organizing communities. I begin this chapter with a history of the evolution of the term, which will illustrate ways in which hacking and making intersect and how the hacker ethos offers a protocol for understanding how transformative teachers organize for change.

The Hacker Ethos: From F/OSS to Freedom

Technology shapes not only what we make, but also how we think about making and, ultimately, our ethos about making and participating. For example, when a child sits with a pencil and paper to write a story, the idea of writing is something that many view primarily as a solitary act. Yet if two children, sitting at opposite parts of the world, use a computer to collectively compose a story, new forms of social negotiation develop and new ideas about the act of writing as a collective endeavor emerge. Our tools and contexts (in this example, pencil and paper or computer) mediate our culture and ethos. The hacker ethos emerged from a particular technological context in which skilled computer coders had access to free and open-source software (F/OSS) that they could use and manipulate ("open source" means that anyone can copy the code and make new versions of the programs).[5] Furthermore, these coders had access to forums and spaces in which they could share, discuss, learn about, and build upon F/OSS.

In this context, the original hackers developed an ethos that served to help them negotiate socially, advocate for their needs and rights, and reinscribe their own identities within the hacker community. In fact, the hacker community is known for its cultural self-awareness; innumerable hacker manifestos that state the ethics and practices of hackers are available for viewing on the Internet.[6] These ethics include a commitment to sharing, open access, and free "speech" (i.e., code); a work ethic that values passion and joy in one's occupation; endeavoring to master a craft and/or tool; failure as an important part of learning; autonomy and self-improvement; mutual aid and caring; and collective work to build upon or improve systems and experiences for the greater good.[7]

The story of the evolution of Linux F/OSS programming exemplifies these ethics in action. Linus Torvalds created Linux, an open-source version of the

Unix operating system in 1991 and shared it with hacker colleagues to adapt and build upon.[8] The hackers created multiple forums, spaces, and communities in which they earnestly worked pro bono (some spending years on single programs) to create iterations to share with the altruistic intentions of offering free alternatives to privately owned technology. The ongoing collective tinkering, problem solving, and sharing over the last thirty years has resulted in a vast collection of programs and codes that technologists have praised as more stable than commercial operating systems and integrated into numerous technologies, from NASA international space station computers to Android phones.[9] This ethos is even evident in the way that coding is now taught to children. MIT's Scratch program, which teaches basic coding to youth online, encourages learners to copy the code sequences of others' projects and remix (hack) them to make them their own.

While hacking has come to have a more sinister meaning in mainstream media, in reality, the more notorious and illegal (or "black hat") acts of hacking are generally regarded as unethical, and such hackers are often ostracized as "crackers."[10] One well-known black-hat figure is Julian Assange, accused of espionage by the American government for his role in WikiLeaks, a public repository of leaked classified government documents. Gerard Briscoe and Catherine Mulligan, two computer science professors who have argued for a more nuanced understanding of hacking computer education, offered a metaphor for the difference between hackers and crackers: hackers are like doctors who work to heal patients, and crackers are the people with medical knowledge and skills who use it for illegal and dangerous purposes.[11] Both have the same skill set, but they have different ethics and purposes. Much of the popular media has focused on the work of crackers, such as Assange, who have skill sets similar to hackers, but not the same ethical orientation.

What is the skill set of a hacker? A hacker has a complex understanding of an entire system and can identify the assumptions, failures, and vulnerabilities that exist within the authoritative power structures that control the system. Briscoe and Mulligan described this as "the skill to question trust and control assumptions expressed in software and hardware, as well as in processes that involve human(s)-in-the-loop (aka 'social engineering')."[12] Likewise, scholar Rafi Santo argues that "hacker literacies" require a critical understanding of how a technological system controls or shapes human interaction and civil liberties.[13] To illustrate this concept, Santo gave the example of how individuals reacted to changes to Facebook privacy settings in 2014. Those with "hacker literacy" had a critical understanding of how the Facebook platform gathered personal data and how the algorithms affected the ways in which individuals received and shared information. These individuals maintained an awareness of how the private company's access to their personal information could be used to influence their decisions about what to buy, how to act, and what to believe.

Furthermore, hackers are not simply expected to be able to develop utilitarian changes to a system, but also to make creative and artful transformations of the system.[14] Many hackers (both coders and those who use the term more broadly) bristle at the idea of hacking being defined as just "disrupting" a system; hacking is about creation, not obstruction. This belief has also been articulated by the transformative teachers and organizational allies I have interviewed for this book. One organizational ally I interviewed was Chris Lehmann, the cofounder of Inquiry Schools, a network of educators and administrators that promotes transformative teaching practices, and the cofounder of Science Leadership Academy, which has gained national recognition for its innovative, inquiry-oriented educational model. Lehmann suggested that the concept of disrupting is more a corporate, top-down approach to change, while bottom-up creation reflects the hacker approach to change: "[The top-down model] is this idea that we're going to do something to people, and the other is we're going to do something *with* them—I think that's the difference . . . Being intentional about this work and not being quite as quick to embrace disruption as a strategy I think is hugely important." As such, the hacker ethos is framed within the perspective that all hackers must (1) understand how complex systems or structures work and what powers them, and (2) learn to play with, tinker, and innovate these systems in order to transform them from the bottom up into something useful *and* carefully crafted.

Last, hackers have historically been a niche group of individuals that relies on social networking and collaboration to sustain its work. Participation in online forums, hackerspaces (similar and sometimes the same as makerspaces), and hackathons or hacking conventions is a vital piece of the computer hacker lifestyle. Hackathons, in particular, are a place where hackers can become immersed in what hacking scholar McKenzie Wark calls "deep hack mode" together with other hackers, sometimes for several days (sustained by energy drinks and convenience food).[15] All these elements relate to the concept of "productive freedom" described by Gabriella Coleman in her ethnography of hackers: she asserts that hackers build agentive tools, systems, and opportunities that enable them to freely exchange information and support each other to build upon their work and craft for the systems in which they work.[16] In the same vein, transformative teachers develop agentive tools to collaborate, innovate, and reimagine teaching together. These tools are structures, routines, and spaces, such hashtag communities or teacher-led "unconferences," that enable them to leverage the power of their larger community to bring forth change.

The hacker ethos evolved and matured within the hacker community over the last thirty years, but by the mid-2010s, the word "hack" began to proliferate in circles outside of code hackers.[17] Terms such as "life hack" began to expand the meaning of the word to a broader audience. This did not happen without some critique from the hacker/maker community, which some members disparage for the diffusion of the meaning of the word. For example, transformative teacher Allison Frick suggested that the term has become diluted in the maker community, noting, "I'll read about 'hacking your hair scarf' to tie it different way . . . no—it's still a scarf and you didn't hack it. That's not what hacking is. That's the opposite of what it is. Taking things and using them in a new way is what I consider [hacking] . . . We made musical instruments with [cigar boxes], and that was a way of hacking the cigar boxes." Yet despite these disagreements, the idea of hacking has developed beyond that of "enthusiastic computer programming" to using a systemic and creative approach to reworking or remixing an idea, object, or system to meet a need.[18] Considering that the current social contexts of the general public (such as digital communication, the ability to make and share creations with broad audiences, and easy access to a plethora of information) are now quite similar to the contexts in which the hacker culture evolved, it makes sense that this concept and the general ethos has been adopted in broader society.

The general public's accessibility to F/OSS and social media has had a particular impact on social movements and grassroots organizing. Manuel Castells noted that the most recent large-scale social movements (Tunisia, Iceland, Egypt/Arab Spring, Spain, Occupy Wall Street) have been what he calls "networked social movements" that use F/OSS as "technologies of resistance" and transmedia organizing across multiple social media platforms to connect with others.[19] He contends that these movements have been influenced strongly by digital culture and the hacker ethos: "The technology of the Internet embodies the culture of freedom, as shown in the historical record of its development. It was deliberately designed by scientists and hackers as a decentered, computer communication network to withstand control from any command center."[20]

While the hacker ethos has met a broader audience and definition, it has also changed the ways in which people organize for change. In some cases, the adoption of the hacker ethos and digital culture is intentional, and in others, the ubiquity of the technology drives the shift toward these ideals. For example, the Badass Teachers Association (BATs) used social media technologies to rewrite (hack) narratives around teaching and testing in the media, using many of the same ideas and principles guiding computer hackers, yet did not realize it had done so until after reflecting on its work. Two BATs organizers noted, "Unconsciously, and through no direct strategy implementation, the members of this grassroots movement utilized the tools of media convergence and smart mob theory to communicate their message and enact change."[21]

For teachers with a social justice orientation, the hacker ethos can serve as an empowering framework and disposition for working to innovate or solve problems in their practice and larger systemic issues with other educators. Further, hacking, as understood from the broad interpretation of the word, can be a transformative act that enables teachers to rethink curricula in new ways, revamp spaces and resources for students to make them relevant to their needs, rewrite negative and culturally derogatory media narratives about students and teachers, and reform inequitable institutions and systems through a grassroots approach to organizing change.

The Hacker Ethos and Transformative Teaching

Drawing from the literature on hacker ethos and practices as well as the research I have conducted on transformative teachers, I identified five core characteristics of the hacker ethos in transformative teachers' organizing work:

1. *Collective work.* Teachers' work is not solo; they work with a network or community of practice to hack systems.
2. *Open and public engagement.* Teachers share their work in public forums and invite others to participate in the work.
3. *Intentional, systematic approach.* Teachers are attentive to the underlying systems and structures in which social power operates and look for openings, vulnerabilities, and possibilities of change in the systems.
4. *Producer orientation.* Teachers see themselves as makers and builders rather than simply receivers and consumers. Teachers engage in remixing, rewriting, and rethinking systems.
5. *Use of specific agentive tools.* An agentive tool is a cultural practice (way of speaking, process, ritual, etc.) that enables agency for a group or an individual in the group. In this case, transformative teachers develop specific agentive tools, such as forums or protocols for collaborative public work that support their ability to work collaborative and make change.

In this chapter, I use these characteristics as the basis for a protocol to describe how transformative teachers adopt many aspects of the hacker ethos to organize for change. Hacking is about making changes in or to a system, and any system—from computer code to language—can conceivably be hacked. Social systems, such as political systems and discourses, are constructed via relationships of social power. Thus, to hack a social system, one must have a critical understanding of how power operates in that system and between people or groups. Here I provide examples of how transformative teachers hack three kinds of systems that are rooted in social interactions: discourses, physical spaces or tools, and institutional and political systems. In all cases, I focus on hacking that serves to change systems in ways that empower those who have been marginalized, give voice to those who are not being heard, and bring resources to those who are under-resourced.

Organizing to Hack Marginalizing Discourses

I draw from work by scholars of New Literacy Studies, multiliteracies, and critical literacy on relationships between literacy, language, and power to define the concept of "discourse."[22] In particular, James Gee's definition of discourse, which offers an expansive perspective on the concept of literacy and highlights relationships between language, social structures, and power, forms the basis of this framework. Gee has defined discourse in the following manner: "[As] ways of behaving, interacting, valuing, thinking, believing, speaking, and often reading and writing that are accepted as instantiations of particular roles by specific groups of people . . . [discourses] are thus always and everywhere social and products of social histories.[23] Elsewhere, Gee has pointed out that some discourses come to be taken as "normal" and others as "marginal."[24]

Thus, my examination of "discourse" here rests on the idea that certain discourses and the narratives or stories circulating within them tend to be privileged in our society as more legitimate or valuable than other stories. For example, the oft-told story of Christopher Columbus coming to the Americas often privileges the European point of view and marginalizes the indigenous stories and perspectives, which has led to a greater value placed on Columbus's story and worth (e.g., Columbus Day), than those of indigenous people. Narratives shape what people believe to be true and right, and guide their life trajectories.[25] When a person or group introduces a counternarrative to a discourse, they are seeking the power to reshape how we think and behave. A discourse hack rewrites and disrupts marginalizing narratives within discourses. Going back to the Columbus example, recent efforts by a coalition of indigenous people of America to rename Columbus Day as "Indigenous People's Day" and teach their story in school curricula are examples of efforts to hack the original marginalizing discourse. Narratives range from being "grand narratives" (stories or ideas that a society ascribes to, like the Columbus example) to narratives that flow through smaller communities, from cities and towns to classrooms and families.[26] All narratives are inscribed through discourses, which are complex social systems of communication.

To hack a discourse, one must have a critical understanding of the cultural and linguistic codes that shape the discourse and use agentive cultural tools that provide access and opportunity to rewrite narratives.[27] The indigenous people who worked to hack the Columbus narrative recognized that celebration was a key mode in which the Euro-centric views of American history proliferated, so they hosted parades to celebrate indigenous people. They used the parades as an agentive tool; through celebrating the holiday together in a public space, they both mobilized their community and amplified their message to change the discourse.

For teachers, this approach is related to the "transformed practice" approach to multiliteracies pedagogy described by the New Literacies Group in which teachers help students to apply their critical understanding of discourse to produce alternative narratives.[28] In a classroom, this could be students critiquing a classic text for the ways that it marginalizes or misrepresents a social identity and rewriting the text to be more inclusive. One teacher I observed in the course of my research facilitated a critical conversation about the story of Cinderella in how it positioned girls to depend on men to be happy and rewrote it with her students to make the main character more independent.[29]

However, I suggest that the hacker ethos offers two other aspects beyond that of the transformed practice approach that lend to the transformation of discourses in a networked era. The first is the collaborative nature of the hacker ethos: an underlying assumption is that hacking cannot occur alone, and that all must contribute their knowledge and skill toward the end goal. This collaborative aspect helps to address the issue raised by Allan Luke and others: that to develop a critical understanding of discourse, one must be exposed to a diversity of cultures, discourses, and narratives (akin to the idea that a fish does not know that it is wet until it arrives on dry land).[30] The second aspect is a community's development of an agentive tool to enable collective work and building—in this case, building means constructing greater social equity through voice and representation in discourse about education. Thus, to truly hack the marginalizing narratives about women's roles in Cinderella, the teacher would develop a tool, process, or space that would help students to critique, reimagine, and rewrite the story of Cinderella and share this exercise or tool publicly as a way to invite and organize other teachers and students to join in building more empowering ways to characterize females in children's books.

HACKING MARGINALIZING DISCOURSES AT THE NATIONAL LEVEL

Grand or metanarratives occur at the national or international level. In his book *Networks of Outrage and Hope*, Manuel Castells conducted an analysis of how power operates in networks to spread a narrative. He argues that mainstream narratives are generally driven by a small group of powerful corporations and political groups, yet can be hacked by organizations of marginalized peoples when they share their messages on a mass scale:

> By engaging in the production of mass media messages, and by developing autonomous networks of horizontal communication, citizens of the Information Age become able to invent new programs for their lives with the materials of their suffering, fears, dreams, and hopes. They build their projects by sharing their experience. *They subvert the practice of communication as usual by occupying the medium and creating the message.* [emphasis added] They overcome the powerlessness of their solitary despair by networking their desire. They fight the powers that be by identifying the networks that are.[31]

This type of organizing is what Sasha Constanza-Chock calls transmedia organizing, in which organizers are involved in "the creation of a narrative of social transformation across multiple media platforms, involving the movement's base in participatory media making, and linking attention directly to concrete opportunities for action."[32] Transmedia organizing, then, is an agentive tool that can be used to hack mainstream narratives about education and schooling. A good example of this national-level discourse hack can be seen in the story of the #EduColor movement, which uses Twitter as a medium to hack into existing narratives about race and education and provide an alternative discourse (see José Vilson's profile in chapter 3). Table 6.1 shows how hacker ethos characteristics are reflected in the #EduColor movement.

TABLE 6.1 Hacker ethos characteristics of #EduColor practices

HACKER ETHOS CHARACTERISTICS	#EDUCOLOR PRACTICE
Collective work	#EduColor community members work to introduce new discourse around race and education.
Open and public engagement	Use of Twitter as a primary medium. Also use of websites and blogs.
Intentional, systematic approach	Specific work to reshape discourse on race.
Producer orientation	Building a new discourse
Use of agentive tools	Hashtag Community (#EduColor hashtag)

HACKING MARGINALIZING DISCOURSES AT THE DISTRICT AND SCHOOL LEVELS

Narratives and stories come in all sizes. In a school or district, narratives exist about topics such as the characteristics of student populations, how particular students learn, and the best approaches for teaching them. In a hierarchical structure such as a school, these narratives are given legitimacy and power by administrators and are echoed through networks of communication from teacher to students.[33] For example, in a school that uses academic tracking, there may be an enduring narrative that students in the lowest track do not have valuable knowledge. This narrative is implicit in the policy and ideologies of administrators who measure student knowledge in a limited way, and the story that students in the lowest track lack knowledge emerges and persists through the networks of teachers, students, and school staff. To hack such a narrative, a collection of individuals must develop agentive tools that disrupt the network of communication and introduce an alternative network and narrative.

In practice, this kind of hack appears in various forms. It may appear as a critical friends group of teachers meeting to examine or change their practice, or an effort by teachers and school leaders to put student voices at the forefront of the school by creating opportunities for students to take leadership roles or share their opinions. What is key in these practices is that organizers work together to develop tools and strategies that convert old communication structures which give power and voice to a few people into a different communication structure that facilitates the generation of stories and narratives by individuals who had previously been silenced. Further, they introduce new messages or narratives through this system that reshape discourses about teaching, learning, and identity. Anissa Weinraub (profiled in chapter 3) engaged in this type of discourse hack when she worked with a teacher network and school community to teach anti-xenophobia to youth. She and her colleagues developed a forum for Muslim students in her school community to share their personal stories of marginalization and exclusion and generate a dialogue on Islamophobia.[34] The event was widely publicized on social media and led to several news items about the students' stories. (See table 6.2.)

HACKING MARGINALIZING DISCOURSES AT THE CLASSROOM LEVEL

At this level, narratives develop about student behavior and identity, such as who is smart, cool, or problematic. These narratives emerge from the teacher as the authority, the curriculum, and the student community. A teacher can help to "flip the script" in his or her classroom by changing the ways in which students are able to share their stories, how they listen to each other, and how they interpret the messages that the curriculum sends to them about who they are and their role in the world. On the whole, a classroom-level hack of discourse is a praxis (pedagogy/action) hack. A teacher must consider curriculum,

TABLE 6.2 Hacker ethos characteristics of anti-xenophobia forum

HACKER ETHOS CHARACTERISTICS	ANTI-XENOPHOBIA FORUM
Collective work	School community and teacher networks work to introduce new narratives about Muslim youth
Open and public engagement	Use of public space and social media to showcase storytelling
Intentional, systematic approach	Specific work to reshape discourse on Muslim youth
Producer orientation	Providing new narratives
Use of agentive tools	Public storytelling forum

pedagogy, and social dynamics in a classroom, all of which contribute to narratives that can drive stereotypes or assumptions

A curriculum hack is not a "fix" but, rather, an uncovering and transformation of the narrative of schooling. In their essay on hacking and education, Tyson Lewis and Daniel Friedrich described this difference:

> To tinker with education and hack the curriculum are therefore not clarion calls to actualize the potentiality of tinkering for instrumental ends (to be a better teacher) or to territorialize the virtual dimensions of the curriculum (in order to revolutionize curriculum standards). Instead, what it means is to be sensitive of those moments when the law of the school is suspended, when the good sense of the law of learning is left idle. It is in such moments that a new kind of freedom can be sensed, a new kind of education explored, a new common manifest, which belongs to no one and resists all forms of regulation and assessment beyond its own appearance.[35]

Thus, to hack a curriculum, one must understand curriculum to be a part of the larger discourse on education, and the hack is a creative, curious de/reconstruction of the narratives that drive this discourse via a rethinking of the curriculum. For example, Jenny St. Romain, a high school English teacher, hacked her English curriculum with her co-teacher Cindy O'Donnell-Allen to include a variety of texts to support students' reading of *Hamlet*.[36] Traditionally, *Hamlet* was taught on its own, perhaps with a showing of a *Hamlet* movie or attendance to the play. St. Romain and O'Donnell-Allen used a unit-planning strategy by Sarah Brown Wessling and colleagues to hack the *Hamlet* curriculum.[37] They began with the question: what do students need, emotionally and intellectually, as learners? Then they identified three kinds of text to understand a primary theme in *Hamlet* (resiliency): a fulcrum text (*Hamlet*), context texts (which provided a broader context for the story), and texture texts (texts—many modern—that attended to the theme of resiliency). The teachers later wrote about their work online and in a published book.[38]

Another example is the curriculum hackathon in 2013 facilitated by Sarabeth Berk and Jim Stephens, faculty at the University of Denver School of Education. They described the curriculum hackathon event: "[A] time and space for educators, students and experts to collaboratively deconstruct and redesign innovative learning experiences. The intended outcome is new models of courses and curriculum developed collaboratively by teams of educators, students, and experts."[39]

They used a design thinking approach, which is a cycle of five practices: discovery (gathering data), interpretation, ideation (generating solutions), experimentation (generating prototypes), and evolution (reflect and revise). Their curriculum hacking was informed by KnowledgeWorks Foundation's analysis of the developing characteristics of learning in the twenty-first century, Knowledge 2020.[40] Based on their experience with the hackathon, Berk and Stephens produced a handbook for curriculum hacking that they made available on the web. (See table 6.3.)

Organizing to Hack Inadequate Physical Resources

A physical hack is in some ways synonymous with DIY and MakerEd; hackers seek to understand the basic mechanisms by which an object works in order to tinker, adapt, and transform it, and share their work with others. In this case, a physical hack involves innovating on or building tools to meet specific needs. A subtler thread that exists in the work of physical hacking is that physical objects and space represent capital; when teachers hack an object or space, they are finding new and alternative ways to cultivate social, cultural, or financial capital for their classrooms and schools. At the national

TABLE 6.3 Hacker ethos characteristics of a curriculum hack

HACKER ETHOS CHARACTERISTICS	CURRICULUM HACK
Collective work	Collaborative approach to hacking curriculum
Open and public engagement	Published practices and guides
Intentional, systematic approach	Systematic examination of intentions and purposes of curriculum
Producer orientation	Redesign of curriculum
Use of agentive tools	Maker/studio design process

level, teachers generally need to use connected technologies to share and re-mix their physical hacks, and they generate resources and new ideas through the medium of online platforms. At the local level, there are more face-to-face interactions between teachers to share their tools, hacks, and ideas, producing local resources and tools that support more equity in educational contexts.

HACKING INADEQUATE RESOURCES AT THE NATIONAL LEVEL

At this level, digital spaces and forums can facilitate exchange and connections between teachers in designing resources for their classrooms. Mia Zamora and colleagues studied the outcomes of one such space, the Making Learning Connected MOOC (Massive Open Online Course) or #CLMOOC, a partic-ipant-driven MOOC for teachers that ran for three summers between 2012 and 2015. In her research, she found that when the ethos of remixing, hack-ing, and sharing physical and digital creations was encouraged in this space, it generated a sense of ownership, agency, and democratic participation. (See table 6.4.) Digital spaces that support a collective, production-oriented ap-proach to sharing and hacking physical makes (for example, common house-hold items repurposed as instructional tools) can provide not only ideas for physical resources but also a sense of belonging and enthusiasm.

TABLE 6.4 #Hacker ethos characteristics of CLMOOC practices

HACKER ETHOS CHARACTERISTICS	#CLMOOC
Collective work	#CLMOOC community members work to intro-duce, share, and build on hacks and makes.
Open and public engagement	Use of Twitter as a primary medium. Also use of websites and blogs.
Intentional, systematic approach	Specific work to rethink writing and making in net-worked era.
Producer orientation	Sharing makes and hacks.
Use of agentive tools	Online participatory space/network.

HACKING INADEQUATE RESOURCES AT THE DISTRICT
AND SCHOOL LEVELS

At these levels, teachers can work together to create or develop resources to meet the needs of their students. These actions are especially important for high-need and under-resourced school districts in which teachers often lack access to resources and materials for their job. Often district- and school-level hacks can mirror the processes and practices of a hackathon, where participants join together to collaborate and/or compete toward creating or improving an app. In the educational context, teachers problem solve (hack) to develop context-specific resources to teach.[41]

One example of this kind of collaboration can be witnessed once a month at PhilaSoup gatherings, in which teachers across Philadelphia pitch proposals for classroom resources and projects. All attendees pay a small entry fee and vote on the best pitch of the night. The winner gets the funds from the entry fee. All participants get a great meal, a chance to network with each other, and most importantly, some new ideas for their classroom. At Hive Chicago, another form of district-level physical hacking occurs. This group brings together a diverse array of educators (from K–12 to museum educators and youth program leaders) to support students in using technology to arrive at creative solutions for social issues. For example, several students developed a ride-sharing app that helped them travel to educational programs and events throughout the city. (See table 6.5.) Of course, the hackathon model

TABLE 6.5 Hacker ethos characteristics of hive practices

HACKER ETHOS CHARACTERISTICS	HIVE CHICAGO HACK DAY
Collective work	Collective work to address members' needs.
Open and public engagement	Use of social media, GIS, and other technologies to communicate and share information openly.
Intentional, systematic approach	Specific work to build new solutions for members. Based on hackathon principles.
Producer orientation	Building new apps, programs, and practices.
Use of agentive tools	Hackathon process.

is not limited to hacking physical resources and space; later, in chapter 9, I describe the EdCamp (unconference) model of teacher professional development, which also borrows heavily from the hackathon model.

HACKING INADEQUATE RESOURCES
AT THE CLASSROOM LEVEL

At this level, the focus is on how to adapt tools and space to meet students' needs. Since I addressed making and tools in chapter 4, here I focus primarily on hacking physical spaces. A space and the tools in it shape and reflect how people are valued and how they interact with one another. To hack a space for students, one must be aware of the ways in which the physical environment shapes participation and access. David Kelly, founder of IDEO and Stanford University's Hasso Plattner Institute of Design, known as d.school, talks about the idea of creating "we" spaces versus "I" spaces in his introduction to *Make Space: How to Set the Stage for Creative Collaboration*.[42] He writes, "Reconfiguring the physical relationship [between people] is a powerful signal that participation is truly welcome. The result is that you get better ideas out in the open where they can grow . . . The people using it should be able to transform it themselves, move things around, and create what they need for the work they're doing at the moment."[43]

Likewise, Garcia and O'Donnell-Allen suggest that a social justice–oriented teacher must also pose as a "designer" of equitable learning environments.[44] They argue that teachers should codesign learning environments with their students and "improvise subversively when schooling conditions shunt you and your students to spaces that would limit learning and diminish morale"; in other words, hack their classroom spaces when necessary.[45] For example, Kathleen Melville (profiled in chapter 3) had her students redesign the classroom space to make it more inviting and accessible. (See table 6.6.) Another example is present in the description of the Hacktory, which youth programs coordinator Allison Frick (also profiled in chapter 3) explains as a kind of "feminist" space that is intentionally designed to be accessible to people of all shapes and sizes.

TABLE 6.6 Hacker ethos characteristics of Melville's classroom space redesign

HACKER ETHOS CHARACTERISTICS	MELVILLE'S CLASSROOM SPACE REDESIGN
Collective work	Students worked collaboratively to redesign space.
Open and public engagement	Use of blogs to share news and get feedback on work.
Intentional, systematic approach	Specific work to address social justice issues embedded in space arrangement. Meeting students' needs through changing structures creatively, aesthetically, and practically.
Producer orientation	Building a new kind of classroom space.
Use of agentive tools	Studio design process.

Organizing to Hack Inequity in Institutional and Political Systems

Transformative teachers also hack institutional and political systems to expand and improve opportunities for learning amid limiting or marginalizing structures and systems. Below I describe how teachers hack systems to address inequities at three levels: school, district, and national. These complex systems are outwardly hierarchical and top-down, yet are influenced by informal social networks that cut across hierarchies and communities. Hacking systems to foster greater equity and capability therefore requires the use of agentive tools and strategies that attend to formal and informal social codes. Here I describe examples of teachers who work to change both formal and informal social structures.

HACKING INEQUITY IN NATIONAL-LEVEL SYSTEMS

At the national level, several movements have used hacker-like practices to challenge institutional and political systems. One group already mentioned is BATs, which has worked primarily to question and challenge the move to tie high-stakes tests to the Common Core curriculum standards. This group, which has a membership of more than fifty-two thousand, uses the power of its collective numbers to ferret out, collect, curate, and share information and facts for the public regarding its cause.[46] One agentive tool that the group has used to hack the political messaging and organization is the "ethical spectacle."[47] In this approach, members use popular culture for the purposes of furthering their agenda. They create digital images and videos that are similar to political cartoons to emphasize a point. For example, they might use a well-known meme picture of an individual looking confused and write an ironic message into the image that addresses their frustration or disappointment at a policy maker's decision, thus using the spectacle of the meme to raise ethical issues. Another popular agentive tool is the "swarm tactic," in which rotating calls for specific, uncomplicated, and local actions are posted on social media outlets to invite members to participate.[48] (See table 6.7.) The group prides itself on the ways in which members' actions have served to shift the debate and focus on teachers in education: "Prior to our founding, teachers' voices had essentially been silenced and marginalized by corporate reformers who routinely characterized them as responsible for all of our social and economic shortcomings. Joining forces with the Badass Teachers Association has given thousands of teachers across the country a place to realize they are not alone."[49]

This group exemplifies many aspects of what Castells calls "networked social movements," such as a focus on transmedia organizing, on networking online and off-line, on being self-reflective, and on changing social values,

TABLE 6.7 Hacker ethos characteristics of BATs practices

HACKER ETHOS CHARACTERISTICS	BADASS TEACHERS NETWORK (BATS)
Collective work	BATs community members work to include more teachers in decision making regarding education policy.
Open and public engagement	Use of Twitter as a primary medium. Also use of websites and blogs.
Intentional, systematic approach	Focused and organized to address specific policy issues.
Producer orientation	Building new roles for teachers in policy-making.
Use of agentive tools	• Transmedia organizing • Ethical spectacles • Swarm tactics

horizontal leadership (at the local level, in this case), and viral messaging or communication (see also Wolfson and Costanza-Chock for new structures of movement leadership in the digital age).[50] The characteristics and practices of the group, and networked movements in general, share a striking resemblance to the characteristics of the original computer hackers. This may be due in part to the use of connected technologies and, in particular, to the use of F/OSS as technologies of resistance, which Kate Milberry argues are "intended to support grassroots struggle online, remaking the internet as a more democratic and humane communication medium in the process."[51] While much of the work that this group and other networked movements engage in is similar to hacking discourses, groups that work to change policy and political structures go beyond narratives to hacking formal social structures.

HACKING INEQUITY IN DISTRICT-LEVEL SYSTEMS

Such organizing work also occurs on a more local level; a good instance of localized system hacking is the example in the introduction of this chapter of WE disrupting the long-standing leadership structures of the union. (See table 6.8.) However, while WE's work was overtly political, many examples of educators and educational allies organizing to hack dysfunctional districts by becoming involved in grassroots professional networks address systemic

TABLE 6.8 Hacker ethos characteristics of Caucus of Working Educators' practices

HACKER ETHOS CHARACTERISTICS	CAUCUS OF WORKING EDUCATORS
Collective work	Works to reshape and influence teacher union and practices
Open and public engagement	Website, Twitter, engagement with media, frequent use of social media
Intentional, systematic approach	Targeted actions and campaigns
Producer orientation	Building a new union
Use of agentive tools	• Listening campaigns • Inquiry groups • Community book clubs

issues through offering alternative models and approaches to school structures. One example is the development of the Harvest Collegiate High School in New York City, a teacher-led and designed school that originated in a summer teacher leadership institute. The group met over several summers and together to design the school, which incorporated structures that supported teacher leadership (see the profile on John McCrann in chapter 3). In the examples of WE and Harvest Collegiate, members openly and collectively uncovered dynamics of power and communication in the current systems, and introduced an alternative to the system in order to increase capacities for equity and voice.

HACKING INEQUITY IN SCHOOL-LEVEL SYSTEMS

Finally, at the school level, teachers can hack the policies and practices that are dysfunctional and disempowering to students in their schools. Antero Garcia and Cindy O'Donnell-Allen suggest that when a teacher embodies the stance of a hacker, he or she inherently disavows the "banking model" of education, "critically reading one's teaching context and pushing back against systemic constraints that might limit students' learning."[52] To do so takes careful maneuvering and awareness of the micro-political structures of power in the school.[53] Teachers alone rarely have the political power to change policy; they must work together to create a collective agency and develop agentive tools for change. To illustrate these concepts in action, I mention a two-year ethnographic study Leif Gustavson and I conducted of teachers who took part in a critical friends group (the Cavanaugh-Astin Teachers Collaboration, or CATC) that transformed the ways in which students were taught in their school. The group developed a unique agentive tool—"asking permission"—that allowed them to transgress an ultra-standardized, high-stakes testing environment in their school to provide space for individual inquiry and expression for their students.[54] (See table 6.9.)

Organizing with a Hacker Ethos

I have provided examples of how the hacker ethos has evolved as a broad term for collective, systematic problem solving and can be used to understand the organizing practices of transformative teachers. Not every transformative

TABLE 6.9 Hacker ethos characteristics of CATC practices

HACKER ETHOS CHARACTERISTICS	CATC PRACTICES
Collective work	Group works to rewrite curriculum and school policies.
Open and public engagement	Invited teachers, student teachers, university faculty, and administration to participate.
Intentional, systematic approach	Strategic work around locating support for curriculum and policy changes.
Producer orientation	Building a new curriculum and school policy.
Use of agentive tools	• Strategic permissive moves • Inquiry group

teacher will explicitly describe his or her organizing approach as having a "hacker ethos." Yet, whether the approach is referred to by the exact term I use here or by a different term, clear patterns of organizing for change connect to or reflect this ethos, which is captured in many aspects of the foundational roots of transformative teaching. The public, open, and collective nature of hacking is part of participatory culture—in fact, one could argue it is the basis for participatory culture. Hacking is also grounded in exploring possibility, tinkering, and progressive experimenting, all elements of inquiry practice. Furthermore, the agentive tools reflect many of the signals of transformative teacher movements and networks that were highlighted at the end of chapter 2, including new models of professional development, transmedia and networked organizing, and the creation of spaces and networks for participation in shared making and storytelling. Finally, and most important to address, are the links between the hacker ethos and organizing for social justice. The early hackers knew that the skill set of hacking is corruptible without a guiding moral ethic to do good in the world. This is perhaps why so many hacker manifestos exist: to reaffirm that hacking is work that benefits the social good and is not an activity that profits the actor at the expensive of the community. The focus on social justice and organizing for equity in education is what drives transformative teachers' work, and the hacker ethos offers a means to understand how we transgress against oppression, marginalization, and dehumanizing systems.

Reflecting on the work of transformative teacher hacking, I am deeply aware of both the enduring challenges and the joys of the work. Hacking, even its original form, is a balance of frustration and exhilaration. Gabriella Coleman wrote, "Hacking is characterized by a confluence of constant occupational disappointments and personal/collective joys."[55] Teaching itself, even without the aspect of hacking, can seem like this. However, transformative hacking requires not only a critical understanding of the social contexts in which one works, but also an intense courage and commitment to social justice that will aid one to work through trying times. I am also reminded of bell hooks' closing statements in *Teaching to Transgress*: "The classroom, with all its limitations, remains a location of possibility. In that field of possibility we have the opportunity to labor for freedom, to demand of ourselves and our comrades an openness of mind and heart that allows us to face reality even as we collectively imagine ways to move beyond boundaries, to transgress. This is education as the practice of freedom."[56]

Just as the original hackers saw their work as rooted in a freedom to learn and explore, the work of hacking by transformative teachers is similarly rooted.

Voices from the Field: Hacking and/in Education

Below are two profiles of lead voices in the hacker ethos of technology and education. These profiles help put some of the concepts discussed in this chapter into a larger context and conversation about technology and society.

Audrey Watters: Hacking Education

Audrey Watters is a journalist, writer, and public speaker on issues of education technology, particularly about the ways in which technologies mediate our learning and social interaction. She is the host of a popular blog, *Hack Education* (hackeducation.com), and the author of several books, including *The Monsters of Education Technology*, *Revenge of the Monsters of Education Technology*, and *Claim*

Your Domain (And Your Online Presence). Watters is known for her critical stance in examining both the potential of new technologies for promoting democratic discourse and participation and the dangers of the same technologies in becoming corporate tools for surveillance and profit making. Her nuanced and in-depth knowledge of these issues reveals the complex role that technology increasingly plays in our lives, and the ways in which individuals can develop greater agency over these tools. She uses the lens of hacking to interrogate and problem solve around these issues.

I asked Watters to explain more about her knowledge of the history of the term "hacking" and the ways in which it can serve as a critical or problem-solving lens. Watters noted that the term had many meanings, which was one reason she liked it so much. She explained that while the term has been associated with hacker culture for some time, she sees it has having more power as a lens to analyze systemic, societal issues:

> I'm really fascinated by the way in which the word contains so much. I think it has been appropriated to talk about the ways in which technology is going to infiltrate and disrupt institution-like education . . . For me it's the question of how do we . . . look, take apart, and analyze and interpret? I'm really interested in scrutinizing these systems and being able to take them apart and look at the pieces of them and understand why the world works the way it does. Then we can do a better job perhaps of addressing some of these systemic issues, and not with an app.

We also discussed the history of technology in education and grassroots organizing. According to Watters, progressive educators' use of computers has a long history, beginning in the 1970s with Seymour Papert's introduction of the constructionist concept, in which he encouraged teachers to help children learn how computers worked by taking them apart and creating code. However, more recent moves by school and district administrators to consolidate and standardize control over technology use in schools has led to rising tensions about the purposes and uses of technology in teaching. Watters elaborated on this point:

> [A]dding a network to these individual computers actually moved the control to the district office and moved the control out of the hands of academic purposes and really made the computers more about these administrative tools that someone else was in charge of using . . .
>
> [A]t the same time many of these early advocates for technology really had to make arguments again and again about why computers were going to be transformative.

In some ways, a lot of those folks are still doing what they need to do to advocate for technology in general, and not . . . what we want to be advocating for—those progressive educational opportunities that computers can enhance. Not just simply technology.

Watters contends that we often have "historical amnesia" about technology, leading us to forget the history of the development and original purposes of technologies; she believes we need to do a better job at developing a critical understanding of the history of technology in education.

There is also a tension in the use of connected technologies and social media for education organizing that requires more critical examination, says Watters. In looking at grassroots organizing today, we see teachers using these technologies as a means to connect, but at times they use them without a critical understanding of the spaces and tools. Watters cited Twitter as an example, stating that it has been a powerful tool for grassroots organizing that allowed disparate groups to come together from afar. Watters mentioned #EduColor as a group that has found success in generating diverse connections through Twitter, noting:

It has the ability to put up a Bat[man] Signal and have a lot of people respond on issues that in the past probably wouldn't have even made it out there . . . It would have been a small blurb in the local paper but they wouldn't have been able to get more eyes and more conversations around these issues . . . To be able to document [racist practices] and to have this potential for virality around it does change the conversation from just a little blip on the evening news.

She also acknowledges two dangers of the tool: Twitter is a private company (as are many social media platforms), which owns all the data and can use that data in the ways it prefers; Twitter posts are public, which makes all participants vulnerable to attack or even to being fired by their schools.

Both of these issues are major challenges that any publicly engaged educator faces. I asked Watters her advice for how to address them. On private company ownership, Watters suggested teachers first develop a strong critical understanding (or "hacker literacy") of the tools they use and that they seek out open-source and personal domain spaces which are not owned by large companies, such as ReclaimHosting, an open-source hosting site developed by her colleagues Jim Groom and Tim Owens. On the issue of vulnerability, Watters acknowledged that anyone who takes a leadership role for social justice in a public space has to stand in the face of fear at times; this is an issue for all activists. Yet she also notes that there is strength in numbers; when groups like #EduColor come together, it creates a safer community to speak up and transform discourses.

Antero Garcia: The Teacher-as-Hacker Pose

Antero Garcia is an assistant professor of education. He researches literacies and connected learning with an eye toward critical participatory practices in youth participatory action research (YPAR) and game-based curriculum design. Before moving to higher education, Garcia was a high school teacher in South Central Los Angeles. His praxis is rooted in progressive education and social justice pedagogy, which he credits to his teacher education program at UCLA.

Garcia and his colleague Cindy O'Donnell-Allen are coauthors of *Pose, Wobble, Flow: A Culturally Proactive Approach to Literacy Instruction*. Garcia and O'Donnell-Allen dedicate a chapter to the "pose" of "Teacher-as-Hacker," arguing that "thinking of yourself as a hacker . . . can help you claim and retain a sense of agency . . . [and] can keep you from seeing yourself and your students as no more than cogs in a system beyond your control."[57]

Garcia told me about the ways in which teachers who adopt a "hacker pose" incorporate connected technologies into their practice and how it shapes their work. He noted that these teachers remix text and images and share them on the open web, which provides them and their students a larger audience to "interrogate issues of race, power, gender, sexuality." Garcia pointed out that teachers who engage in this practice and the hacker stance must be willing to model vulnerability and mindful engagement in connecting with others, whether in person or online:

> We need to recognize that to be our whole self means part of our identity is in these online spaces and part of it is in these off-line spaces, and we need to educate young people and teachers mediating both of these and recognizing that we need to be present wholly in whatever we bring.
>
> That means bringing our vulnerability . . . We need to allow teachers to feel vulnerable in their class, as well as students to feel vulnerable, and to be a thriving and loving community, it means being able to hold each other up, being able to do those kind of check-ins, *"How are you doing? What's happening?"*

Without engaging in a pedagogical stance that embraces vulnerability and community support, teachers may be apprehensive about using the web as a platform for sharing because they fear that others will steal their ideas.

Garcia is now working with a research team at University of Colorado, Boulder, and self-professed teacher-hacker Bud Hunt on a study of project-based learning and socio-emotional learning called Compose Our World (http://ComposeOur World.org). He is also examining how young people engage in tabletop role-play games. You can learn more about his work through his blog, *The American Crawl* (http://TheAmericanCrawl.com).

SEVEN

Leading by Connecting

To live with courage, purpose, and connection—to be the person whom we long to be—we must again be vulnerable. We must . . . show up, and let ourselves be seen.

—Brené Brown, *Daring Greatly*[1]

TRANSFORMATIVE TEACHERS ARE LEADERS who work in the public eye. At a time when teachers are carefully scrutinized for test scores, choice of curriculum, and pedagogical approaches, why do transformative teachers engage in public "knowledge work"?[2] Why do so when protecting one's privacy and going it alone is a historically ingrained aspect of teaching culture? Perhaps most importantly, *what* sustains them? This chapter addresses these questions and presents important insights about the relationship between teacher leadership and connecting, examining the ways in which various forms of connecting enable teachers not only to navigate the bumpy terrain of this connected world, but to be sustained through the public spaces and networks in which they work.

I use the term "connecting" with a particular understanding of the word in a networked era. In this case, I use it to mean the pursuit of greater *authentic human connection* through mindful and strategic relationship building and outreach. Ironically, in an era in which everyone is easily linked to others through technology, building authentic human connections can be more difficult. Carrie James, author of *Disconnected*, identified eight characteristics of connectedness in the networked era that are new "social facts": scalability, persistence, replicability, searchability, anonymity, constant connectivity, asynchronous connectivity, and text-dominance.[3] In her book, *Alone Together*, Sherry Turkle describes how these kinds of characteristics have enabled individuals to carefully craft personas that are very different from their real-life identities, which makes it difficult to connect with others in fulfilling and meaningful ways.[4] Such inauthentic connections serve to further isolate people rather than bring them closer to others.

Connecting in a networked era requires what Howard Rheingold has called "digital mindfulness," which, he argues, is exercised through the development of five key "literacies": an awareness of network dynamics, "attentional discipline" (the ability to focus), critical "crap detection" (the ability to critically interrogate ideas and information), net savviness (similar to Santo's "hacker literacy"), and collaborative know-how.[5] Ultimately, Rheingold urges us to be authentic and deliberate in the ways in which we learn and collaborate with others. While Rheingold's approach is especially useful for navigating the digital domain, it is also useful for face-to-face collaboration and communication. In the following sections of this chapter, I provide stories, examples, and concepts to help readers become more critically conscious and authentic connectors in this networked society. Further, I answer some of the key questions posed earlier by examining the reasons and ways in which transformative teachers engage in connecting.

Connect to Lead:
The Fourth Wave of Teacher Leadership

Why do transformative teachers connect? Transformative teachers are the teacher leaders of the networked era. They work to elevate their profession through fostering meaningful connections and change within and beyond the walls of their school communities. Key to their efforts as leaders is their ability to connect across boundaries and communities. Leadership and connecting are almost synonymous for transformative teachers because their leadership is defined by relationship building. I begin the exploration of connecting with a brief history of teacher leadership.

Until recently, the idea of leadership was not readily associated with teaching, certainly not in the way I have just described. Many new ideas and concepts have been introduced over the past forty years in terms of professional development, school reform, and even the culture of teaching itself. Yet these new concepts reside alongside older, deep-rooted models of schooling that persist in an educational system that is slow to change at its core.[6] Therefore, it is important to understand both the new models within and the older models, and the tensions that exist between them today.

There is little argument among scholars that there have been several waves of school reform, cultural change, and teacher leadership practices over the past several decades in the United States.[7] In many ways, they are part of a broader societal shift from an industrial model of work to a postindustrialist, networked, knowledge society.[8] The traditional industrial model of US schooling is based on the premise similar to that of Henry Ford's car production model: all parts must be standardized and workers engaged in technical work on a moving production line.[9] For teachers in this model, their role was that of technician; there was no room at all for leadership, and no reason to collaborate and connect.[10]

The first wave of major change was initiated in the late 1980s when industries began to migrate from many Western nations and a focus on scientific knowledge and achievement emerged in policy and practice. Such knowledge could not simply be delivered in standardized packages, and teachers required more training on how to develop future inquirers. Thus, this wave resulted in an increase of top-down policy mandates and training. Some teachers were placed in hierarchical roles not dissimilar to factory managers. While teachers were repositioned as leaders in the hierarchical sense, the industrial framework of the model did not shift very much.

In the 1990s, the second wave of school reform in the United States saw a transition from top-down policy mandates to an emphasis on decentralized school management and increased teacher professionalism.[11] Decentralization required some collaborative work and increased autonomy for teachers to implement reforms based on their school contexts and needs. This wave introduced more hybrid leadership roles for teachers, such as mentors and coaches.[12]

Further, some teachers began to develop their practice in teacher inquiry groups, and some scholars, such as Ann Lieberman, began to identify this as teacher leadership as well.[13] Teacher leadership, though still grounded in hierarchy for the most part, began to shift in this wave to a more relational concept.

In the early 2000s, the third wave of school reform arrived with a more ambitious goal of whole-school transformation involving community partnerships and professional collaboration.[14] Teachers were encouraged to collaborate and develop relationships across their school community. Researchers introduced new conceptions about teacher leadership that revolved around action and relationships, with less emphasis on hierarchical roles. For example, J. P. Spillane and colleagues introduced the idea of *distributed leadership*, which conceptualized a leader as a person who played an active role in a social network to effect change in his or her school community.[15] At the same time, in the United States and elsewhere, standardization was emphasized through increasing focus on high-stakes testing and a scripted curriculum. Teacher leadership stood at a crossroads; while these news ideas about the relational notion of leadership emerged, they were couched within a culture shaped by decades of the industrial model and the ever-present emphasis on teaching to the test.

At this crossroads, notions of teacher leadership seemed to grow into two tracks: relational and hierarchical. Dorothy Andrews and Frank Crowther coined the term *parallel leadership* to describe the ways in which teacher leaders operated in both realms.[16] During this time, research and theorizing around the relational aspect of teacher leadership expanded. Ann Lieberman and Lynne Miller, Desiree Pointer-Mace, and others shared models of teacher leadership that involved out-of-school collaboration and teacher-led professional development.[17] But until the widespread use of social media and Web 2.0, many examples of these actions were limited to academic journal articles, static websites, and books.

In the 2010s, use of connected technologies, such as blogs, Twitter, and Facebook, exploded. Teachers had new forums in which to tell their stories on their own, which provided new and nuanced pictures of teacher leadership. A new wave of leadership was born. In this fourth wave, the buildup of ideas around relational teacher leadership was released in a flood of narratives and stories. Definitions of teacher leadership became even more situated as relational. Further, the global stage of the digital sphere allowed teachers to set their sights on something bigger than just leading in their schools; they could leverage connected technologies to build relationships and share stories beyond the borders of their city, state, or even country.

In addition, the digital sphere celebrated innovative thinking, entrepreneurship, and exchange of ideas, giving rise to notions of teacher leadership that aligned with these shifts, such as the *teacherpreneur*, a concept introduced by Barnett Berry and colleagues at the Center for Teaching Quality (CTQ).[18] The teacherpreneur is a classroom teacher who seeks time and opportunities to take leadership roles and innovate on educational practices. In many cases, teacherpreneurs take "hybrid" roles, spending part of their time in the classroom, and part developing new curricula, practices, and tools for teaching, which they share and collaborate on. Likewise, James Pounder suggested that the fourth wave of teacher leadership could be called *transformational leadership* and observed that, in this definition, teacher leaders were seen as intellectuals open to new ways of doing things, as nurturers of relationships, modelers of professional growth, encouragers of change, and challengers of the status quo.[19]

In the fourth wave of teacher leadership, the focus is on how teachers' connections across boundaries build what Andy Hargreaves and Michael Fullan call "professional capital," a combination of social and human capital that fosters professional growth, support, new ideas, and change.[20] While this concept of teacher leadership continues to develop, it resides in tension with the former, more industrial, hierarchical ideas. When I interviewed transformative teachers about leadership, some were proud to call themselves leaders in the fourth-wave sense, but others were hesitant to identify as leaders in the hierarchical sense. Noga Newberg described this feeling: "[It feels] hierarchical. When I think of a leader, I think of my bosses. That doesn't feel right." On the other hand, Annie Huynh suggested that "when you give teachers a voice, when teachers exercise their voice, that is a form of leadership."

Teacher leadership is a complicated concept. If one were to use the industrial, hierarchical model to define leadership, many transformative teachers would not fit the description. However, their characteristics reflect the fourth-wave conceptualization of teacher leadership; they use connecting to build knowledge and change across boundaries of multiple communities.

Why Collaboration and Connection Works:
Evidence from Research

While connecting may be the basis for fourth-wave teacher leadership, the question remains, what good does connecting do? The role of teachers' collaboration and connection in teaching and learning has been studied from many angles since the second wave of teacher leadership initiated an emphasis on learning communities and mentorship. The majority of research has examined the ways in which teachers' collaboration within a school community shapes their practice. Studies that have examined student learning and achievement at this level have repeatedly found correlations between high levels of teachers' collaboration and students' achievement.[21] However, this evidence is tempered by cautions about the nature of teachers' collaboration; when it is forced or structured in a way that does not value teachers' inquiries and autonomy, it can have negative consequences.[22]

Student learning is important, but another important aspect of teachers' practice is their own sense of self-efficacy, joy, and commitment to their workplace or profession. We know that teachers' satisfaction and self- or collective efficacy have a high correlation with student engagement and achievement.[23] Several studies have shown that teachers develop greater self-efficacy—a sense that they can accomplish their work effectively—when they work in collaborative teams and when the school culture supports collaboration.[24] Turnover is also affected by the degree to which teachers have strong ties in their school community.[25] Finally, when teachers build strong learning communities and collaborative networks, they are more likely to innovate and take risks in trying new approaches.[26]

Other studies have focused on the outcomes of teachers collaborating with others beyond the school community. In my previous research on teacher networks, I found that those who built connections with "diverse professional allies" outside their school community were more apt to innovate in their curriculum and construct student-centered learning experiences.[27] This finding relates to research on teacher leadership. Spillane found that when teachers brought in new ideas and resources from their out-of-school networks, they were perceived as leaders (in the relational sense).[28] Lieberman's extensive research on members of the National Writing Project, a formal network of literacy teachers across the United States, has repeatedly shown how the collaborative work and processes of the network support teacher leadership and innovation.[29]

Connecting enables teachers not only to better support student learning, but also to be brave in their practice, innovate, create, and take the lead in their school communities and beyond. Perhaps most importantly, it helps sustain teachers by fostering collegiality, joy, mentorship, and trust among colleagues. In 2015, I contributed a chapter to an edited book about international research on the quality of teachers. Rather than focus on human capital (quantifiable experience and skills) to conceptualize teacher quality, I focused on social capital or the resources that exist in teachers' social networks.[30] I provided an overview of recent research showing that teachers are not isolated figures in their work, as much as our traditional industry-based culture would like us to believe. Who we know matters just as much as what we know. Teachers' work is, as my colleague Lauren Anderson says, "embedded and emboldened" amid the networks of relationships in which they live and work.[31] Knowing this, transformative teachers make the most of these connections to improve the educational experiences of students in their classrooms, schools, and broader communities.

How Transformative Teachers Connect

Through my research and work with transformative teachers, I have observed three major ways in which they build connections for their work. The first is by going public. Transformative teachers understand that their voices can make a difference in shaping the professional knowledge base of teaching and educational policies. They take on the role of public knowledge workers to improve education. The second is by cultivating connections through participating in and organizing gatherings or opportunities for teachers to build stronger relationships with each other and exchange ideas and experiences.

The third is by curating connections through a critical understanding of how to build networks and relationships and shape social contexts. In the following section, I review these three approaches.

Going Public: Being Public Knowledge Workers

As the United States shifted away from industrial manufacturing in the late 1980s, the "knowledge economy" began to grow. Instead of tangible goods, ideas and specialized ways of knowing (such as how to problem-solve technological systems) became the valued commodity of Westernized economies and societies at large.[32] In this way, the concept of the "knowledge worker," a person who seeks, analyzes, produces, or transforms information and knowledge, emerged. At the same time, how we thought about the job of being a teacher was beginning to change. Teachers straddled and continue to straddle this liminal role of being an industrial-model technician (with decision making about curriculum and pedagogy set by administrators or the state) and being a knowledge-society professional (with the autonomy to make informed decisions about their practice).[33] Similar to the way in which lawyers run the American Bar Association and oversee the bar exams for entry into the profession (and doctors set standards with the American Medical Association), teachers must be able to set the standards for their practice and contribute to the developing knowledge base about the profession to make teaching a fully recognized profession.

In order to elevate teaching to a profession, teachers must be its designers. They must be knowledge workers and do their work in public in order to shape the discourse, systems, and structures. Transformative teachers unite and build the profession primarily through engaging with the public about their practice.

Public engagement is a form of connecting on a broad scale; connected technologies are particularly good at supporting such engagement. Platforms such as blogs, wikis, Facebook groups, and Twitter enable teachers to broadcast their expertise, ideas, and experiences; connect with others; and work together to effect change. José Luis Vilson is a prime example of a teacher who has become a public knowledge worker and has generated powerful connections through his regular blogging about educational issues and his work with #EduColor colleagues to shift discourses around race and education. His public blogging and guest posts or articles in various media publications and, most recently, a book based on his blog posts, *This Is Not a Test*, have generated important discussions and thinking about how teachers and schools can talk about and wrestle with racism and prejudice.[34] Vilson focuses primarily on two things when he makes his work public: making education better and uniting teacher voices. As he noted in our interview, this work is not about talking out loud, but instead about talking *with* and *building* a community of public knowledge workers.

Vilson's work has made an impact on the political level. For example, in 2014, he was invited to a presidential summit on education at the White House to meet Secretary of Education Arne Duncan and provide feedback on several education initiatives. Consider the likelihood of this type of meeting just a decade earlier: a teacher being invited to advise the secretary of education. Without the ability to broadcast, rally, and connect others through technologies, it would have been very unlikely indeed. Many teachers now blog, so what is different about Vilson? The technologies enabled him, but it was his mind-set, focused on connecting and building together with others, that created such a deep impact. This harkens to Carrie James's discussion in her book *Disconnected* about the ethics of digital connection.[35] She suggests that we are prone to develop ethical "blind spots" in our online engagement when we practice "bounded ethicality" (focusing only on our self-interests) and "ethical fading" (lessening the ethical dimensions of an issue or problem). As Vilson's story illustrates, to build authentic, ethical connections in the digital public sphere, it is critical to be aware of these blind spots and to focus on uniting and developing when using these tools.

While Vilson has worked to develop powerful networks of transformative teachers, another way that teachers have engaged in going public is through participation in formal professional networks. For example, the National Writing Project (NWP) has constructed opportunities for teachers to share and develop professional knowledge and expertise and has encouraged them to go public with their practice. As with Vilson, the driving focus of being public is to connect with others and develop the profession. The NWP hosts several web platforms to support such connections. One online platform, *Digital Is*, encourages teachers to blog, curate collections of teacher resources, and participate in public forums. This teacher-generated site is a hub for innovation and discovery for teachers and the public at large. This and other work has captured the imagination and interest of politicians, administrations, and even superstar musicians (R&B singer John Legend sponsored a grant project in 2015 with *Digital Is* for teacher-led learning initiatives[36]).

Teachers can also go public without digital technologies. Scott Storm, a teacher in New York City, goes public by writing academic papers about his collaborative teacher inquiry projects. While the audience is slightly different, his goals are the same: to connect with others who have similar interests and contribute to the development of the profession. His academic writing takes him beyond his school community and allows him to provide grounded, informed perspectives on teaching and education. As mentioned earlier, when teachers build connections beyond their school walls, they bring back new ideas and are positioned to take relational leadership roles in the school as informal mentors or advisers.

Despite the benefits of going public, it should not be romanticized. Going public requires being vulnerable by exposing your thoughts, views, and experiences to others who may disagree with you or challenge you (or your job). In digital spheres, there is a heightened sense of vulnerability, since publications live permanently on the net and can be easily replicated. Yet going public is not a choice these days; being a public knowledge worker is the choice. We are all public; our identities and information are available on the web, and in many cases, they are in places beyond our control. Just like teachers in a classroom, our work is public and scrutinized in a multitude of ways and by many stakeholders. The choice is how we choose to shape our participation and voice in the public realm, and to what end. Brené Brown, a social scientist who studies vulnerability, has argued that vulnerability and sharing one's story is how humans connect in authentic ways; it is vulnerability, she says, that generates creativity, innovation, and change.[37] Transformative teachers build authentic connections through their vulnerability and, in this way, develop themselves and their profession.

Cultivating Connections Through Active Gatherings

In literature on networked social movements of the twenty-first century and participatory practices such as making and hacking, one characteristic is very clear: these practices rarely occur *fully* online; most are hybrid, occupying physical as well as digital spaces.[38] In digital spaces, individuals can and usually do operate asynchronously, rarely joining en masse for a collective moment. However, in physical spaces, individuals join together in shared moments or gatherings—moments in which people join with the intention of connecting and being a part of a larger "we." A gathering is not just network building; it is culture building.

Transformative teachers participate in and organize gatherings in order to cultivate authentic connections, professional knowledge, and collective agency. In examining the types of gatherings in which these teachers tend to participate, I identified several shared characteristics that enable them to meet their purposes. These characteristics include expertise coming from experience, not position; authentic, participant-led conversations; an inquiry stance to learning; democratic participation; and integration of digital tools to extend conversations and make the work public.

Gatherings range from yearly events to weekly meetings. Meenoo Rami was one of the founding teachers to organize a unique teacher conference called EduCon. Hosted by Science Leadership Academy, a public school in Philadelphia, EduCon has been occurring yearly since 2007, with educators from several nations attending the conference.[39] Sessions are based on discussion topics rather than formal presentations. This discussion-based format enables participants to be active members in the sessions. Discussions can develop and transform into actions. For example, several years ago at EduCon, the #EduColor movement was initiated at a session about diverse racial representation in discussions of educational innovation. Participants are encouraged to tweet to the EduCon hashtag, and sessions are often linked to shared Google docs or web resources. Further, many sessions are videotaped and people can attend the conference virtually. Another unique aspect of the event is that it showcases the work of students at Science Leadership Academy, and many students and parents attend the event as volunteers. Events akin to EduCon, but on a slightly larger scale, are EdCamps, participant-initiated and -led conferences about teaching and education (see chapter 8).

Teacher-led networks across the United States host regular local and national gatherings to lead their own professional development and strategize on issues of concern. On the West Coast, the Association of Raza Educators (ARE), a coalition of teachers, community members, and scholars committed to raising critical consciousness and supporting democratic education, hosts "PRAXIS PDs" and an annual statewide conference. In their literature, they describe the PRAXIS PD (professional development) as:

1. Led and developed for social justice educators by social justice educators who teach culturally relevant curriculum and are actively involved in organizing campaigns outside their classrooms and in their communities.
2. Provides a critical pedagogy lens to teacher training and combines it with strategic campaign organizing.
3. Challenges the for-profit PD industry by providing an affordable alternative for professional development that funds the movement in lieu of paying consultants.[40]

In the Midwest, the Educators' Network for Social Justice in Milwaukee and the Teachers for Social Justice (TSJ) network in Chicago both hold regular gatherings related to professional development, including TSJ's Curriculum Fair, in which teachers convene around questions and curricula they have developed for their classrooms. Finally, on the East Coast, the New York Collective of Radical Educators (NYCoRE) and the Teacher Action Group (TAG-Philly) host similar gatherings.

Transformative teacher gatherings help to bridge the physical and the digital, deepen connections, and support the development of the characteristics and culture of transformative teaching for participants. Essentially, communities of practice, which engage in an intense level of apprenticing new attendees, move from legitimate peripheral participation to full membership in the community.[41] Many transformative teachers are not just attendees of gatherings; they are the organizers, planners, and active participants.

WHAT ABOUT DIGITAL GATHERINGS?

While digital tools allow individuals to gather together, developing a digital space that nurtures deeper relationship building and trust among participants can be more challenging. It not impossible, though, to construct such a space, as long as several key components are put in place. First, a small group of organizers must be committed to preserving and maintaining the space and the work of those who gather there. Second, a shared understanding of the norms and modes of interacting must be established. It is helpful to have clear and explicit descriptions of the community's beliefs and practices. Third, there must be a shared goal that group members are working toward. This can be a collective project or a skill for which individuals are connecting to exchange ideas and experiences on their work. Finally, new members should be initiated into the norms and practices of the space.

A good example of such a digital gathering is the Peeragogy project, run by a collective of educators and scholars, which is a gathering of colleagues who work together to develop a handbook of collaborative learning, or "peeragogy" (see Rheingold's profile in chapter 5).[42] Participants are invited to weekly gatherings via Google's hangout platform, in which they discuss aspects of the handbook and their work. Through this project, participants are constantly thinking about the norms and practices of working collaboratively and are collectively working toward a shared goal as well as individual learning goals.

Curating Connections: Being Critical Networkers

The previous two sections of this chapter are illustrative of how transformative teachers can build what social network theorists call "social ties." Social ties are generally categorized by network theorists on a spectrum from "weak ties" (social relationships in which people do not know each other well, such as acquaintances) to "strong ties" (deeper relationships, such as family or close friends). Going public generally builds weak ties, while participating in gatherings supports the development of strong ties. Transformative teachers may be unable to quote social network theory, but the ways in which they connect reflect a strategic understanding of networking. In this section, I'll explain how social network theory can provide a way to describe how to be critical and strategic in curating the kinds of connections that support transformative teaching.

There are five aspects of the dynamics of social networks that are important to understand in order to strategically curate connections: (1) the quality of social ties, (2) the ways network structures support needs, (3) network metacognition (4), the way social ties are nurtured, and (5) connected learning. Social network theory is based on the assumption that relationships shape how we think, feel, make decisions, and can access resources. One of the primary concerns of research in this area delves into the qualities of social ties. What has become apparent in research on networks is that it's not *how many* people you know, but *who* you know and the quality of the relationships that matter.[43]

For example, teacher A might work diligently to create a network of 1,000 Twitter connections, while teacher B concentrates on building close relationships with 3 teachers in his or her school and maintains an online network of about 150 people. Which teacher has more social capital (resources and support in one's network)?[44] One might initially think the answer is teacher A, but even though this teacher has many connections, they are all weak ties (socially distant, and not very interconnected).[45] Weak ties help to bring in new resources and ideas, but rarely offer socio-emotional support such as mentorship.[46] Teacher B has a balance of strong ties (close relationships, often interconnected with others) and weak ties. In this case, teacher B has socio-emotional support in his local community, which helps him to navigate the micro-politics of his school and a broader network of weak ties to introduce new ideas and resources. Sherry Turkle, author of *Alone Together*, has noted that with the increased amount of online networking, we rarely think about the type of ties we build, noting, "[W]e celebrate its 'weak ties'—the bonds of acquaintance with people we may never meet. But that does not mean we prosper in them."[47] While public knowledge work generally builds weak ties, gatherings build strong ties. Engaging in both forms of connecting helps teachers to build a balance of strong and weak ties.

The structure of a network as it relates to need is another key aspect of understanding the dynamics of social networks. Teacher A may actually benefit from focusing solely on building Twitter connections if her purpose and need is just to get exposed to new ideas. An important aspect of being a critical connector is reflecting on one's professional needs and participating in and building networks of support that meet those particular needs. For example, Annie Huynh was really interested in taking a leadership role in education. She sought opportunities for new ideas and collaborative actions across the school district. She devoted many of her efforts to participating in citywide teacher networks and going public with her practice. She developed a large base of diverse weak ties, which enabled her to meet her needs. In contrast, another teacher may find that her needs are more focused on issues at the school level. In this case, fostering strong-tie connections at a local level would support these needs.

Identifying our networks and needs can prove difficult because we all have network biases. We tend to ignore or forget about the people in our networks who we consider "lower status" than ourselves.[48] This is why network metacognition is key to being a critical connector. We must consider how we think about our networks. Are we focusing only on connecting with people we see as cool or high status in our fields? If so, it may be time to rethink. Often the people we don't see are those who will help us change and grow the most.[49] Networks, especially closed (densely connected) networks, can become echo chambers. When individuals cultivate awareness not only of *how* they are networking, but of how their networks *shape* their thinking, they can gain different perspectives and solve problems from new angles.[50]

Next is the issue of *how* to nurture connections and develop networks. Relationships are built through shared experiences and are strengthened particularly when there is a mutual purpose and project on which to focus efforts.[51] Inviting others to work with you on a task, question, or project will result in more generative relationships than chatting in the break room. While it is important to take opportunities to connect with others informally, relationships take time to develop, and a shared commitment to a project or activity ensures that everyone will invest his or her time in the work and the relationships.

This is also where the maker mind-set becomes an important aspect of connecting; focusing on collective production builds authentic connections. The successful teacher advocacy and support groups I have worked with usually bring teachers together around a shared goal or project, and invite them to contribute in some way. For example, the Boston Teacher Residency (BTR), a highly successful program that supports new teachers in their first few years, has a private web space for its teachers in which it invites them to coproduce through articles and examples of practice (see the profile of Sarah Langer from BTR at the end of this chapter). This activity helps to connect teachers and gives them something tangible to use and contribute to.

Finally, we come to the issue of learning. Humans are social learners; therefore, networks matter a great deal in learning. Connected technologies and online tools have extended our abilities to collaborate across distances and build broad networks. Before the rise of connected technologies, our understanding of how social learning occurs had been based primarily in sociocultural and critical models of learning by scholars such as Lev Vygotsky and Paulo Freire. More recently, Mimi Ito and colleagues developed a learning approach that builds on sociocultural and constructivist/constructionist models and incorporates what they discovered about informal learning practices of youth in this connected world.[52]

The approach, known as connected learning, comprises three learning principles and three design principles.[53] The learning principles are that learning should be interest powered, peer supported, and academically oriented. The design principles are that learning environments and practices should be production oriented, openly networked, and centered on shared purposes. Two principles that are particularly relevant to critical connecting are shared purposes and openly networked learning. The notion of shared purposes relates to the aspect of network dynamics I mentioned earlier: authentic relationships are developed through shared work. Openly networked learning relates to the hacker ethos (described in chapter 5), which focuses on sharing and collaborating on work publicly and freely. When Ito and colleagues looked at how youth are learning today, they found that youth used openly networked tools and spaces to develop skills, knowledge, and practice about their own interests.

One example of how the openly networked design component can cultivate meaningful relationships was described in a 2014 publication on connected learning in schools.[54] Elementary teachers Gail Desler and Halie Ferrier from the Elk Grove Unified School District in California designed a language arts unit in which students studied the history of the United States' Japanese internment camps. Students envisioned what it must have been like to be in the camp and wrote letters from an internment camp. To build in the openly networked design feature of the project, teachers posted the letters online using a platform called VoiceThread, which allowed people to comment and share their stories. This resulted in hundreds of comments, some from individuals who had spent time in the camps, and allowed students to connect directly with others who had an interest in the topic. Desler described the outcomes of the project in terms of student learning and engagement:

> Within a matter of days, responses to the Letters from the Internment Camps VoiceThread began trickling in. Students, teachers, parents, and the community at large contributed content and compliments. Several former internees shared their memories of the camps. A project that started as students creating historical fiction now included primary source accounts. For a classroom of students too often confined to the physical boundaries of their neighborhoods, technology had leveled the playing field, providing them with a global microphone for speaking out against social injustice, creating a powerful example of what writing for change looks and sounds like.[55]

The connected learning approach is based on how young people learn in a networked world. When teachers learn what it is like to live as a young person in a world made more complex by the digital realm and find ways to connect their experiences with what and how young people learn at school, they can have a strong impact on student learning.[56] A recent study by Danielle Filipiak and Isaac Miller on teachers' use of a connected learning approach in a classroom showed that students thought the curriculum was more relevant to their lives and were more engaged in their work.[57] Young people need models of authentic participation and connection in this networked era. In my own research on connected learning and teacher education, I have found that when teaching the connected learning approach, teachers develop more diverse and extensive support networks themselves.[58] Connected learning is important to understand and embody in order to develop supportive relationships with students and for one's own professional learning.

Why Connecting Is a Transformative Teacher Practice

Connecting is at the heart of transformative teacher practice. Participatory culture is rooted in connecting and sharing to learn and make. Teachers build stronger and more authentic connections when they engage in a shared project, and often this project is inquiry about their work. Thus, teacher inquiry and connecting reinforce each other. Community organizing is about fostering connections and social power through social networks. Community organizers engage in public knowledge work, cultivating networks through gatherings and curating networks to build power for social change.

In this chapter, I have tried to distinguish between inauthentic and authentic connecting and emphasize that authentic connecting happens when individuals build together toward a greater purpose. This marks a critical difference between being a passive consumer of information and being an active producer and transformer. Transformative teachers are not passive. They are actively working to elevate the profession of teaching, build better educational systems and opportunities for their students, and continually develop as lifelong learners.

Voices from the Field:
On Connecting, Leading, and Learning Together

The profiles below are of educational advocates and leaders involved in nurturing connections between teachers, students, and community members. Their stories help to illustrate the ways in which theories of networking and connecting have been applied to real-world contexts.

Mimi Ito: Stories of Connected Learning

Mimi Ito, a cultural anthropologist at the University of California, Irvine, is known for her research on youth, new media, and participatory practices. She and a team of colleagues conducted research on how youth engage in learning in out-of-school contexts in the twenty-first century. Their research revealed that youth were enabled by connected technologies to make, remix, and collaborate on shared interests and projects.[59] These findings informed the development of the connected learning framework, an approach for engaging twenty-first-century youth in authentic and expansive learning experiences (described earlier).

In my conversation with Ito, we discussed the growth of connected learning, how it has been translated into the classroom, and the ways in which it has shaped teacher practice. The connected learning team has worked closely with the National Writing Project (NWP) and other educator groups, and thus formal teacher networks have played a role in educating teachers about the approach. However, the process took time and continues to be organically codeveloped by educators and researchers. Several early-adopter teachers began inquiring about connected learning as a result of the connectedlearning.tv site that offered demonstrations and examples. NWP teachers became more active contributors and an audience for the site. In order to expand beyond early adopters to a broader population, Ito and colleagues found that anchoring workshops and information in particular technologies and software programs, such as Minecraft (a popular collaborative online game), opened doors to teachers in other networks and communities.

While technology is a draw, it is not the main focus of connected learning. For Ito and colleagues, the main focus is the authentic learning that comes from building relationships based on interests. When conducting workshops with teachers, she has found that many teachers experience transformative moments when they intentionally build opportunities for learning around shared interests, including their own. For example, a teacher interested in Minecraft might start an afterschool club about it. Ito described the outcomes:

> Even though the math teacher is running a Minecraft club and the club is not about math, what's really interesting is what happens is the relationship towards the teacher changes because of the student's engagement in a shared interest. That seems genuinely transformative in ways that are not totally predictable, but that are just strengthening—especially when you're talking about kids who have an alienated relationship to the school. Just that ability to connect with a teacher on a genuine interest, teachers have described this as . . . transformative.

Ito is aware that a multifaceted approach such as connected learning can seem daunting to those who are unfamiliar with it, but she notes that "every little bit counts . . . Something as simple as starting an afterschool gaming club or starting your morning meetings with something that's about students sharing things they are involved in outside of school. Little things make a big difference in kids' lives when it is centered on their interests and identities." Her research on connected learning supports this argument. In almost all of her cases, she has found that even one connection with a person around a shared interest can make a difference: "It only has to happen once. It's not like teaching a really basic skill or something. It's like the brokering the opportunity, that one connection that lets the kid jump from point A to point B, lets them see an opportunity; that is life changing for these kids' trajectories."

Furthermore, it is most often a teacher who is the catalyst for this shift in trajectory. She calls these catalysts "learning heroes"—people who have made an important impact on a child's learning path. Teachers, she suggests, can become students' learning heroes if they connect in authentic ways to students' interests and affinities and help them build their own learning networks around these interests: "teachers are in a uniquely privileged position to make a difference."

Sarah Langer: Holding Space for Teachers to Connect

Sarah Langer is a teacher coach with the Boston Teacher Residency (BTR) program. She has been instrumental in designing the website, BTRGrad.org, which provides content on teaching practices and is coproduced by teachers in the program. This website is part of a larger support structure that facilitates both online and face-to-face support and networking opportunities for teachers in the program.

I asked Langer to describe how BTRGrad.org was developed and how teachers used the resource. Langer said that initially she and her team of instructional coaches wanted to create a site that would provide resources for teachers she was coaching. She had to make a lot of new content, which took quite a while to develop. After the site was launched, she began to share not only her suggestions, but also practices that BTR teachers were using and that seemed to work well in their own classes. For example, one teacher developed the idea of a "Reset Day One," in which students and teachers rewrote norms and rules for their class and even worked with administrators to start again when the classroom began to feel a little chaotic. When she shared this strategy on the website, it became popular throughout the network, and many BTR teachers tried it with much success. Based on this success, Langer and other program coaches began to write descriptions of successful practices in BTR classrooms that she could post on the site. The website has become an important tool for BTR teachers and graduates and has also garnered interest from the broader teacher community in Boston.

In addition to the website, Langer facilitates two types of face-to-face meetings. One, called a "planning party," is an informal gathering in which individuals can share ideas for curriculum planning and get feedback. The other is a more formally organized gathering around an inquiry or action research topic. Participants in this group read shared articles or books and discuss how these resources relate to their own teaching and inquiries.

Langer described how the combination of an online resource that reaches BTR graduates and beyond, as well as smaller face-to-face gatherings, supported the exchange of resources and ideas among teachers:

> Last year I saw two different teachers I was working with doing a "class challenge." One was doing it around following expectations for starting off class. One of them was doing it around completing class work. I wrote that up as a page, and that has been spreading, and lots of people are trying all sorts of class challenges around whatever they want. Someone this week is doing one around the interruptions . . .
>
> People can write [a need] on the board, or they'll tell a coach and we'll say, "You should go talk to this person." That happens in almost every planning party. Someone will say, "I want to start standard-based grading, but I don't really know where to start?" And [others] will say, "That math teacher over there is doing it, go talk to them." Fifteen minutes later, the person has some really good ideas about how to start.

These spaces for connection have nurtured an interwoven community that has grown in influence and impact over the ten years since the organization was founded. The presence of this support network has an impact not only on the current teachers in the program, but also on the schools in which program alumni are teaching.

PART III

Transformative Teachers and Educational Change

EIGHT

The Impact of Teacher-Led
Networked Social Movements

"I T ALL STARTED WITH INQUIRY," said Samuel Reed, as he described how he came to be a leader in several teacher networks, helped to launch a new school, organized summer youth programs for students, and joined advisory councils of major foundations. "I just wanted to design a way to help my students get excited about writing. I started an inquiry and started networking, and everything I did spurred some new connection or opportunity."

Reed's recollection symbolizes the work of transformative teachers in the ways in which their efforts are grounded in fundamental principals related to teacher inquiry, community organizing, and participatory culture, fostering not only professional growth, but also impacts on students' learning, institutional culture, policy, public discourse, and teacher agency. This chapter traces how transformative teachers influence educational change. While most of this book has thus far focused on transformative teaching as an individual act, here I examine the collective, interconnected aspects of transformative teaching.

I contend that transformative teachers are the drivers of teacher-led, networked social movements in educational change. This can only be understood by looking more broadly at educational movements and communities that reflect the principles and practices of transformative teachers, so here I describe the collective influence and impact of transformative teachers in and across various social arenas. In the process, I reveal a less tangible type of transformation: a transformation in teacher agency or in the way teachers and their communities understand and value teachers' roles in shaping educational policy and practice.

Teacher-Led, Networked Social Movements and Educational Change

The phrase "a movement, not a moment" has become a pervasive motto since it was first coined by organizers of the #BlackLivesMatter movement in 2014. It has since been taken up by other groups (e.g., #EduColor) and even appears in popular song (e.g., Lin-Manuel Miranda integrated it into lyrics for a song in the *Hamilton* musical to describe the American Revolution). The widespread use of this phrase is likely due to the rise of transmedia organizing and networked social movements that leverage connected technologies to amplify voices and build broader coalitions for social change. While these types of movements have been questioned for their ability to sustain momentum and change, they have proven to have a significant impact on our society, from our discourse to our politics.

Transformative teaching is a paradigm shift in teacher leadership and learning that has led to the emergence of teacher-led, networked social movements for equity and justice in teaching and learning. It is not just one movement; multiple social and educational movements that embody the principles, practices, and cultural tools of transformative teachers have been driven by this shift. In chapter 2, I described several signals of transformative teaching: new forms of professional development, increasing numbers of teacher-led professional networks, teachers' use of social media to publish professional work, and new forms of pedagogical practices that reflect the principles of transformative teaching. Further, I highlighted several specific movements and practices as examples of these signals, including the maker movement, unconferencing, youth-led participatory action research, connected learning, the Opt-out movement, social justice unionism, and game-based learning. These are just a few examples of a growing number of teacher-led movements to transform education. Other movements, such as sustainable "green teaching," restorative justice, and mindfulness are also taking root in schools. In this chapter,

I attempt to capture the impact of just some of these movements to demonstrate the educational changes brought about by transformative teachers.

Transformations in Policy: Social Justice Unionism

Changes in educational policy are perhaps the most difficult for teachers to effect. This is primarily due to long-ingrained institutional and political structures and cultures that are sometimes disconnected from grassroots movements. Furthermore, as a part of the educational system, teachers feel a tension between enacting policies and changing policies. The foundational principles of community organizing are an important aspect of transformative teachers' work in this arena because they center on building coalitions of stakeholders and uniting disparate voices. One networked social movement that has effected policy change and that reflects the principles and practices of transformative teachers is social justice unionism. The work of this movement provides examples of the collective influence of transformative teachers on policy and the connections between ideology and action.

The term "social justice unionism" was established by a collective of teachers and academics in the early 1990s in the United States who were seeking to address issues of social, racial, and economic justice, have a greater voice and democratic participation in teacher unions, build coalitions with other community organizations and social justice activist groups, and redefine the role of teacher unions to reposition teachers as more active and transformative members of their own profession.[1] In the two decades that followed, the concept seemed to give hope to some, but did not catch fire as a movement until about 2010.[2] Bob Peterson, a teacher, activist, and one of the original members of the group that defined the term, described this new surge of involvement in a 2014 article: "A revitalized teacher union movement is bubbling up in the midst of relentless attacks on public schools and the teaching profession. Over the next several years this new movement may well be the most important force to defend and improve public schools, and in so doing, defend our communities and our democracy."[3] Peterson documented a range of efforts across the country since 2010 to reconceptualize the role of union members as "social justice patriots," including efforts in Los Angeles,

Portland, Oregon, St. Paul, and Chicago. Several of these efforts resulted in union contract renegotiations that called for more resources and assistance to under-resourced communities and schools.

On the East Coast, teachers and educational scholars also noticed a shift toward increased interest in social justice unionism. Kathleen Riley studied the work of WE campaigns to focus on social and racial justice in their unions and noted that WE took many cues from the Caucus Of Rank and file Educators (CORE) social justice union members in Chicago, and from organizers in their network in East Coast cities such as New York and Boston.[4] In many of these cases, the union members had an impact not only on district and state policies, but also on internal union policies, practices, and goals. This trend is not just occurring in the United States, but is a global phenomenon. Teacher union historians Cindy Rottman and coauthors suggested that the global surge in participation and the parallel and collaborative actions of various social justice unions worldwide could be attributed to increased networking and information sharing by teachers: "International solidarity networks between teacher unions in the global north and south have allowed teachers to learn from and support colleagues facing similar conditions across educational jurisdictions . . . These solidarity networks have reduced teachers' isolation and allowed them to share activist strategies."[5]

The example of the social justice unionism movement not only demonstrates the ways in which a teacher-led social movement can create policy change, but also highlights the growth of a *networked* social movement and how increased connectedness propelled a concept into a global phenomenon.

Transformations in Institutional Culture: Inquiry Practices and Maker Activities

The rising number of makerspaces and Maker Faires in schools is evidence of the impact that transformative teachers involved in the maker movement have had on the institutional culture of schools. As described previously, the maker movement embodies all three of the foundational cultures at the roots of transformative teaching: inquiry, community organizing, and participatory culture. The Maker Media foundation has been documenting the organizations and institutions that have held affiliated Maker Faires. Between 2015 and 2016, over 160 schools worldwide have hosted a Maker Media–affiliated Maker Faire, from China to Turkey to the United States.[6] Kylie Peppler et al. conducted a study of 450 makerspaces and fabrication labs across the United States both in and outside schools in 2015. They found that about 35 percent were in schools and were being used by approximately eight thousand students each year.[7]

A specific example of a shift in institutional culture by transformative teachers is the story of Science Leadership Academy's (SLA) makerspace. SLA has been nationally recognized for its innovative approaches to teaching and is viewed as a model of excellence in the district. The school has been successful in partnering with community organizations to build grants and programs for the school. It received a $100,000 grant to develop a makerspace at SLA Bieber (its newest sister school), which founding SLA principal Chris Lehmann calls the "physical representation of what we believe." He sees the maker movement as historically related to the progressive education movement. He credits some part of the movement's rise to the increased ability to share creations and ideas about making through social media.

Lehmann's school and the network of schools that are invested in fostering inquiry-driven, project-based learning are cultivated by administrators but driven by the teachers who work inside them. When I described the concept of a "transformative teacher" to Lehmann as a social justice–oriented teacher who leverages connected technologies to organize for educational equity and change, he said, "That sounds like an SLA teacher!" He suggests that one of the more unique aspects of the teachers at his school is that they see themselves as "organizers" and use connected technologies to take the lead in developing the field of inquiry-based teaching. For example, for the past eight years, SLA teachers and their students have organized EduCon, a national unconference about innovation and inquiry-driven learning.

Lehmann's story reflects the role that transformative teachers play in schools with makerspaces and inquiry-driven learning. As self-described "organizers," they spread the word about the work they are doing and build interest in the practices through public storytelling and network building. A good example of teacher organizing and networking in the broader maker movement is the "Resources for K-12 Fab Lab and Makerspaces" Google Plus community website, a hub in which teachers gather and discuss maker-related work.[8] It sources feeds for more than thirty teachers' blogs about maker education, and members can share news about events, books, tools, and questions of practice. The discussion forum is active and has about fourteen hundred subscribers. Teachers build connections with each other through the site and help each other organize maker activities.

Transformations in Teaching and Student Learning: Looking at YPAR and Genius Hour

Youth participatory action research (YPAR) and Genius Hour are two new pedagogical practices that transformative teachers have adapted, experimented with, and developed. The practices reposition students as agents of their learning and thus provide a very different educational experience and outcomes than traditional schooling. Both practices reflect the principles and roots of transformative teaching in that they foster inquiry, engage students in collaboration and organizing, and encourage participatory learning.

Studies that have examined teachers' use of YPAR with students have found positive impacts on their civic and academic engagement, sense of agency, critical thinking, social capital, and interpersonal skills.[9] While this approach was developed mainly by scholars such as Michelle Fine, Julio Cammarotta, and Ernest Morrell from 2005 to 2007, it has been practiced and further developed by teachers since. The YPAR hub (yparhub.berkeley.edu), maintained by associate professor Emily Ozer and colleagues at the University of California, Berkeley, highlights the dozens of examples of YPAR activities in schools that are designed and facilitated by teachers. Antero Garcia (described in chapter 6's Voices in the Field) learned of YPAR through collaboration with Morrell and used it as a teacher; he spoke with me about its trends and uses. He noted a steep rise in YPAR research since the mid-2000s when he was working with Morrell: "The fact that we're able to have a conversation about YPAR and we don't get kicked out of [an education research conference], and that people were actually able to discuss it, I think we've seen that change. That was language that didn't exist prior to 2006–2007."

Garcia also talked about teachers' use of YPAR and its impact on schools. He suggested that through YPAR, "teachers and students are equipping themselves with a discourse to label issues of power in ways that they would not traditionally be able to do." He described how he brought his high school students to the American Educational Research Association conference to present their YPAR findings. He noted that, initially, the students were not treated as legitimate researchers, but once they started talking about theory and how it connected to their work, there was a tangible shift in the way they were perceived. Furthermore, their work resulted in real policy change at their school; after presenting findings about the impacts of suspension policies on student engagement and suggesting alternative approaches to discipline, the principal adopted several of their recommendations. Through YPAR, he and his students not only changed policy, but also hacked enduring narratives about students' knowledge and academic research paradigms, such as the notion that students are unable to contribute to discussions about discipline and classroom management in constructive and critical ways.

Genius Hour is another new pedagogical approach being spread through networked collaboration and sharing between transformative teachers. The approach, sometimes called "20 percent time," came from a Google workplace policy in which employees are allowed to spend 20 percent of their time working on a project or idea of their choice. This practice was described in behavioral science writer and innovator Daniel Pink's TED Talk and subsequently adapted by teachers for the classroom (generally allotting one hour per week of school for students to work on projects of their choice); some called it Genius Hour or 20 percent time. Angela Maiers, a former teacher and education advocate, was one of the first to formally call for Genius Hour in schools in her blog.

The practice is a new phenomenon, though the concept of promoting student-driven learning during a "choice time" or "project time" has been popular in progressive education since Dewey, and is still implemented by teachers (although predominantly by private-school teachers). The difference is that Genius Hour has become an acceptable form of teaching in more traditional public schools that have the pressures of high-stakes standardized testing and are often under the yoke of scripted, mandated curricula. Perhaps the increasing acceptance of Genius Hour is due in part to its flashy name, but I suggest that it has become accepted and more popular due partly to the increased online presence of teachers' stories in blogs, media, and websites that share resources and ideas. One such popular resource site is the Genius Hour Wiki, which includes categories such as Genius Hour teacher blogs or posts, student resources, testimonials, chat archives, presentations, and (harkening back to the hacker manifesto) a "Genius Hour Manifesto." Since it is a wiki, anyone can add to or edit the document, thus inviting collaborative development of the approach.

Teachers blog, create resource sites, and write books about Genius Hour with a sense of altruism in sharing resources that reflects the maker mind-set and hacker ethos. These efforts have a domino-like effect, promoting the concept to broad audiences.[10] For example, teacher Joy Kirr's "LiveBinders" site offers Genius Hour resources and project examples for others. She grants much inspiration to engage in the work to Maiers's call. Another teacher, Terri Eichholz, maintains a blog called "Engage Their Minds," on which she shares a plethora of resources for Genius Hour. On the blog, she notes, "This page is devoted to sharing some of the resources I've collected over the past two years with anyone else who is interested in starting a classroom Genius Hour." As teachers write about their own experiences, they inspire others to do the same.

In 2014, CNN reported on Kirr's and several other teachers' Genius Hour practices, framing Genius Hour as a new, popular educational movement: "The concept is now catching on in schools, usually rooted in the idea of student-led passion projects with a focus on creating and sharing. Teachers said it's part of a larger movement in education to promote student-driven learning."[11] In an interview with Kirr, CNN noted that she had been inspired by "design-systems thinking" and that one of the "commandments" of Genius Hour is that "failure IS an option"—that is, students can learn from failure. These mind-sets and beliefs reveal a relationship between Genius Hour and transformative teacher cultural practices, and demonstrates how the mind-set has both grown in popularity and had real impact on how students are supported as learners in schools.

The blogs, sites, and online resources that teachers create do not stand alone; they are a part of a discussion between teachers about the practice. In blogs, teachers will often refer to others' practice through a link or reflection and build on it. For example, teacher Denise Krebs refers to blog posts by Joy Kirr and A. J. Bianco in her curated collection of Genius Hour resources.[12] She also collaborates with Kirr on a Genius Hour wiki, which is constructed by a network of teachers who have Genius Hour in their classrooms.[13] Through these kinds of interchanges in networked third spaces, the teachers build a shared discourse about their practice that is brought into the school arena, influencing colleagues at the school and shaping student learning.

Transformations in Public Discourse: Education Chats

Jerry Blumengarten's website of Twitter education chats, cybraryman.com, lists about 350 different weekly chats. A quick sampling of such chats gives some insight into the variety of participation. #EdChat, an educational chat that covers a range of issues in education, claims an average reach of over 2 million viewers per week (based on analysis by Keyhole, a net analytics application) and has about 100 active users per weekly moderated chat session. #EngChat, which focuses on English teaching, has been hosting weekly chats during the school year since 2011 and has an average of 15 to 30 active users during weekly moderated chats. #EduColor, launched in 2015, has about 40 to 50 active users during weekly chats. #NTChat, or "New Teacher Chat," was launched in 2010 and exists on several social media platforms—Facebook (about 2,000 members), Google Plus (about 450 members), and Twitter (average number of moderated chat participants is about 40). Taking a loose average of about 30 unique users per weekly chat session for each of the 350 chats listed, that comes to approximately 10,500 users per week. Multiply that by 35 weeks of school per year and you get about 13 million chat participants per year. This does not include a calculation of chatter outside the moderated sessions and is thus a relatively low estimate. Further, it is an estimate of users, not tweets. The average user tweeted about ten times in the one-hour moderated session that I analyzed, which, when taken into the calculation, would lead to an estimated 130 million education-related tweets appearing online each year. That's a lot of tweets.

My dear friend Meredith Broussard, one of the leading experts in data journalism in the United States, would be careful to remind us that there really is no way to capture the true number of users and tweets that relate to education on Twitter. There are "bots" that are not really human at all, just programs designed to capture data, and there are humans who have three different accounts and thus can appear as three different "users." Yet, that low-estimate calculation of 130 million tweets does offer a good hint of the amount of chatter coming from teachers into the Twittersphere and, thus, into the laps of those who use it most voraciously: journalists.

Journalists use social media to look for stories. Teachers can use Twitter and other forms of social media as a direct means to connect with a journalist about something happening in their school or classroom, as several of the teacher networks that I have studied do, and teachers can have an influence in more subtle ways just by contributing to the development of an idea or artifact. Surveys of transformative teachers support this assertion as well. Over 51 percent of participants in a 2015 study of teacher-led network members found that educators engaged in "remixing and creating content" for their classrooms in a Pew national survey.[14] As with Henry Jenkins's studies of participatory culture in fandom, transformative teachers play a different role than the typical media consumer. They don't just consume ideas and information; they hack, remix, transform, and create new ideas and share them publicly. Furthermore, this level of involvement in online public spaces does not just introduce novel practices to the mainstream media; it builds communities of shared interest among practitioners. These networked communities then further refine, critique, and build on new practices through their ongoing discourse.

Transformations in Collective Teacher Agency

Participation in online chats is just one of the ways in which teachers are increasingly taking advantage of connected te chnologies for their professional development *and* the development of their schools and profession. For example, teachers are bringing resources to their schools by using crowdfunding applications. According to a 2013 crowdfunding industry report, teachers raised over $2.7 billion for their classrooms through crowdfunding software.[15] Also, teachers are increasingly organizing their own forms of professional development outside school, with the assistance of connected technologies to promote the events. Between 2010 and 2016, approximately two thousand teacher-led unconference events were organized by teachers worldwide through networked movements such as EdCamp and TeachMeet and by organizational allies such as nonprofit education advocacy organizations.[16] The EdCamp Foundation has begun to research the impact of EdCamp unconferences on classroom teaching. According to Kristen Swanson, a principal investigator for the study, the most significant finding thus far is how the event fosters social capital for teachers.[17] Hence, teachers' increased connectivity and networking reinforces an agentive shift toward building connections to share ideas and resources between educators.

These increased levels of connectivity and participation have also been identified in surveys on teacher collaboration and leadership. A 2010 MetLife survey of teachers' views on their roles in schools showed a majority of teachers (67 percent of the 1,003 teachers surveyed) believed that collaboration and networking is an important part of being a good teacher, an increase from previous years.[18] Furthermore, another MetLife survey on leadership in schools showed that more teachers (about 51 percent) are taking on formal, hybrid leadership roles in schools, and many are interested in holding informal leadership positions outside the classroom.[19] Marilyn Cochran-Smith and Susan Lytle highlight the growth of practitioner research in their 2009 *Inquiry as Stance: Practitioner Research in the Next Generation*, a follow-up to their original 1999 book, which brought to light many of the inquiry practices that teachers were engaged in during the 1990s.[20] Not only has this approach become popularized over time, it has also become *more teacher-led*, which has resulted in more nuanced understandings about teaching and learning. They described this change and its impacts: "Until relatively recently . . . most of the literature about practitioners was written by university-based researchers . . . Since 2000, a wider range of participants in the movement has been involved in the development of frameworks that involve more emic understandings of the practice of teaching and emanate from practitioners constructions of their diverse experiences in the classroom and within and across communities."[21]

Thus far I have described how teachers are transforming institutions, policies, and student learning. Yet transformative teachers not only alter contexts, but also change their own sense of *agency*. They transform the way that they perceive themselves as actors in the system of education, and how others perceive them as well. Jerusha Conner and Sonia Rosen conducted a study on youth organizers and the ways in which their actions had an impact on change in their schools.[22] They argue that one of the most important aspects of the organizers' work was in changing the way others perceived them: were they scrappy troublemakers with little power, or were they thoughtful and strategic organizers with a powerful network? When they were able to shift others' perceptions of them (as well as their own self-perception), they were then able to make substantial change in their schools and communities. In the same way, teachers going public with stories and leveraging connected technologies to organize and network has influenced public perception of their agency and transformative teachers' own sense of agency, which is just as important as their impact on policy, institutions, and student learning.

A Holistic Perspective on Transformative Teaching and Change

Although I have organized my descriptions of these various transformations according to several different arenas, in reality, they are all interconnected and each affects the others. A transformative teacher who inquires about implementing a Genius Hour in her classroom may indeed have an impact on the students' learning experience, but she also has an impact on the school culture: by offering a new model of teaching and learning, or of public discourse; by sharing her work or seeking funding; and by altering or augmenting the sense of agency and the public's perspectives on teacher agency. Thus, these transformations are woven throughout all the arenas and have an impact on all.

Furthermore, one teacher who tries Genius Hour in her classroom has a localized impact, but if we consider the impact of the networked community of educators who are working together, that impact becomes much larger.

While looking at individual transformative teachers gives us a good picture of the work they do, it is important to understand that the power of transformative teaching comes from the networks, communities, and movements such teachers build.

This understanding is embedded in the three building blocks of transformative teaching: teacher inquiry, community organizing, and participatory culture. For each, a community is required in order for the work to exist. The cultural tools that grow from these foundational ideologies—making, hacking, and connecting—are also, at their core, a part of collective work and endeavor. When we think about the impact, influence, and professional growth of transformative teachers, we must take a holistic view of their work and the networks they build.

Change for What?

In this chapter, I have outlined some of the many ways that transformative teacher movements have influenced schools, practices, pedagogies, research, and discourse. Innovation and change is exciting to see. Yet, it is important to recall the central ethical purpose of this change: social justice and equity. This purpose is what distinguishes transformative teachers' work from other movements to introduce innovative technologies and practices. An example is the story of a professional development event initiated and facilitated by Gamal Sherif, a transformative teacher leader in Philadelphia.

Sherif brought together a range of teachers and allies from his PLN to think about how to develop a grant for a green teacher network in the region. The event was organized as a "design charrette," or a hackathon-like structure in which individuals worked in small groups to develop an idea to present to the larger group. In the beginning, Sherif framed the work with the following question: "How is this work helping to conserve energy and water, foster wellness, and integrate social, economic, and environmental justice?" Sherif's event reflected many elements of transformative teacher leadership: he leveraged his social capital and PLN, he adopted a participant-led format of professional development, and he fostered connections and collaboration among participants. The event resulted in the establishment of a formal partnership between several organizations to develop a large-scale grant for a teacher network reflecting the ideas generated at the event. However, what made this event distinctly transformative was its social justice framing. While the objective of the event was to build a green teacher network, the underlying purpose was to address issues of environmental justice and wellness for children living in under-resourced environments. Sherif was facilitating the group members to articulate what they believed about the conditions of learning that students deserve in schools (and their communities), and building power through their unified network to transform their beliefs into reality.

Organizations and advocates that want to support transformative teachers must remember this central purpose. In the next chapter, I examine how we can support the learning and growth of transformative teachers while keeping these fundamental purposes in mind. I use the developmental framework of transformative teaching introduced in chapter 3 to provide a focus for this question and offer three in-depth case studies of organizations and institutions that have successfully supported transformative teachers' work and growth.

NINE

How Institutions and Organizations Support Transformative Teachers

TRANSFORMATIVE TEACHERS WORK with a complex network of community partners and advocates to organize for educational change. There are many strategies and approaches that these allies can take to support such teachers. Here I provide suggestions for individuals and groups that work in teacher education, educational institutions, and community organizations to support transformative teachers. I use the organizing framework of transformative teaching development described in chapter 3 to identify what we should do to help teachers develop and highlight key strategies that allies can use to support transformative teachers. I also offer three examples of organizations and institutions that have successfully supported the teachers' work and professional development: EdCamp, the Connected Learning Alliance, and the Philadelphia Education Fund's Teacher Networks project.

In many ways, the transformations described in chapter 8 emerged organically as a result of the cultural shifts in technology, collaboration, and learning that have supported a paradigm shift in education, positioning teachers as the designers of their profession. There is a tension for institutions and organizations that want to support transformative teachers: how to give them space and freedom to take charge of their learning and, at the same time, focus their energies and work on the mission and goals of the whole group. The suggestions and examples highlighted here explain how organizations and institutions can design programs that support transformative teaching and maintain a partnership that honors the expertise, voice, and leadership of participating teachers. Rather than use traditional top-down models of teacher training, they use a variety of innovative strategies and practices to cultivate teacher-led professional networking and development. These organizations are examples of partnerships that reflect the new paradigm of the teaching profession.

Supporting Transformative Teachers' Development: What and Why

In Chapter 3, I introduced a developmental framework (see table 3.1) that showed the spectrum of growth in transformative teaching across eight domains: learning, techno-social development, modalities of learning and production, voice and storytelling, sociopolitical development, social capital and agency, role of the teacher, and hybridity and third spaces. While I do not suggest using this framework as an evaluative tool, it does offer a good way to think about how to support the development of transformative teachers. Furthermore, I contend that supporting teachers to develop their capacities in these domains is simply supporting good teaching. In this section, I offer a review of the domains and the core traits of a "leader" on the framework, and highlight some previous research that demonstrates why they are important for high-quality teaching. Later, I describe how to support teacher development in these domains through analysis of three case studies.

The first domain, *learning*, is concerned with how teachers think of themselves as learners and make efforts to learn. Previous research on teacher development and learning shows that a disposition toward inquiry and a "growth mind-set" are important factors in fostering self-efficacy, resiliency, and continuous learning.[1] Furthermore, teachers who use inquiry practices to initiate changes in their teaching or school communities develop a strong sense of agency and empowerment through their work.[2]

The second domain in the spectrum is *techno-social development*, or the ways in which teachers understand and use technologies to facilitate and mediate social interaction and learning. Previous research has been conducted on teachers' knowledge of how to integrate technology into their pedagogical practices effectively, and while these studies support the argument that this type of knowledge is important for effective teaching, much research still needs to be conducted on teachers' techno-social understanding and how this influences their work.[3] Yet, preliminary research on teacher learning and social media has been very promising. Andrea Forte et al. studied the professional growth of teachers who used Twitter as a learning tool. They found that teachers' use of social media allowed them to expand their learning horizons and share information more easily:

> Through Twitter, teachers forge and maintain professional ties outside their local schools and, in doing so, become conduits for new practices and ideas to move in and out of their local communities . . . Our findings portray teachers on Twitter as progressive thinkers who are in a position to build the trust and support networks necessary to strengthen leadership in educational communities and increase the effectiveness of reform efforts that serve their shared interests in appropriating social media for the classroom.[4]

Furthermore, in my research on preservice teachers who participated in a course about connected learning and social media, the participants found that their use of openly networked social media for inquiry and professional development in the course resulted in diversification of their learning networks and increased opportunities to locate resources and support through the networks that they developed.[5]

The third domain, *modalities of learning and production*, considers how teachers integrate multiple modalities of literacy into their work. Studies of the maker culture in teacher education show that the outcomes from the hands-on, multimodal, constructivist aspects of makerism have effects on learning in students similar to those they have on teachers.[6] That is, while students tend to experience a sense of agency, empowerment, and what Sean Justice and Sandra Markus call the "cognitive effect . . . of the feeling of knowing," so too do teachers.[7] Similarly, research shows that arts-based education for teachers provides powerful opportunities for reflection and self-expression, particularly in issues of social justice.[8] The allotment of space for making and arts-based learning in schools or universities allows teachers to feel safe to collaborate with others and deepen their inquiries into practice.[9]

Voice and storytelling, the fourth domain of the framework, concerns both descriptive inquiry and the craft of communicating one's story. In her book, *Teachers Practice Online: Sharing Wisdom, Opening Doors*, Désirée Pointer-Mace shared stories of teachers who went public with their practice by using the web to showcase their inquiries and work. She discussed the impacts on teachers.[10] Not only did "going public" create more opportunities for learning through reflection, but also growth through connecting with the community around their work. In her article coauthored with Ann Lieberman, both scholars reflected on the ways in which going public, and teacher voice, can have an impact on the profession of teaching beyond just the single teacher: "We propose that the advent and ubiquity of new media tools and social networking web resources provide a means for networked learning to 'scale up.' These important conceptual hooks present some new possibilities for thinking differently about the codification of professional knowledge, the conditions for its evolvement and the ways that professional development is organized."[11]

The fifth domain, *sociopolitical development*, can be one of the most challenging yet important aspects of development for transformative teachers. Learning about critical theory and pedagogy requires a lens for understanding social power and structured social experiences that allow for critical conversations and collaboration. Beliefs about diversity, equity, and knowledge are difficult to articulate, and research in teacher education has demonstrated that many individuals resist discussing these topics.[12] Several scholars of ethics in teacher education have noted that, although morals and moral choices are a central aspect of the work of teaching, many teachers do not have the language or practice in articulating their own moral or ethical stances.[13] This disconnection between moral stance and practice leads to what Matthew Sanger calls a "schizophrenia" of teaching in which teachers try to make moral decisions about teaching in a context that does not recognize the moral nature of the problem.[14]

The sixth domain, *social capital and agency*, has been a central theme in this book. Research on the effects of teachers' social capital on teaching, learning, and school community has become quite popular since the mid-2000s.[15] These studies have shown that teachers with high levels of professional social capital have positive effects on student achievement, are more likely to feel efficacious in their work, have greater access to resources, and are more often positioned as leaders and innovators in their schools.[16] Sara Van Waes and colleagues in Belgium explicitly taught a cohort of preservice teachers about social network theory and dynamics, and found that this cohort developed higher levels of social capital than the cohort that did not learn about how networks function.[17] Therefore, these studies show that knowledge of how social networks function is important for teachers to develop.

In 2014, Andy Hargreaves and Michael Fullan introduced the concept of "professional capital," a combination of human capital, social capital, and decision-making capital.[18] They argued that it is critical for schools and districts to support the development of teachers' professional capital by fostering opportunities for teacher leadership and collaboration. The concept of professional capital speaks to the relationship between social capital and agency: that transformative teaching requires that teachers have access to rich and diverse sources of social capital and the agency to apply these resources to the work they do in schools.

The *role of the teacher* is the seventh domain in the framework. This domain focuses on how teachers define their occupation (as technical or professional work), and the positions they place themselves in for developing a knowledge base for the occupation. As transformative professionals, teachers see themselves as key agents in shaping curriculum, educational practices, and policies that affect student learning experiences. They actively seek out opportunities to collaborate in inquiry about student learning with other teachers not only to improve their practice, but also to contribute to the profession. A wide range of research has indicated that collaborative teacher learning and inquiry supports and sustains teachers in their practice.[19] Furthermore, the grounded, classroom-based research that transformative teachers contribute to the knowledge base about education is extremely valuable.

Finally, the last domain in the framework is teachers' understanding of cultural *hybridity and third spaces*. Third spaces, or spaces in which diverse individuals and cultures intersect and communicate, are vital for teachers to develop the cultural competence to connect with and support their students' learning, as well as to develop a well-rounded understanding of their professional world. Research efforts in teacher education to foster third spaces for collaboration and learning have demonstrated the tremendous growth in cultural understanding and connections.[20] For example, Ken Zeichner and colleagues fostered a partnership between his university and a local school in which all participants learned together in the third space that was created through the partnership.[21] This was different than typical school partnership because there was no top-down hierarchy of expertise. Rather, everyone learned to value the knowledge and expertise that every individual brought from his or her own context. Spaces such as this, which recognize individuals' funds of knowledge or the unique life view and expertise of each person, help to generate a sense of tolerance and respect among all participants in the space, which fosters a greater exchange of information and learning.[22]

Case Studies of Transformative Teacher Support

The preceding overview provides a reminder of the key domains of the developmental framework and research about why the domains are important for good teaching. In the following section, I share three in-depth case studies of organizations in order to highlight specific strategies and approaches that support teachers. I describe how these strategies support the development of transformative teachers across the eight domains of the framework. These case studies represent a variety of types of organizational allies. The EdCamp Foundation is a national educational nonprofit that supports the work of a networked social movement. The Connected Learning Alliance second is a partnership of several educational organizations. Lastly, the Philadelphia Education Fund is a community-based educational advocacy organization and foundation.

Case Study One: EdCamp and the EdCamp Foundation

EdCamp is a model for teacher-led professional development rooted in the "hackathon" tradition. The first EdCamp was organized by a small group of teachers in 2010 in Philadelphia. Between 2010 and 2016, over a thousand

EdCamps were organized by teachers worldwide (about two hundred internationally and about eight hundred in the United States). With an average attendance of about a hundred fifty teachers, it is likely that at least a hundred thousand teachers have attended an EdCamp since 2010. In 2013, the EdCamp Foundation was established as a 501(c)(3) to support organizers through grant funding, supplies, and networking. By 2015, the foundation had received over $2 million in grant funding from major foundations and organizations.

An EdCamp is an annual "unconference" or participant-led professional development event. In a traditional educational conference, the agenda is preset and participants attend sessions often led by scholars or researchers. When participants arrive at EdCamp, the schedule ("session board") is blank, and over the course of an hour, participants develop it by suggesting session topics. Sessions are generally conversations about a topic of mutual interest, instead of the "sage on the stage" approach of traditional workshops and presentations. For example, a participant might propose a discussion on how to use podcasts in the classroom. Individuals who are interested in discussing the topic attend the session. The participant who proposed it facilitates discussion; he or she does not need expertise in the area, just interest. Another important aspect of EdCamp is the "rule of two feet," which means that participants freely travel between sessions and attend multiple sessions during one period. The idea is that time is precious, and participants should attend what interests them. The result is that the remaining sessions are those that people are most interested and engaged in. It's a kind of Darwinian survival of the fittest for session topics.

EdCamp has some other unique features. First, all EdCamps are free, and no sponsors are allowed to attend the event. Companies that want to be sponsors typically give "swag" such as subscriptions to software, technology tools, and T-shirts that are raffled off. Given EdCamp's strong history and connection to educational technology, many ed-tech companies are frequent donors. Second, EdCamps tend to end with an "Ed Tech Smackdown," a timed, speed-drill session in which participants share suggestions of websites, apps, and instructional technology to use in the classroom.

Third, behind the scenes of the EdCamp event is constant networking and back-channel discussion. EdCamps are generally promoted through hashtags on social media such as Twitter and Voxer, and through a posting on the Ed-Camp wiki. The first EdCamp was organized entirely through Twitter, which set the precedent for using hashtags as a key organizing strategy. During an EdCamp event, participants use the hashtag of the event to talk about what is happening in each session and post news. This helps to facilitate travel between sessions and allows participants to get information about sessions that they decide not to attend in person.

Another unique feature of EdCamp is the session board, which is hosted online through a networked collaborative writing application (such as Google Docs). Changes are made immediately online, and all attendees can see the changes. If a session is canceled due to low attendance, it is removed from the schedule. Also, the session boards generally contain links to collaborative writing spaces for each session that all participants use as a collaborative note-taking tool that lives on after the event (so participants stay in contact after the session).

EdCamps have been organized based on location (e.g., EdCamp Boston) or topic or area of interest (EdCamp Leadership). In most of the events, technologies are used to connect and document work. Many sessions focus on innovative uses of technology, making and maker education, inquiry, and creativity. This focus is likely due to the population of attendees (most participants learn about the events through social media and are thus somewhat versed in connected technology), the technology roots of EdCamp (it originated as a teacher version of BarCamp—a hackathon), and the fact that many of the biggest questions teachers now face are in using new and different forms of technologies in teaching. The event becomes a moment when teachers can inquire and solve problems about new teaching methods, as well as build their professional network.

Behind the structure of the EdCamp model is a philosophy about teaching, learning, and leading. Hadley Ferguson, one of the original EdCamp organizers, is the founding director of the EdCamp Foundation. When I spoke with Ferguson about the history, mission, and growth of EdCamp, she described

EdCamp as "democracy in action" or a free space where everyone can share voices and perspectives, and that encourages cross-pollination of people from different kinds of schools and positions. Ferguson says that a core value of the culture is in "honoring the voices and choices of teachers." She described how this value plays out through the event's structures and practices:

> What's core to EdCamp folks is that teaching is a *profession*. Teachers care deeply about their work and they are not children. A lot of professional development is just people talking at them. People coming here want to be lifelong learners. At EdCamp, you can go to the sessions that are right for you. If you have gone to an EdCamp and not found anything interesting, then add a conversation that is one you want to take part in: there is an open door for you to create new sessions that are interesting to you. The learning is on you, but it is a responsibility that is liberating, not onerous. It honors who they are as educators.

Ferguson's goal for the EdCamp Foundation (and greatest challenge) is that it supports the grassroots work of organizers without being too controlling or taking agency away from them. She has sponsored several initiatives that are open ended, facilitated by the EdCamp community, and create resources or spaces for EdCamp leaders to develop. The first initiative is a summit in which all EdCamp organizers in a region join an event to plan other EdCamps. They share questions and resources, swap stories, and build support networks for each other. Another initiative is the "EdCamp in a Box" mini-grant, which provides key materials and starter funds for an event. The only request is that grant recipients share outcomes and stories of the events with the foundation. Finally, Ferguson documents examples and develops resource guides for future EdCamp organizers.

As part of its documentation work, the foundation has been collecting stories and data about the impact of EdCamp on teachers, schools, and students. The endeavor is challenging, mainly because of EdCamp's open-source attitude to use of its concept and materials; anyone can start an EdCamp by using the logo (freely available on the wiki) and organizing a free, participant-led professional development event. In my discussion with Ferguson about the research team's ongoing work, it is clear that an important aspect of EdCamp is the way it shapes teachers' social capital. That is, teachers develop strong professional networks and connections through the events. Many teachers repeatedly attend the EdCamp because the experience is so positive. Ferguson shared the anecdote of one teacher who was determined to go to an EdCamp in every state. She created a map and posted her travels online to share everything she was learning.

Perhaps the greatest indicator of EdCamps' success as a powerful source of teacher learning is simply the sharp increase in events over time. Figure 9.1 shows the increase of *documented* events each year between 2010 and 2015.[23] Ferguson noted that the number of undocumented events (events not posted on the EdCamp wiki) is unknown, which could add significantly to the total numbers.

Ferguson suggested that the EdCamp movement has also had a direct impact on the classroom. Not only do teachers develop new ideas and plans for their classroom, but participants have documented instances in which there is a ripple effect influencing their colleagues' ideas about student learning as a result of some of the ideas they bring to their schools. For example, Glenn

FIGURE 9.1 Increase in EdCamp events listed on EdCamp wiki, 2010–2015

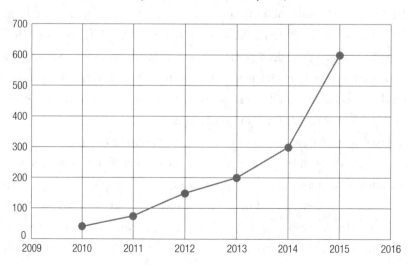

Robbins, a regular participant, decided to create a weekly EdCamp event in his school for students. The event quickly became one of the most valued activities of the community. On his school district blog, Robbins shared that students responded with increased engagement, parents wrote letters about how much more engaged their children were in school, and several teachers who had been peripherally involved in the event even began to rethink their practice when they witnessed students that they thought were disengaged or had weak academic performance become highly motivated and demonstrate strong academic performances in the EdCamp event.[24]

While Ferguson's aim is to nurture teacher leadership and innovation through the foundation, she also remains conscious of diversity issues and participation in a movement led primarily by individuals who have the opportunity and disposition to speak up and connect with others. Therefore, the EdCamp Foundation has also sought opportunities to create space and time for members to openly discuss issues of equity, voice, and participation and strategize ways to be inclusive. Ferguson works to make sure there is diverse racial and ethnic representation among leaders at the EdCamp organizers' summits and convenes meetings specifically about issues of diversity and inclusion for leaders. The commitment to inclusion, diversity, and equity is made explicit through such strategies and are part of the EdCamp language and ethos.

The EdCamp Foundation, and the movement it supports, helps to develop transformative teachers. Table 9.1 outlines the ways in which the characteristics of the organization support the eight domains of the transformative teacher development framework. For the first domain, learning, the EdCamp ethos supports teachers taking control of their own learning and developing a lifelong mastery of their craft. EdCamp provides a process for teacher inquiry and collaboration, and physical space in which the work can occur. The second domain, techno-social development, is supported by the integration of social media and connected technologies as back-channel discussion, curating, and follow-up communication tools and intentional conversations about participation online and face-to-face. EdCamp highly supports inquiries into multimodal forms of learning and exploration, and makes this possible through

TABLE 9.1 Characteristics of EdCamp that support the development of transformative teachers

DOMAIN	CHARACTERISTICS OF EDCAMP
Learning	• Inquiry process • Open-ended "mastery" • Spaces for sharing innovations/work
Techno-social development	• Integrated as social tool for use as back channel, documentation, or follow-up • Integrated as resource-curating tool • Intentional conversations about ethics/participation
Modalities of learning and production	• Recognition/celebration of multimodalities • Grants development • Modalities drive connections/ relationship building
Voice and storytelling	• Invites all voices; democratic participation as central theme • Promotes teachers going public
Sociopolitical development	• Critical questioning/social justice as ethos • Intentional discussions on diversity • Identifies problems; works to solve them.
Social capital and agency	• Open membership, encouraging affinity subgroups • Primary purpose as organizing/sharing tool • Inviting diversity • Connecting to group resources and grants
Role of the teacher	• "Leadership" as relational and supported. • Valuing expertise from the "ground"
Hybridity and third spaces	• Face-to-face and online spaces • Functioning as bridge between spaces

grant support and the community's interest in promoting good ideas about the use of multimodal tools.

A central theme of EdCamp is teacher leadership and voice. Broadcasting or sharing one's ideas is considered a way to contribute and care for the community, which promotes storytelling and voice. Alongside this, the foundation is careful to be transparent about its work to make EdCamps inclusive and inviting. This intentionality supports sociopolitical development. The combination of open membership with the opportunity to meet in affinity groups based on shared interests and questions helps to generate strong social capital, the sixth domain. Furthermore, the EdCamp Foundation uses its connections to help EdCamps share resources or ideas to support each other and to connect to grant opportunities.

The role of the teacher as a professional is supported by the organization's recognition of the central need for teachers to lead the movement, and the redefinition of leadership from a hierarchical position to a relational, action-oriented position. Furthermore, expertise is redefined in EdCamp—the expertise is from teachers who have honed their craft in a particular area or practice, rather than from outsiders. Finally, the domain of hybridity and third spaces is supported by two characteristics: the hybrid nature of EdCamp (face-to-face and online), and the ways in which it functions as a third space, bridging school and personal interests or passions.

Case Study Two: Teacher Professional Development in the Connected Learning Alliance

The Connected Learning Alliance is a coalition of nonprofit educational organizations and institutions that use the connected learning approach to guide and inform the work they do with educators and youth. The alliance was coordinated at the Digital Media and Learning (DML) Research Hub of the University of California Humanities Research Institute (based at UC Irvine and originally funded by the John D. and Catherine T. MacArthur Foundation). Key members of the alliance include the National Writing Project, the Institute of Play, the Digital Youth Network, and the Mozilla Foundation. These members, as well as associates, scholars with the DML Research Hub, and individuals, work to integrate connected learning into programs, projects, and research on learning. In this case study, I focus primarily on the ways in which members of the Connected Learning Alliance have supported transformative teacher development through the National Writing Project and the Connected Learning Certificate Program at Arcadia University.

As I described in chapter 7, connected learning is an approach that supports participatory, interest-driven learning toward greater equity in education and civic participation. In the core publication that defined connected learning, the authors made this connection between equity and education explicit:

> Connected learning centers on an equity agenda of deploying new media to reach and enable youth who otherwise lack access to opportunity. It is not simply a "technique" for improving individual educational outcomes, but rather seeks to build communities and collective capacities for learning and opportunity . . . Without this focus on equity and collective outcomes, any educational approach or technical capacity risks becoming yet another way to reinforce the advantage that privileged individuals already have.[25]

Thus, equity and participation are central aspects of connected learning and drive many of the practices and design features of organizations that use it to guide their work. In this way, the connected learning approach offers a pedagogical guide for transformative teaching. Therefore, professional development in connected learning supports the development of transformative teaching.

The approach was created primarily through collaborative efforts led by the MacArthur Foundation that brought together a diverse collection of scholars and practitioners who were all working at the leading edge in their fields. In 2011, leaders of this work decided to examine whether there were crosscutting principles emerging from their efforts in digital media and learning. They called themselves the "Decemberists," because they met in December 2011 to design what would become the connected learning approach. I spoke with Elyse Eidman-Aadahl, executive director of the National Writing Project, and one of the Decemberists to learn more about the birth of Connected Learning, and how the National Writing Project, a long-standing, national, teacher-led professional network, came to take a central role in helping teachers learn about and engage in connected learning practice.

In December 2011, Mimi Ito and colleagues in the Connected Learning Research Network were disseminating their large-scale study on youth learning in the twenty-first century and pondering how to use their findings for actionable change. Their thinking was that connected learning needed to be fully developed, tested in real projects and programs, and fully fleshed out. The National Writing Project had been developing a set of practices consistent with the approach and was eager to build on its efforts to engage teachers in digital media and storytelling. Together with colleagues from the Institute of Play, Quest to Learn, Youth and Participatory Politics, the Digital Media Hub, the Digital Youth Network, and the Mozilla Foundation and with support from the MacArthur Foundation, the Decemberists met to transform the theory of connected learning into a fully developed design approach and subsequently worked together as the Connected Learning Alliance in order to implement and disseminate the approach.

NWP, a central member of the Alliance, has had a very long history of leveraging technology to connect teachers and support teacher voice. In the early 1990s, NWP helped teachers learn to use modems and e-mail, creating communities such as UrbNet using early community tools like First Class as a way to communicate with NWP teachers. During these early times, the NWP conceptualized websites on Mosaic and Netscape as "digital paper." In the early 2000s, NWP created a website called Digital Is to share teaching resources and practices. Having fostered a growing network of NWP teachers who were exploring the integration of digital media into their teaching and professional development, NWP began working with others to build the connected learning approach and think about how to use it to support teacher leadership and learning.

NWP used a range of tools, spaces, and events to help teachers not only explore connected learning, but take leadership roles in the development of connected learning practices (several of the teachers featured in this book are NWP teachers). A primary tool and space was the Digital Is website, an open platform that allowed members to share, curate resources, and blog about teaching. Christina Cantrill, associate director of national programs at NWP, developed the site to encourage users to take the lead in building the resources on the site; behind the scenes, Cantrill reached out to particular NWP educators that she knew might have important work to share and just needed a nudge to write about it online. Cantrill and NWP associates also helped to amplify teachers' writings on the site by sharing it on social media and through networked communities of educators.

Another important aspect of the NWP structure that supports teachers to explore and lead in connected learning is the local nodes, also known as

NWP local sites. As of 2016, 185 local nodes have been established across the United States. Each node is associated with an institution of higher education so that the organization has a strong connection with education scholars and an institutional home base. At the local node, membership comprises mainly "teacher consultants" (or TCs), teachers who have attended the intense four-week summer institutes that are orientations and gateways to the network. New members are introduced to the norms and practices of the community, which revolve mainly around teacher inquiry, writing, and leadership, and are then expected to take active roles as TCs in organizing and leading events and summer institutes afterward. Framing membership in the network as an opportunity to be an active leader in the professional community and orienting all members around a set of shared practices and beliefs have helped to sustain (and grow) NWP membership for over forty years. When the connected learning approach was introduced through NWP summer institutes and professional development, it offered another way to develop a shared language and set of practices through which to innovate and lead.

Within the events and workshops led by local nodes, the work of "developing teacher voice" occurs. Eidman-Aadahl distinguishes "*developing* teacher voice" from simply "teacher voice." In our conversation, she noted that without the opportunity to develop the ability to articulate a complex stance about their work, teachers' voices can be diminished or discounted. Therefore, teachers need private spaces, or what she calls "studio spaces," to develop their work and their voice, and public spaces ("gallery spaces") in which to share their crafted messages and stories: "Everybody needs their studio space, their working space, their opportunity to iterate, reiterate and really discover what they think and how it works for different audiences. The internet needs to give us that, as well as the public sphere."

Furthermore, the summer institutes and smaller groups offer opportunities for newer members to become coached and mentored by longtime members of the network, which creates a type of apprentice model for leadership and greater voice:

> I think that's a big piece of what we try to do, when we have people we supported in summer institutes, or in small nested working groups, the same

opportunity as an emerging leader teacher to investigate research, to talk to experts, to battle on an idea, to consider if the switched metaphor really works for you, why and why not . . . It's like the think tank. Everybody who is a pundit, has a think tank. Teachers need the same think tank as well.

The NWP also leads national project campaigns to encourage all teachers (not just NWP members) to participate and lend their voices to the professional community. In 2015–2016, the NWP led the "Letters to the Next President 2.0" campaign, in which teachers were given a publication venue for publishing their students' writing about issues concerning them in the presidential election. NWP teachers took the lead in sharing news about their projects, which spread into a broader phenomenon in school districts around the United States. In the Letters 1.0 version of this project conducted for the 2008 election, students and teachers wrote over ten thousand letters. NWP projects that the 2.0 version will have even broader impact. Furthermore, the 2.0 version involved intentional use of collaborative writing technologies and social media to share ideas and outcomes. The campaign highlights not only the NWP's strategy to encourage transformative leadership and action, but also how it uses connected learning as a lens to frame the project.

One NWP project that explicitly aimed at fostering broader teacher engagement in connected learning practices was the Making Learning Connected MOOC (or #CLMOOC) that ran for three summers between 2013 and 2015. The #CLMOOC was facilitated by teams of NWP teacher consultants, called Connected Learning Ambassadors, and was open to anyone on the web. Using the connected learning approach as a pedagogical guide, it provided an eight-week experience in digital writing that encouraged participatory practices such as making and hacking. Another important aspect of the #CLMOOC was the opportunity and space to reflect on one's own work and others' in an open and connected space.

Cantrill also designed a core class of the Connected Learning Certificate Program at Arcadia University (an alliance partner) modeled after the #CLMOOC. In the course, the syllabus, projects, and discussions are publicly shared; web visitors are invited to join class projects and conversations. In addition to this course, the design of the four-course graduate certificate program for educators is modeled on the central tenets of connected learning. For example, all students who enter the program become part of a sustained network of current and former program members, and are encouraged to build professional networks within and beyond the network as a part of their practice. Also, the one-credit, one-week "Connected Learning Camps," in the program are proposed and led by either program graduates or leading educators in their field, and rotate based on interest and topic year-to-year. Finally, participants are taught how to make, hack, and share inquiry projects in openly networked spaces and how to design makerspaces.

While the majority of research on connected learning has focused on youth development, research on educator learning and engagement has been conducted on the NWP #CLMOOC and the Arcadia Connected Learning Certificate program. Anna Smith et al. studied the outcomes of the #CLMOOC on discourse practices among participants and found that the connected learning ethos and approach led to a high level of collaboration and democratic discourse among participants.[26] Instead of a typical online learning experience in which participants are isolated learners and are admonished for borrowing others' ideas or work, in the case of #CLMOOC, participants were free to borrow, remix, and remake others' work, which spurred new conversations and connections among them about the nature and meaning of their ideas and their background and contexts. In short, it encouraged an awareness of the ways that participation shapes thinking and learning. Similarly, my research on the connected learning program at Arcadia has demonstrated that participants began to think of themselves as networked learners, rather than isolated thinkers, after they were encouraged and taught how to remix and share their inquiries online.[27]

Table 9.2 lists the characteristics of the Connected Learning Alliance and the two members featured here (NWP and the Arcadia Connected Learning Certificate program) that support transformative teacher development. In the learning domain, a unique characteristic of the Connected Learning Alliance is the pedagogical structure that centers the work. The structure is open to interpretation, which allows educators to apply it in a wide variety of contexts, yet is clear enough that the ethos and design features are recognizable and

TABLE 9.2 Characteristics of the Connected Learning Alliance members that support transformative teachers' development

DOMAIN	CONNECTED LEARNING ALLIANCE
Learning	• Orientation to shared norms and practices around inquiry • Offers open pedagogical framework • Open-ended "mastery" • Space for sharing innovations/work
Techno-social development	• Integrated as social tool for use as back-channel, documentation, or follow-up • Integrated as resource-curating tool • Intentional conversations about ethics/participation
Modalities of learning and production	• Recognition/celebration of multimodalities • Writing as multimodal
Voice and storytelling	• Promotes teachers' stories/writings • Studio space and gallery space
Sociopolitical development	• Intentional discussions on politics, equity, and participation
Social capital and agency	• Participation opportunities available to many • Apprentice model • Connecting to resources in network
Role of the teacher	• Membership is leadership • Expectation is to transform profession
Hybridity and third spaces	• Face-to-face *and* online spaces

resonate across any projects or programs that apply it. Teachers in the NWP network receive an orientation to the NWP's ethos, which incorporates the connected learning approach, along with its commitment to teacher inquiry and writing, through its summer institutes. Spaces such as Digital Is and its next-generation online publication called the *The Current*, allow teachers to see models of others' learning take the lead in sharing their own work as well.

The connected learning approach highlights the techno-social understanding that connected technologies mediate our social worlds. Many of the members' strategies, such as using it as a social and voice-amplifying tool, as well to make space for connections and conversation are present in the Connected Learning Alliance organizations described here. Further, there are several instances of explicit reflection on participation and equity in these examples.

For the multimodal domain, the connected learning approach itself encourages production-oriented learning and, thus, multimodal practices. The NWP in particular describes writing as a form of making to include multiple modalities of expression. The Connected Learning Certificate program also recognizes and emphasizes multimodal learning, with the incorporation of making as a central practice in several courses, as well as opportunities to engage in making, such as the course on maker education and project-based learning. The various outlets and structures that invite teachers to share their writings and "makes" in both programs support teacher storytelling and voice. Another aspect of the NWP model to support voice is the distinction between more private studio spaces, in which teachers receive mentoring and support to coach them in developing their public voice, and gallery spaces, which provide open, public spaces for teachers to share their stories and ideas.

The focus on equity in the connected learning approach can be witnessed in the programming and structures of the alliance organizations. For example, the NWP's focus on the presidential election was an intentional move to help teachers and students think together about politics and voice in a constructive way. During political campaigns, many citizens are driven to express their views or engage in discourse through writing and multimedia. This project capitalizes on this desire to converse, which reflects the connected learning tenet of interest-driven learning, and provides a guided venue to explore different perspectives and issues.[28] In the Connected Learning Certificate program, Cantrill's course, "Seeking Equity in Connected and Networked Learning," offers an explicit examination of equity in the connected world and educational spaces.

Regarding the social capital domain, the alliance organizations helped foster social capital through several structures: (1) through open participation opportunities; (2) through apprenticing models, in which new members were coached and supported to develop their voice and craft; (3) through intentional work to connect participants with each other and help them seek resources through each other. While the organizations described here are not as open as the EdCamp model, they do provide opportunities and spaces for the broader public to participate and engage with them in their work. For example, while the title "teacher-consultant" might be restricted to individuals who attended the summer institutes, any teacher could participate in the Letters to the Next President 2.0 campaign, and any teacher could contribute to the Digital Is website or participate in NWP public programs like #CLMOOC. Further, in the connected learning program, the syllabus and weekly activities of several courses were available for drop-in learners to participate in.

In terms of the role-of-the-teacher domain, the role of NWP member is clear and explicit: members are leaders who facilitate peer learning for other teachers and members. In other alliance organizations, such as the Connected Learning Certificate program, leadership is encouraged through sharing and (re)using others' ideas. For example, in one class, each student kept an individual blog that fed into a central blog everyone followed. Students were encouraged to read each others' work and build off of one another's projects and ideas. This ethos and structure supported relational leadership opportunities.

Finally, these organizations provided multiple platforms and spaces for teachers to meet and connect, ranging from more private studio spaces in which members or select groups of individuals meet (such as summer institutes) to gallery spaces in which there is open, public participation (such as the #CLMOOC).

Case Study Three: The Philadelphia Education Fund's Teacher Network Project

The Philadelphia Education Fund (the Ed Fund) is a nonprofit, educational advocacy organization with a thirty-year history of supporting teacher professional development and creating college and career pathways for public school students. In the 1980s, an early version of the Ed Fund was founded through a federally funded grant as a program to support professional development teacher networks in the humanities and sciences (then called the PATHS/PRISM program). In 1995, the program merged with the Philadelphia Schools Collaborative program, which focused on high school reform, to become the Ed Fund. Today, the Ed Fund continues to have an impact on Philadelphia teachers by offering a range of programs offering preservice and in-service professional development opportunities and network support.

My case study of the Ed Fund's programming focuses on the Teacher Network program that it initiated around 2013 to convene and connect teacher-led professional development networks. The Teacher Network project came about as a result of the Ed Fund's inquiry into the best ways to support teacher professional development in the city. It started from the core beliefs that teacher collaboration fosters learning and that teachers should take the lead in designing their professional development because they know their needs best. The Ed Fund already sponsored several professional development networks for teachers based on these beliefs, and when it looked further, it discovered that over fifteen teacher-led such networks existed autonomously in the city, and that many of the teachers in these networks were actively transforming educational practices in their schools and communities. Rather than remake the wheel, it sought to understand what made these networks successful and how to support them. Here I document some of the processes and strategies that the Ed Fund used to support teacher leaders in the networks.

As a first step, the Ed Fund members worked with research partners at the University of Delaware to study the landscape of teacher networks in Philadelphia, including where networks existed, what network teachers needed, and what strategies the networks used to build their networks. They interviewed over 180 teachers in fifteen city schools. They found networks both inside and outside schools and decided to focus primarily on the out-of-school networks.[29] When they looked more closely at the strategies that teacher leaders used to build and sustain networks, they saw that these strategies were very similar to, if not the same as, community-organizing strategies. Marina Fradera, one of the Ed Fund program designers, noted: "Basically what we've realized is that . . . it's become a form of organizing—nothing like the labor connotation, but in the mobilizing resources connotation, and so all the same practices that are successful for organizing, we found are also successful for network building. Things like consistency in terms of communication, distributed leadership models, shared language, norms."

They also found that many teachers were members of multiple networks. However, despite the overlaps between networks, there were no formal opportunities for the networks to convene on key educational issues in the city or leverage their collective power. Furthermore, many networks spoke of needed space and time to meet.

Based on its community research, the Ed Fund developed a plan of action that involved working with multiple constituencies. It met regularly with a core group of teacher network leaders to build a solid partnership. Together, they wrote a white paper for the school district with suggestions for partnering with and supporting teacher leaders through existing networks. They also urged that the network focus on expanding opportunities for teacher-led professional development. The suggestions were adopted by the Philadelphia School District in its 2015 "Action Plan 3.0" on items related to teacher professional development. The Ed Fund also published its research in academic journals for the teacher educators and the education research community.

Throughout this process, the Ed Fund continued to host quarterly gatherings for teacher network leaders to meet with each other and with school district officials, local teacher educators/academics, and policy makers. The meetings led to a series of "Teacher Convenings," in which members of all the teacher networks joined to lead professional development events for each other and any teacher who wanted to attend. While the Teacher Convenings were led and organized by network leaders, the Ed Fund helped locate space, organize logistics, and source grant money for sponsorship. After many months of meetings, events, and collaborative actions, a "network of networks" established its own identity as the Coalition of Teacher Networks, as well as its own hashtag: #PHLCTN.

One challenge that organizations face when they are trying to support large, diverse coalitions is creating unity while celebrating and supporting the unique missions and qualities of every coalition partner. Ami Patel Hopkins, an Ed Fund staff member who led the effort to organize the teacher network meetings and convenings, noted that an important part of creating this balance was in making space and having time to ensure all members felt known. She described the importance of slow, intentional partnership development and growth in the work:

For a year and a half, we brought these out-of-school teacher networks to-gether on a quarterly basis, and what we've found from that is there's such a rich landscape of teacher networks and a lot of them don't know about each other. We . . . spent that year and a half . . . getting to know each other, so part of the meeting and the quarterly meetings would be focused around that, but also a piece would be focused around information of the teacher networks might need, and action items.

From this intense partnership building and the Teacher Convenings emerged a collective agenda and set of goals that all the networks could agree to work together on: (1) celebrating and empowering educators, (2) establish-ing policy and advocacy, and (3) enhancing teacher network landscape (tools that teacher networks need).

Another important strategy that the Ed Fund used to help unite the net-works was to act as a bridge between the school district and policy makers and the networks. While teacher networks can generate strong internal unity and group power, it can sometimes be difficult to break through the institu-tional policies and structures set in place by schools without a brokered con-nection between teachers and administrators. The Ed Fund invited district administrators and leaders to quarterly meetings to hear teacher leaders share news and concerns, and also to connect and partner in solving problems. Its neutral stance, transparency, and even physical location helped create a space for these conversations to occur.

The Ed Fund's efforts to offer grant opportunities and foster collabora-tive grant-writing work both united and engaged network members. With funding from the Gates Foundation, the Ed Fund developed mini-grants for supporting new and existing teacher networks based on its understanding of what the networks needed from the research. Some recipients offered their own mini-grants to teachers, and the Ed Fund promoted news of these grants through e-mail lists for the quarterly meeting attendees. At quarterly meet-ings, attendees could connect with others to discuss potential collaborations and updates on projects. For example, Samuel Reed (see chapter 3) discussed his BoysWriteNow project and eventually partnered with another network teacher to cofound and develop funding for Girls on Fire, a writing program for middle school girls. Both projects were primarily funded through an online crowdfunding campaign. Reed and his colleague had a large network of teachers and educational advocates to reach out to due to their connections through the teacher networks in the Ed Fund's coalition.

Finally, the Ed Fund created an online hub (http://philadelphiateachernetworks .org) for participating teacher-led networks that helped to distribute important information and updates about the networks, and give a platform for network teachers to discuss their work, and create opportunities for the various networks to collaborate. The major components of the online hub include a live calendar that members can update with upcoming events, a comprehensive list of all teacher-led networks in the area that describes their foci and provides contact information, blog posts written by network teachers, resources (such as information on grants), and a discussion forum. The hub also shares news from the #PhlEd (Philadelphia education) and #PHLCTN hashtag communities.

Table 9.3 shows the strategies the Ed Fund used to develop the Teacher Network project that support transformative teacher development. In the first domain, learning, the Ed Fund used its institutional power to conduct research that it then translated to clear, actionable information and approaches for teachers to use in leading and organizing networks, such as network self-assessment tools and asset maps. It also provided space for teachers to develop their thinking and work. The web hub provided an online social space in which to connect, supporting teachers' techno-social development. Network members that previously did not know about hashtag communities or how blogs worked were introduced to these concepts through the online portal. Furthermore, network members who were actively using social media had access to another tool and community through the web hub.

The Ed Fund's support of teachers' work to develop grants in their interest areas fostered multimodal teaching and learning. Storytelling and voice were promoted through the web portal as well as by quarterly meetings. Teachers were encouraged to share their concerns and stories with each other and with administrators and education advocates. The Ed Fund's role as a broker between communities also supported members' sociopolitical development. While each network had its own agenda and stance, the Ed Fund supported

TABLE 9.3 Characteristics of the Philadelphia Education Fund's Teacher Network Project that support transformative teachers' development

DOMAIN	PHILADELPHIA EDUCATION FUND
Learning	• Providing research data, conceptual frameworks, and informational tools • Space for sharing innovations/work
Techno-social development	• Integrated technology as curating and connecting tool • Connected to networked communities beyond the organization
Modalities of learning and production	• Recognition/celebration of multimodal efforts • Grants development
Voice and storytelling	• Invites all voice; democratic participation as central theme • Promotes teachers' stories/writings
Sociopolitical development	• Transparent • Mediator role • Identifies problems; works to solve them.
Social capital and agency	• Open meetings • Primary role is to connect teachers/groups • Connecting to grants/resources • Social capital lens on teacher learning
Role of the teacher	• "Leadership" is relational and supported. • Valuing expertise from the "ground"
Hybridity and third spaces	• Face–to-face *and* online spaces • Functioning as bridge between spaces • Slow, ongoing work to build partnership

them to engage in problem solving together and learn more about each others' perspectives and experiences.

The Ed Fund's explicit lens of social capital development through teacher professional development helped it to construct experiences that supported both strong ties within networks and brokerage between networks. It also supported collaboration that led to outreach beyond the networks, cultivating groundwork for partnerships and structural change in institutions, as well as access to grant funding. Another explicit stance taken by the Ed Fund was in positioning teachers as leaders and designers of their profession. It worked to empower networks and teacher leaders to promote teacher-led professional development.

The Ed Fund's transparency and stance as an ambassador to teachers and the school district supported teacher growth in the domain of hybridity and third spaces. The Ed Fund created a space in which real restructuring could take place by brokering conversations between administrators and teachers and between teacher networks. Also, its deliberately slow partnership development created multiple spaces in which members felt acknowledged and able to contribute.

Learning from these Case Studies: Lessons and Takeaways

EdCamp is a teacher-led movement to reinvent professional development. The Connected Learning Alliance is a coalition of organizations to promote the connected learning approach. The Ed Fund's Teacher Network project is an effort to connect teacher-led professional networks in one city. Each of these organizational allies has very different aims and goals, yet all share certain characteristics that support the development of transformative teachers. These case studies offer lessons for transformative teacher allies and educators to draw on in their work to support teachers' work and development. Here I describe some of these lessons using the developmental framework as an organizing lens. Table 9.4 provides of a summary of the key strategies and lessons across the domains.

Supporting Teacher Learning

In the case studies, a common factor in the learning domain was that the organizational allies offered third spaces for teachers to meet and learn together. Also, they offered teachers research and approaches to help them think about their work. They do not use this information to tell teachers what to do, but rather to support critical and constructive thinking about their work. Furthermore, the structure and practices support inquiry and a growth mind-set regarding professional development.

TABLE 9.4 Summary of case study characteristics that support transformative teacher learning

DOMAIN	CHARACTERISTICS OF LEADERS	WHAT ORGANIZATIONAL ALLIES AND TEACHER EDUCATORS CAN DO
Learning	• Collaborate with members of their professional networks on common projects or issues. • Use inquiry-based professional learning to enact change.	• Promote inquiry process and open-ended work toward mastery. • Offer spaces for sharing innovations/work. • Orient members to shared norms and practices. • Provide research data and conceptual frameworks. • For teacher educators: develop assessment systems that allow space for teachers to learn through failure and trial/experimentation.
Techno-social development	• Use connected technologies as producers to design, facilitate, and share social learning opportunities. • Understand the social contexts and issues that shape equity in the digital era.	• Integrate technology as social tool for back-channel and follow-up conversations and as a resource-curating tool. • Connect to networked communities beyond the organization. • Have intentional conversations about ethics and participation in digital spaces. • Provide both private and public online spaces to connect.
Modalities of learning and production	• Shift from focus on end product to process when thinking about learning and knowledge development. • Value the processes of making, and hacking art, crafts, hardware, software, text, and digital media in learning.	• Recognize and celebrate multimodalities. • Promote grants development for multimodal work. • Modalities drive connections/relationship building. • Communication is understood as multimodal.
Voice and storytelling	• Demonstrate strong skills as storytellers. • Use storytelling to empower learners to address social issues and injustices.	• Invite all voices; democratic participation is a central theme. • Promote teachers' stories/writings. • Provide "studio" space and "gallery" space. • Support teachers going public.

DOMAIN	CHARACTERISTICS OF LEADERS	WHAT ORGANIZATIONAL ALLIES AND TEACHER EDUCATORS CAN DO
Sociopolitical development	• Achieve a critical consciousness of systems of oppression in society. • Work as change agents for social justice in education.	• Promote discussions on politics, equity, and participation. • Transparency regarding roles/stance. – Mediator role – Explicit stance • Identify key problems and support teachers to solve them.
Social capital and agency	• Connect with others to organize for learning and change. • Seek diverse perspectives. • Develop a sense of agency through their professional communities.	• Offer open membership or multiple ways to participate. • Support affinity subgroups. • Model a network mind-set that values diversity. • Have an apprentice model. • Serve primarily to connect and organize teachers. • Connect teachers to grants/resources. • Design programming using a social capital lens.
Role of the teacher	• Facilitate culturally responsive learning experiences that empower learners to be civically engaged. • Have a critical understanding of the political dimensions of teaching.	• Promote membership as (relational) leaders. • Expect that teachers can transform their profession. • Value expertise from the "ground." • Study the history of teacher role and agency.
Hybridity and third spaces	• Consciously seek to connect authentically with students. • Blend interests and passions of home, third spaces, and school life. • Participate in professional communities in third spaces as regular members or leaders.	• Provide various forms of spaces: – Face-to-face and online – Diverse and affinity – Public and private • Function as bridge or broker between institutions. • Promote slow, ongoing work to build partnerships. • Identity mapping • Invite (vs. impose) and model vulnerability.

These findings have implications for preservice teacher education. Teachers need permission and a supportive community to take risks, make mistakes, and learn from failure. For teacher educators, this may mean rethinking how evaluation happens in the classroom. Is there space and room for preservice teachers to fail (note, failure is not the same as laziness)? Are students being "held" safely in a way that they can experience and explore discomfort? Are relationships nurtured in a way that builds networks of support among students? All these questions are important to consider for teacher educator programs and administrators who seek to cultivate transformative teacher leadership in their schools. Furthermore, school administrators need to make explicit the norms of permission to experiment and create real spaces, such as makerspaces or learning labs, that encourage inquiry-based work and thinking among students and teachers. Finally, everyone, from teachers to administrators, can seek mentors and models beyond the classroom that inspire, support, and sustain their learning, especially through the use of connected technologies.

Supporting Techno-Social Development

In the techno-social domain, the transformative teachers' organizational allies used connected technologies as way to continue or add to conversations, connect ideas, curate resources, and expand dialogue about an issue of interest. Connected technology was a natural part of the collaboration and work that took place; it was not an add-on and the only tool for communication. Yet, the role technology played in shaping participation and voice was interrogated by the organizational allies, and they aimed a critical eye at the way members were engaging in digital spaces. They were clear to identify the ethical issues bound in the use of technology and social media, and set expectations for behavior or participation. Finally, connected technology was used as a way to link members beyond the borders of their group or network to expand horizons and access to resources and information.

Therefore, in order to support teachers in their techno-social development, the move to connect must be driven by a need, interest, or passion that a teacher would like to explore. Encouraging teachers to make and share their questions, inquiries, and *final* work in open, online spaces helps them to understand connected technologies as primarily a social learning tool, a way to learn from and with others. More private group spaces are important as well for teachers to develop their voice and thinking as a part of the process toward public sharing or publication. Alongside this production process, it is also important to uncover the ways these tools mediate and shape social issues such as privilege, social power, privacy, and equity through explicit conversation and activities that illustrate the ways in which participation and sharing in online spaces mediates our relationships and power.

Supporting Modalities of Learning and Production

The case studies revealed a range of ways in which organizational allies can support the modalities of learning domain. The first and most straightforward approach used by all of the organizations was to acknowledge the work and value of teachers' multimodal learning and practices. Another approach, used in the EdCamp Foundation, was to help teachers build connections through their multimodal, maker-related projects. Finally, a third approach used by allies was to help teachers and teacher networks locate funding opportunities that helped them continue to build their practice in these areas. Organizational allies played an important role as advocates for multimodal approaches to teaching and learning by amplifying news about teachers' work and helping teachers access resources and spaces to create multimodal projects.

Therefore, as with the previous domains, the analysis of these cases suggests that teachers need a supportive space in which to explore and develop their multimodal interests, and a place or community that not only values the work, but challenges them to continually improve. Resources and space are particularly important for this domain. Teachers need access to not only materials and locations for this work, but also connections with arts and community organizations that can support them (and their students) in practicing their crafts.

Supporting Voice and Storytelling

To support teachers' voice and storytelling, these organizational allies modeled democratic participation by structuring their own meetings and events with the same participatory practices that they espoused. They helped teachers to develop their voices through coached, small-group experiences (studio spaces) and offered opportunities for teachers to share their work and inquiries in broader public spaces (gallery spaces). Teachers' stories were valued as a source of empowerment, agency, and information for the public, and they were used to inform the professional community about the grassroots transformations that were happening in education.

In teacher education, exploring such questions as, "How are stories being told today?" "What makes stories powerful?" and "How have stories transformed people and communities?" are good initial inquiries for teacher educators or teachers interested in developing their voice and storytelling abilities. Second, not only are studio and gallery spaces important for developing voice, but also opportunities to cross over between face-to-face and online communities. For example, a small critical friends group at a school might provide a safe community in which to conduct teacher inquiry and begin writing or work that they later post in a public, online space.

Supporting Sociopolitical Development

The organizations studied here faced challenges in bringing together a diverse group of individuals or groups that sometimes had differing goals or perspectives. In order to support teachers' sociopolitical development, the organizational allies developed an understanding of their positionality and power in relationship to the stakeholders with whom they engaged. Some chose to take a mediating stance between stakeholders—for example, of the Philadelphia Education Fund—and others chose to take a more marked stance on social issues, such as the way in which the EdCamp Foundation chose to address issues of diversity and inclusion directly. In both cases, transparency was a very important aspect of helping members and participants relate to and trust the organization. To address issues of social justice and equity as a collective, participants must trust that they understand each other's intentions and perspectives. In addition to transparency, another way that the organizational allies unified diverse groups was through identifying a shared problem (or problems) that members could organize to solve together.

These findings can also translate to formal teacher education programming. Schools of education that offer clear, transparent stances on issues of social justice, diversity, and inclusion help preservice teachers understand immediately that teaching is inherently moral and political. Furthermore, in such programs, preservice teachers should work to uncover their own beliefs and develop a lens for understanding by beginning with *comparative* self-reflection of their views or perspectives on learning, difference, and knowledge. However, these understandings do not become realized without dialogue. Alison Cook-Sather's Teachers Learning Together program at Bryn Mawr College is a good example of this practice. Cook-Sather created what she called "liminal spaces," in which preservice teachers learned from and with high school students about schooling.[30] In her research on the program, Cook-Sather found that preservice teachers developed a strong sense of critical pedagogy and ability to develop learning experiences for students that were empowering and engaging.[31]

In addition to liminal spaces, teachers who may be marginalized due to race, ethnicity, or gender identity need safe spaces to meet as affinity groups to debrief and support each other.[32] Jesse Tauriac et al. studied the use of affinity groups to enhance intergroup dialogue for high school students and found that the process of allowing affinity groups to meet before initiated intergroup activities helped to facilitate discourse among everyone.[33] Likewise, Stephen John Quaye and Shaun Harper's study of men's racial identity development in a college black student union revealed that the participants developed a stronger sense of racial identity, which enabled them to cross cultural boundaries with greater confidence.[34] While diversity helps to create critical dialogue, affinity groups can be sites of healing and strength for individuals who are frequently the minority or experience micro-aggressions daily. Furthermore, white teacher identity scholar Ali Michael suggests that white teachers can also benefit from affinity groups that focus on becoming antiracist allies, exploring white identity, and understanding white privilege.[35]

Supporting Social Capital and Agency

The organizational allies had a big-picture understanding of social capital and used this lens to design programming to support teachers' social capital development. The strategies they used, such as cultivating diverse membership, developing apprentice models, encouraging affinity groups, and leveraging the network to seek resources, were all rooted in social network theory. The organizational allies saw that their greatest power was in their ability to assist teachers in connecting and collaborating with others so that the teachers could lead. They worked to foster such collaboration, not to do the work of the teachers. They advocated for transformative teachers by making room for them to connect and build.

Using some of the newer models learning collaborations such as unconferences, participatory action research (PAR) groups, teach-ins/hackathons, and online collaboration events or groups (for example, hashtag communities) can also create spaces that foster connections between teachers and encourage leadership. In the case studies, EdCamp and the EdFund were able to successfully create such spaces for teacher networking and collaboration. For teacher educators, often the in-classroom communality-building work limited by the size and experience of its community members; preservice teachers need to be encouraged to attend existing, active groups in their areas to truly understand the value of networks and begin building them. If they have difficulty attending physically, simply participating in a hashtag community chat can help them connect with and understand the ways networks shape practice and education.

Another lesson learned from these case studies is that fostering connections between teachers doesn't simply come from the activities; mind-set matters as well. The three organizations actively invited a diverse array of people with multiple perspectives and views to develop and implement their programs. Their networking mind-set valued diverse thought and opinion, and in doing so, it became a norm for group participation. In her work on teacher learning development, Eleanor Drago-Severson writes about mind-sets for teacher leadership and notes that the most advanced form of professional learning is demonstrated when teachers intentionally seek a variety of opinions on a subject and challenge themselves to consider others' perspectives.[36] Technical teachers may not even recognize the homogeneity of their network, whereas transformative teachers are aware of their network diversity and seek to learn from building greater diversity in their network. Therefore, the case study organizations supported teachers to build mind-sets that fostered diverse networking and social capital for their professional learning.

Supporting the Role of the Teacher

In the case studies, strategies to support social capital went hand-in-hand with strategies to support the teacher role as relational leader. While, in some cases, traditional (hierarchical) leadership was valued, it was not the primary language of leadership in these organizations. In EdCamp, the teachers who brought people together for an EdCamp event were considered the leaders. In Ed Fund, the teachers who showed up for quarterly meetings or worked on designing the Teacher Convenings were seen as the leaders. At the programs in the Connected Learning Alliance, the teachers who jumped in to share their work on Digital Is or their blog were making a move toward being leaders. This redefinition of leadership widened the gate and broadened the road for teachers to take steps toward being transformative leaders in their profession.

Preservice and early-career teachers may need to seek mentors and role models who engage in transformative work in order to understand the nuances of this domain. Certainly this book offers some strong examples of teachers that may spark some thinking for beginning teachers; however, interviewing or work with transformative teachers can have a long-lasting influence on emerging or participatory teachers. Another recommendation for teachers in the beginning stages of this domain is to develop a richer understanding of the history of teachers' work, especially as it relates to curriculum development and teacher agency. There are two important facets to examine in the history. First is the way in which teaching emerged as a "women's profession" in the mid-nineteenth century, and how roles, the value of the profession, and the treatment of teachers was established in this pre-feminist era. The second facet is understanding the school as an organization and how it shapes teachers' agency. Looking back on this history may help teachers to develop more agentive understanding and goals for their professional work.

Supporting Hybridity and Third Spaces

Finally, the stories of organizational allies demonstrated the importance of third spaces to transformative teacher development. Transformative teachers needed many different kinds of spaces to do their work. They needed face-to-face and online spaces, public and private spaces, and diverse and affinity spaces. The organizational allies had the time and resources to create and support stable spaces for them. What these spaces had in common was that they were places in which teachers could explore and express themselves differently than they did in school or with friends. These were the places where teachers could safely, slowly, and transform and become transformative over time. Also, the spaces were places of listening and negotiation between stakeholders.

Preservice and beginning teachers would benefit from participating in networked third spaces and connecting their personal passions with their teaching; however, many need help learning to work in hybrid spaces. This can prove to be difficult due to the long-held belief that teachers should not show their human side in schools. Think of the infamous adage that pervades teaching communities: "don't smile 'till Christmas." The belief can be difficult to change because technical teachers see it as a source of strength, even though it is the quite opposite—it is a disempowering weakness. To constantly hold up the façade of the false or tough personality is emotionally exhausting. Furthermore, it creates a negative relationship between teachers and students; students can have no empathy or connection with a teacher who is, essentially, emotionless.

Thus, to begin working on this domain, one must start by examining the idea of vulnerability, an inherent factor in teaching and learning. Geert Keltchermans, a scholar who has extensively studied teacher vulnerability, suggests that we should think of vulnerability as a structural condition instead of an emotional condition.[37] He notes that teachers experience negative repercussions from being vulnerable when vulnerability is imposed, often by an authority. Yet, positive emotional and pedagogical experiences arise when vulnerability is invited or embraced. Likewise, in my research with Leif Gustavson on a teacher inquiry group, we found that when teachers *modeled* and *invited* vulnerability in their classrooms, they expressed joy and a sense of fulfillment that several had never experienced before.[38] Thus, to help preservice and technical teachers "smile before December," teacher educators must develop communities that invite, rather than impose, vulnerability. Most often, this is done through modeling one's own vulnerability. Also, being attentive to group norms by developing them together and talking about participation openly with sensitivity to those who may feel silenced are critical to structuring spaces for vulnerability in a positive way.

Another way to help preservice and beginning teachers learn to traverse multiple spaces and identities is to do some identity-mapping work. Invite teachers to map out the spaces where they spend time (virtual or face-to-face), what they look like, how they are positioned, and what their passions and interests are in these spaces. Taking a look at the many identities and spaces we occupy in our lives helps us to not only see the many (often overlapping) spheres of our lives, but also the potential for new connections.

Organizational allies and teacher educators can play a key role in connecting teachers, developing resources, and making innovative ideas become realities for transformative teachers. Their ability to act as brokers between institutions and safe harbors for teachers is paramount to the development of transformative teachers. Organizations that make space for teachers to take the lead and connect operate in a fundamentally different way than those that use traditional professional development approaches to lead and impose from the top. The alternative approaches shared here foster innovation, teacher agency, and a sense of joy for teachers doing the work.

TEN

Growing the Next Generation

When institutional conditions create more combat than community, when the life of the mind alienates more than it connects, the heart goes out of things, and there is little left to sustain us.
     —Parker J. Palmer, *To Know as We Are Known*[1]

L IKE THE TEACHERS FEATURED in this book, as a teacher educator I am part of a larger system of education. I see and take part in the traditional practices and structures of my profession. I teach courses on content, methods, and occasionally classroom management. Yet, as I have taught, I have noticed a gaping hole in teacher education coursework. Missing from our programs are classes and experiences that help preservice teachers learn how to be publicly engaged, collaborative, critical professionals in the digital age. Or, simply, to learn how to become transformative teachers for the connected era. And, just as the teachers I have described here have done, I am going public with my inquiry in hopes of making a change in teacher education and the broader education community. My hope here is to spur a recognition in these communities that teachers need more than content and methods; teachers need community.

The transformative teacher movements that are gaining ground have grown like wildflowers in concrete. In the midst of a harsh and denigrating environment of high-stakes (yet often invalid) accountability measures, lack of funding and resources, and disrespectful media discourse, transformative teachers have persevered to design, organize, and lead positive change. I ask readers to imagine what schools would look like if transformative teachers were cultivated in schools of education and through the support of educational advocates rather than having to fight their way up through the concrete? What if we committed to connecting preservice teachers with existing teacher-led networks? What if we celebrated the risks that teachers take to innovate rather than punishing them for not conforming? What if we supported teachers' development as social media–savvy, public intellectuals? What if we recognized the contributions transformative teachers have made to the development of pedagogy, school culture, and even educational theory, rather than see them as people who implement others' ideas?

Here, I call on all who work with and support teachers, and teachers themselves, to challenge old paradigms rooted in isolation and replication. Let us teach teachers how to be transformative, not just for their professional community, but to build within themselves a sense of agency and optimism to keep their hearts strong in their work. Here, I have provided a starting point for this work. I've shared rich portraits of real teachers transgressing injustice and inequity through their work. Their stories help to illustrate the developmental framework of the ways of knowing and understanding critical to teachers to sustain through the joys and challenges of their work. These understandings go beyond traditional ideas of teacher development to include notions such as techno-social development, social capital, and hybridity, capturing the essence of the role of participatory culture and technologies in transforming teaching and learning. They also show that transformative teaching is not a "super hero" phenomenon; it is one that is cultivated when provided mentorship, networked support, and the space and freedom to take risks in learning.

Furthermore, here you have read about cultural tools and practices—making, hacking, and connecting—and the ways in which these practices support transformative teaching. These practices are both old and new. They are rooted in progressive ideals about student-centered, interest-based, authentic learning. However, their processes are more clearly articulated and promoted through the design-thinking maker mind-set, expanded upon through the co-constructive and systematic nature of the hacker ethos, and amplified through increased connectivity and a drive to go public with one's practice and inquiry. Recognizing how teachers employ these cultural tools and practices in their work helps us to better understand the evolution of teaching and learning in the twenty-first century, challenges us to adapt, and most importantly, honors the innovation teachers have brought as leaders in this change.

Threaded through these cultural practices is discussion of digital-age technologies. Here I have not advocated for the use of a particular tool or platform or even that teachers use technology in their teaching. Rather, I have sought to show how digital technology has shaped the way we understand collaboration, public voice, learning, and political engagement, and how these changes have affected the teacher as a leader and professional. Through their embrace of a technology-mediated *culture* of making, sharing, remixing, and connecting to lead, transformative teachers have broken barriers of institutional norms and policies and created new movements of professional learning and pedagogy. Instead of focusing on the ever-changing technological tools, we need to help teachers learn more about the ways technology mediates our ways of learning and doing, to take advantage of these shifts to empower learners, and to be critical of the ways technology can also divide and marginalize individuals and groups.

I have also described how transformative teacher leadership is part of a larger picture of advocacy for educational progress, equity, and social justice, and the ways in which all stakeholders in education can support this work. Fundamental to this picture is the positioning of teachers. When teachers are partnered *with* rather than trained *on*, when they are allowed space and support to develop their professional voices, when they are seen as leaders in the relational sense and encouraged to collaborate for change, and when they have the agency to take risks in their learning and work, then their grounded expertise and understanding can support the positive change sought by them and their advocates. As Parker Palmer noted in the epigraph, institutions are critical to sustaining the connections that foster joy and care in a community.

Finally, the stories and research described here highlight the central role of social capital in teaching. Transformative teachers, like the clutch of wildflowers, are grounded and sustained by a vast, often unseen, interwoven connection of social "roots" between them. It is easy to admire the amazing projects and work they do, but what is most important is to recognize the role of roots or networks of support. Historically, literature on teacher quality has focused on visible achievements, yet perhaps due to the high turnover rate in teaching, scholars have been looking more deeply at what drives teacher quality and commitment. They have begun to examine the roots and have discovered that teachers' social networks of professional support are just as important as more visible measures of good teaching. Transformative teachers survive and thrive because of the roots they build, particularly because they engage in the digital participatory culture and technologies that support connecting. Their making, collaborating, and networking in face-to-face and digital spaces create strong personal learning networks.

To support the growth and development of new transformative teachers, it is essential that teacher educators and advocates recognize the importance of building roots, or social capital, as a part of teacher education. In most teacher education programs, social capital development is limited to building a mentor-teacher relationship during student teaching. I argue that this is not nearly enough. Teachers need to be taught how, where, and why to build professional networks, and be given opportunities to connect with other transformative teachers and teacher-led networks during their teacher education program. Teacher education programs need to cultivate gardens for growing roots rather than scatter unsown seeds to the wind. Then the grassroots leadership and learning movements of the digital era will be supported and nurtured by the institutions that exist to develop them.

APPENDIX

Networked Third Spaces
and How to Join Them

Hashtag Communities

Examples of Hashtag Communities

#ENGCHAT—Created and led by an English teacher in 2012 (Meenoo Rami, profiled in chapter 3), this community emerged from a weekly Twitter chat (Monday nights at 8 p.m.) that focuses on English teaching and literacy.

#EDUCOLOR—Developed and maintained by a team of educators, including José Luis Vilson (profiled in chapter 3) and Chris Lehmann (mentioned in chapter 8) in 2015. This hashtag community is actively organizing as a movement to fight racism and its effects in education.

#PHONAR—A community of amateur photographers that grew from Jonathan Worth's open, online photography course that ran from 2012 to 2014. This maker community focuses on sharing the truths of its members' lives through images.

#CLMOOC (Connected Learning MOOC)—A community of makers and educators focused on developing connected learning practices that emerged through an openly networked MOOC led by the National Writing Project that ran during the summers of 2013 to 2015.

How to Join a Hashtag Community

1. *Geek out.* Begin by considering your passion or an enduring question. What is a topic or issue that you find yourself drawn to? Investigate hashtag communities that are related to your passion. Cybraryman.com provides a list of hundreds of education-related Twitter chats, or you can just search social media platforms using the hashtag for your topics of interest to see the kinds of communities or conversations on the topic.

2. *Lurk and follow.* Once you have found a few communities that seem to meet regularly for chats and have a solid group of followers, be a lurker. That means watch the conversations, but don't chime in yet. Observe the ways in which the community members interact and talk with each other. Each hashtag community is a community of practice (CoP) and has its own norms and practices. Being a lurker, and following a few members, is essential to engaging in what Lave and Wenger call legitimate peripheral participation; it is the way newcomers enter CoPs.

3. *Participate in scheduled chats.* The next level of participation in a hashtag community is to join a scheduled chat. At the appointed time, the moderator will open by asking everyone to introduce him- or herself, and then use a question-and-answer structure to moderate the discussion. In Twitter chats, "Q1" translates as "Question 1" and so on. To reply to Q1, use the hashtag in your response and begin with "A1." You must use the hashtag in all of your responses or other participants will be unable to read them. Some people find particular apps or software, such as tweetbot.com, helpful in participating in chats because they can move fairly quickly. People in the community will likely begin to follow you or reshare your posts if you make some insightful or helpful comments. Hashtag communities may also conduct Google hangout chats or use other forms of software to facilitate conversations outside of Twitter.

4. *Connect with individuals.* You may want to build relationships with individuals once you have spent some time online with the hashtag community. You can message an individual through Twitter if you both follow each other. Or, you can request to have an e-mail conversation with someone you would like to follow up with. Greater trust is built when

individuals have an opportunity to meet face-to-face. Look for conferences, such as EdCamps or professional organizations, at which you can meet members of your community.

5. *Share original content.* Original content is highly valued in hashtag communities and online in general. Sharing blog posts, analysis, ideas, and resources makes you a valuable member of any community and builds reciprocity and trust.

6. *Be a "crap detector."* Howard Rheingold, noted scholar of the digital domain (profiled in chapter 5), urges individuals to be mindful and critical "crap detectors" on the web.[1] Hashtag communities operate in public spaces, and conversations can be derailed or hacked by others, even robots. "Bots" are accounts (primarily in Twitter) that are not people but, rather algorithms set to follow people in order to gain followers for a business or individual or just to disrupt. When someone follows you, read what they share and find out who they are, so that your account is not corrupted by bots.

Online Teacher Spaces

Examples of Online Teacher Spaces

DIGITAL IS (http://digitalis.nwp.org/)—An online teacher space facilitated by members of the National Writing Project, yet open to all educators. Participants can publish guest blog posts, create curated collections of resources, share teaching ideas, and join forum discussions. The site is structured to enable teachers to take the lead in providing content for the site.

CTQ COLLABORATORY (http://www.teachingquality.org/collaboratory)— An online space for connecting with other educators around issues of interest. Members can connect and collaborate by joining "labs" (a collaborative space) focused on particular topics.

CLASSROOM 2.0 (http://www.classroom20.com/)—Hosted on a Ning platform that is similar to Facebook, with friends/member profiles, status updates, and sharing, yet it is a gated community and focused solely on the topic of the Ning, in this case, participatory learning and twenty-first-century technologies.

TEACHER NETWORK PORTAL (http://www.philadelphiateachernetworks.org/)—An example of a localized online teacher space. It is facilitated through the Philadelphia Education Fund (profiled in chapter 9), provides information on meetings and events run by several face-to-face and hybrid networks, and invites teachers to share blog posts and discuss important issues in a forum.

EDCAMP WIKI (https://edcamp.wikispaces.com/)—A collaborative space in which EdCamp organizers can share news and information about their events. The wiki platform allows anyone to edit the posted documents and pages. See chapter 9 for a more detailed description of the EdCamp movement.

How to Participate

1. *Geek out, lurk, and join.* Similar to hashtag communities, you should find a space that meets your needs as an educator. Pay attention to the conversations that happen in the spaces that you discover, and see if they align with your philosophies of teaching and learning. When you decide to participate, many sites require you to register to join in conversations or post content.

2. *Submit content.* Share your inquiries and news of your work. Keep it relevant and authentic; you will build trust and recognition by sharing your true voice and views.

3. *Do crap detection for online teacher spaces.* Know the difference between teacher-led, production-oriented intellectual spaces and commercial or consumer-oriented spaces. Many spaces online offer worksheets and lesson plans. While these websites have their role, they are not spaces that allow teachers to critically express their views, thoughts, and expertise. Ultimately, they do not serve to elevate the profession. Look for spaces that value the teacher as a critical thinker and inquirer.

4. *Respect rules of privacy and ownership.* In online teacher spaces, there may be gated (or private) spaces to communicate; however, you should always assume that what you write in these spaces is publicly available. This can happen in several ways. First, members can share your posts with others.

Second, the owners of the website can use your data in a myriad of ways (usually for selling statistics about users to other companies). Third, search engines may be able to search the site. Never post information that you would not want others to know on these sites. Also, be respectful of others in private spaces and do not share their content unless you have their permission. Anytime you share or remix someone else's content, be sure to give him or her credit for original work.

Hybrid Teacher Networks

Examples of Hybrid Teacher Networks

BADASS TEACHERS NETWORK (BATS)—Emerged as an outgrowth of activism by the Parents and Teachers Against the Common Core (PTACC) and was primarily led by Mark Naison and members of the PTACC. Naison and PTACC organizers started a Facebook group in June 2014, which grew at a rate of a thousand a day over several weeks. The group organized local chapters, each with a Facebook page, and created a website and very active Twitter feed, in which members are invited to post memes and remixed issues that critique standardized testing and the Common Core. In his book on the development of the group, Naison described these efforts: "Many of the teachers who joined the group were computer-savvy, artistically talented, and expert at using social media . . . [W]e encouraged all our members to use multimedia techniques—especially memes and music videos—to get the group's message across creatively."[2] As of 2014, BATs claimed a national membership of twenty thousand. Members participate face-to-face in local and national actions, and are active online to promote their group.

CAUCUS OF WORKING EDUCATORS (WE)—A network of educators and education advocates that supports social justice unionism. The group was initiated at a caucus of the Philadelphia Federation of Teachers by a group of teachers who were disillusioned by the union's continued shunning of their calls to address issues of social justice in schools. The WE invited nonunion members such as parents, education advocates, and scholars to join the caucus and launched a highly successful Opt-out campaign in Philadelphia. Use of social media and networked online spaces was critical to the group for organizing the Opt-out campaign as well as other campaigns.

CHILDREN'S LITERACY INITIATIVE (ON THE WEB) (CLI)—A national network that focuses on helping teachers to teach literacy in grades K–3. CLI uses a "model classroom" approach, in which it locates a few teachers in a school, provides support and coaching for them to develop their pedagogical practices, and then asks them to take the lead in mentoring others in the school. It developed an online space for CLI teachers, as well as parents, preservice teachers, and all educators to learn about CLI methods and connect with others. This space is an extension of its face-to-face community and allows it to expand its audience of learners.

How to Participate

1. *Be an intentional networker.* In my previous research on teacher networking, one of my key findings was that local (especially school-based), face-to-face networks can be extremely helpful to new teachers or people who need help navigating school politics and accessing resources.[3] Purely online networks were more helpful for individuals who craved new ideas and needed help innovating. Consider first what you need as an educator and what type of network would best support your needs. If you find that you are struggling with local or school-based issues, seek local hybrid networks that have many opportunities for face-to-face collaboration. Alternatively, if you wish to innovate or become part of a regional or national dialogue, look for networks that are more broadly networked online.

2. *Show up.* Hybrid teacher networks primarily use social media tools as a way to let others know what they are doing and invite them to join face-to-face meetings and actions, if possible. If you learn of a hybrid network that is sharing resources and information that you find helpful, look for opportunities to meet with members face-to-face.

3. *Be a connector.* Research on social networks shows that the people who act as "bridges" between groups can be powerful sources of social capital and resources.[4] If you are a member of an existing teacher network or

several networks, look for opportunities to create connections between these groups and people.

Teacher-Made Spaces

Examples of Teacher-Made Spaces

THE VIEW FROM ROOM 105 (http://myclassroom105.blogspot.com/)—The View from Room 105 is a teacher-made blog published by elementary school teacher Stephen R. Fleming. Fleming shares updates of classroom projects, views on educational issues, and information about real impacts of school funding cuts and policies on his classroom. He uses Twitter to share his posts with a wider audience.

THE JOSE VILSON (http://thejosevilson.com/)—The Jose Vilson is a website maintained by José Luis Vilson (profiled in chapter 3) that includes a blog, teacher resources, news of events, and connections to the #eduColor community. Vilson regularly publishes blog posts and wrote a book based on a collection of his blog posts called *This is Not a Test* in 2015.

CYBRARYMAN (http://cybraryman.com/)—Cybraryman is a website of curated educational resources maintained by Jerry Blumgarten. Blumgarten describes the site as "[t]he internet catalogue for students, teachers, administrators & parents. Over 20,000 relevant links personally selected by an educator/author with over 30 years of experience."[5]

#EDJUSTICELEAGUE—The #EdJusticeLeague started as collaboration between two teachers, Chrissy Romano-Arrabito and AJ Bianco, and grew to include several other teacher collaborators. The group produces a podcast series on educational innovation and technology, and uses the EdJusticeLeague hashtag as a way to communicate about their podcasts and other work. As to the goal of the EdJusticeLeague, Chris Nesi, one of the organizers, stated, "[W]e want teachers to be more connected and influence more positive change for the world of education."[6]

How to Participate

1. *No teacher-made space is an island.* Teacher-made spaces are meant to be places for people to gather, discuss, and reflect of important educational

issues. As such, you can build connections and conversations by reading and responding to others' blogs, hashtags, and spaces, and developing your personal learning network. To create trust, interest, and reciprocity, you must be as engaged in reading others' work as you are to share your own.

2. *Privacy and FERPA.* The Family Educational Rights and Privacy Act (FERPA) is a federal law that protects students' educational records. Teachers cannot share students' academic records or private information online. Furthermore, if you chose to post pictures of your students or their work, make sure you have written permission from parents, and check into your school's policy on sharing student work publicly.

3. *Organization is everything.* Categories, tags, hashtags, and labels are all ways of organizing information in subjects so that it is easier for people to connect with people and topics of interest. When navigating others' spaces or creating your own, be aware of how you organize your space; categories reflect interest priorities.

4. *Find your model.* Visit others' spaces and find what aspects appeal to you and would be most helpful in fostering dialogue that would support your work. One very helpful resource for learning to blog is the National Blogging Collaborative (http://www.nationalbloggingcollaborative.com), which provides teachers with ongoing writing support, tips, and a network of bloggers who will share your posts with others.

Notes

Foreword

1. http://btulab.com.s200635.gridserver.com/about.
2. Margaret Himley, Ed., *Prospect's Descriptive Processes: The Child, the Art of Teaching, and the Classroom and School* (North Bennington, VT: The Prospect Center, 2002); Margaret Himley with Patricia F. Carini, Eds., *From Another Angle: Children's Strengths and School Standards* (New York: Teachers College Press, 2000).
3. Patricia F. Carini, *How to Have Hope: Play's Memorable Transiency* (talk, Miquon School, Miquon, PA, 2000), 21.

Chapter 1

1. Grace Lee Boggs, *The Next American Revolution*, with Scott Kurashige (Berkeley: University of California Press, 2012), 50.
2. Henry Giroux, "Teachers as Transformative Intellectuals," in *Kaleidoscope: Contemporary and Classic Readings in Education*, ed. K. Ryan and J. M. Cooper (Belmont, CA: Wadsworth Cengage Learning, 2009); James A. Banks, "The Historical Reconstruction of Knowledge about Race: Implications for Transformative Teaching," *Educational Researcher* 24, no. 2 (1995): 15–25; Ann Lieberman and Lynne Miller, *Teachers—Transforming Their World and Their Work* (New York: Teachers College Press, 1999); and Nicole Mockler, "Trans/Forming Teachers: New Professional Learning and Transformative Teacher Professionalism," *Journal of In-Service Education* 31, no. 4 (2005): 733–46.
3. Grunwald Associates, "Education Influence and Influencers: A Market Probe into the New Dynamics in Education" (Stanford, CA: George Lucas Educational Foundation, 2004).
4. M. Frank Pajares, "Teachers' Beliefs and Educational Research: Cleaning up a Messy Construct," *Review of Educational Research* 62, no. 3 (1992): 307–32; Jennifer Gore et al., "Data-Driven Guidelines for High Quality Teacher Education" (paper presented at Australian Association for Research in Education Conference, Citeseer, 2007); and Terry J. Burant, Sharon M. Chubbuck, and Joan L. Whipp, "Reclaiming the Moral in the Dispositions Debate," *Journal of Teacher Education* 58, no. 5 (2007): 397–411.
5. Henry Jenkins, *Fans, Bloggers, and Gamers: Exploring Participatory Culture* (New York: NYU Press, 2006); and Henry Jenkins, "Confronting the Challenges of Participatory Culture: Media Education for the 21st Century. An Occasional Paper on Digital Media and Learning," John D. and Catherine T. MacArthur Foundation, 2006.

6. Eva Gold, Elaine Simon, and Chris Brown, *Successful Community Organizing for School Reform* (Chicago: Cross City Campaign for Urban School Reform, 2002); Dennis Shirley, *Valley Interfaith and School Reform: Organizing for Power in South Texas* (Austin: University of Texas Press, 2010); Dennis Shirley, *Community Organizing for Urban School Reform* (Austin: University of Texas Press, 1997); and Mark R. Warren, "Communities and Schools: A New View of Urban Education Reform," *Harvard Educational Review* 75, no. 2 (2005): 133–73.

7. Patricia F. Carini, *Starting Strong: A Different Look at Children, Schools, and Standards* (New York: Teachers College Press, 2001); M. Cochran-Smith and S. Lytle, *Inside/ outside: Teacher Research and Knowledge* (New York: Teachers College Press, 1993); Ann Lieberman and Diane R. Wood, *Inside the National Writing Project: Connecting Network Learning and Classroom Teaching* (New York: Teachers College Press, 2003); Marian M. Mohr, *Teacher Research for Better Schools* (New York: Teachers College Press, 2004); and E. W. Ross, J. W. Cornett, and G. McCutcheon, *Teacher Personal Theorizing: Connecting Curriculum Practice, Theory, and Research* (Albany: SUNY Press, 1992).

8. Yasmin B. Kafai and Kylie A. Peppler, "Youth, Technology, and DIY Developing Participatory Competencies in Creative Media Production," *Review of Research in Education* 35, no. 1 (2011): 89–119; Eva-Sophie Katterfeldt, "Maker Culture, Digital Tools and Exploration Support for FabLabs," *FabLab: Of Machines, Makers and Inventors* (Berlin, Germany: Verlag, 2014), 139–47; Julia Walter-Herrmann and Corinne Büching, *FabLab: Of Machines, Makers and Inventors* (Berlin, Germany: Verlag, 2014); Paulo Blikstein, "Digital Fabrication and 'making' in Education: The Democratization of Invention," in *FabLabs: Of Machines, Makers and Inventors*, ed. Julia Walter-Herrmann and Corinne Büching (Berlin, Germany: Verlag, 2014), 1–21; Lee Martin, "The Promise of the Maker Movement for Education," *Journal of Pre-College Engineering Research* 5, no. 1 (2015): 30–39; Sylvia Libow Martinez and Gary Stager, *Invent to Learn: Making, Tinkering, and Engineering in the Classroom* (Torrence, CA: Constructing Modern Knowledge, 2013); Shirin Vossoughi and Bronwyn Bevan, "Making and Tinkering: A Review of the Literature," National Research Council Committee on Out of School Time STEM (Washington, DC: National Research Council, 2014); and Erica Rosenfeld Halverson and Kimberly Sheridan, "The Maker Movement in Education," *Harvard Educational Review* 84, no. 4 (December 1, 2014): 495–504.

9. Sergey Bratus, Anna Shubina, and Michael Locasto, "Teaching the Principles of the Hacker Curriculum to Undergraduates" (paper presented at SIGCSE 2010, Milwaukee, WI, 2010), 1–5; Rafi Santo, "Hacker Literacies: Synthesizing Critical and Participatory Media Literacy Frameworks," *International Journal of Learning and Media* 3, no. 3 (July 1, 2011): 1–5; and Pekka Himanen, *The Hacker Ethic* (New York: Random House, 2001).

10. Philadelphia Education Fund, "Teacher-Led Professional Development through Integrated Inquiry" (Philadelphia: Philadelphia Education Fund, January 2015).

Chapter 2

1. Michael Wesch, "Mediated Culture/mediated Education," in *"In Dreams Begins Responsibility"—Choice, Evidence, and Change* (ALT-C Conference, Association for Learning Technology, Manchester, UK, 2009).

2. M. Castells, "Toward a Sociology of the Network Society," *Contemporary Sociology* 29, no. 5 (2000): 693–99; and Manuel Castells, *Rise of The Network Society*, vol. 1, *The Information Age* (Hoboken, NJ: Wiley, 1996).

3. Gerard Delanty, *Challenging Knowledge: The University in the Knowledge Society*, (Buckingham: SRHE and Open University Press, 2001); Suzanna Sherry, "Democracy and the Death of Knowledge," *University of Cincinnati Law Review* 75 (2007): 1053; and Joshua G. Tanenbaum et al., "Democratizing Technology: Pleasure, Utility and Expressiveness in DIY and Maker Practice" (paper presented at the SIGCHI Conference on Human Factors in Computing Systems, Paris, France, April 27–May 7, 2013), 2603–12.

4. David Weinberger, *Too Big to Know: Rethinking Knowledge Now That the Facts Aren't the Facts, Experts Are Everywhere, and the Smartest Person in the Room Is the Room* (New York: Basic Books, 2014).

5. Henry Jenkins, *Convergence Culture: Where Old and New Media Collide* (New York: NYU Press, 2006).

6. Ann Lieberman and Lynne Miller, *Teachers—Transforming Their World and Their Work* (New York: Teachers College Press, 1999).

7. Marilyn Cochran-Smith and Susan L. Lytle, "The Teacher Research Movement: A Decade Later," *Educational Researcher* 28, no. 7 (1999): 15–25; L. Darling-Hammond, "Policy and Professionalism," ed. A. Lieberman, *Building a Professional Culture in Schools* (New York: Teachers College Press, 1988), 55–77; J. W. Little, "The Persistence of Privacy: Autonomy and Initiative in Teachers' Professional Relations," *Teachers College Record* 91, no. 4 (1990): 509–36; and James S. Pounder, "Transformational Classroom Leadership the Fourth Wave of Teacher Leadership?," *Educational Management Administration & Leadership* 34, no. 4 (2006): 533–45.

8. C. L. Paris, *Teacher Agency and Curriculum Making in Classrooms* (New York: Teachers College Press, 1993); and Mark Priestley, G. J. J. Biesta, and Sarah Robinson, "Teachers as Agents of Change: An Exploration of the Concept of Teacher Agency" (working or discussion paper, 2012, https://dspace.stir.ac.uk/handle/1893/9266).

9. Pew Research Center on Global Attitudes & Trends, "Emerging Nations Embrace Internet, Mobile Technology," Pew Research Center's Global Attitudes Project, February 13, 2015, http://www.pewglobal.org/2014/02/13/emerging-nations-embrace-internet-mobile-technology/.

10. Marc Prensky and Bruce D. Berry, "Do They Really Think Differently," *On the Horizon* 9, no. 6 (2001): 1–9.

11. Pew Internet Project and American Life, "Demographics of Internet Users," 2008, http://www.pewinternet.org/data-trend/internet-use/internet-use-over-time/.

12. Grunwald Associates, "Education Influence and Influencers: A Market Probe into the New Dynamics in Education" (Stanford, CA: George Lucas Educational Foundation, 2004).

13. Henry Jenkins, "Confronting the Challenges of Participatory Culture: Media Education for the 21st Century. An Occasional Paper on Digital Media and Learning," John D. and Catherine T. MacArthur Foundation, 2006, 9.

14. John Fiske, "The Cultural Economy of Fandom," in *The Adoring Audience: Fan Culture and Popular Media*, ed. Lisa A. Lewis (London: Routledge, 1992), 30.

15. Matt Hills, "Fiske's 'Textual Productivity' and Digital Fandom: Web 2.0 Democratization versus Fan Distinction," *Participations* 10, no. 1 (2013): 130–53; and Henry Jenkins, "'Cultural Acupuncture': Fan Activism and the Harry Potter Alliance," *Transformative Works and Cultures* 10 (March 31, 2011), doi:10.3983/twc.v10i0.305.

16. Stephen Brown, "Harry Potter and the Fandom Menace," *Consumer Tribes*, 2007, 177–93; and Jenkins, "Cultural Acupuncture."

17. Jennifer Earl and Katrina Kimport, "Movement Societies and Digital Protest: Fan Activism and Other Nonpolitical Protest Online," *Sociological Theory* 27, no. 3 (2009): 220–43; and Jenkins, "Cultural Acupuncture."

18. Fanfiction.net, "FanFiction.net Harry Potter Stories," 2015, https://www.fanfiction.net/search.php?keywords=harry+potter&ready=1&type=story.

19. Julia Walter-Herrmann and Corinne Büching, *FabLab: Of Machines, Makers and Inventors* (Berlin, Germany: Verlag, 2014).

20. Eva-Sophie Katterfeldt, "Maker Culture, Digital Tools and Exploration Support for FabLabs," *FabLab: Of Machines, Makers and Inventors*, 139–47.

21. Mark D. Gross and Ellen Yi-Luen Do, "Educating the New Makers: Cross-Disciplinary Creativity," *Leonardo* 42, no. 3 (2009): 210–15; and Tanenbaum et al., "Democratizing Technology: Pleasure, Utility and Expressiveness in DIY and Maker Practice."

22. Kurt Squire, "Open-Ended Video Games: A Model for Developing Learning for the Interactive Age," in *The Ecology of Games: Connecting Youth, Games, and Learning*, ed. Katie Salen (Cambridge, MA: MIT Press, 2008), 167–98.

23. Mizuko Ito et al., "Living and Learning with New Media: Summary of Findings from the Digital Youth Project," John D. and Catherine T. MacArthur Foundation, 2008; and Yasmin B. Kafai and Deborah A Fields, "Cheating in Virtual Worlds: Transgressive Designs for Learning," *On the Horizon* 17, no. 1 (2009): 12–20.

24. Yasmin B. Kafai and Kylie A. Peppler, "Youth, Technology, and DIY Developing Participatory Competencies in Creative Media Production," *Review of Research in Education* 35, no. 1 (2011): 89–119.

25. Mizuko Ito, Sonja Baumer, Matteo Bittanti, Rachel Cody, Becky Herr Stephenson, Heather A. Horst, Patricia G. Lange et al., *Hanging out, messing around, and geeking out: Kids living and learning with new media* (Cambridge, MA: MIT Press, 2009).

26. David Anderegg, *Nerds: Who They Are and Why We Need More of Them* (New York: Penguin, 2007); and Ito et al., *Hanging Out, Messing Around, and Geeking out.*

27. Earl and Kimport, "Movement Societies and Digital Protest: Fan Activism and Other Nonpolitical Protest Online"; Joseph Kahne, Ellen Middaugh, and Danielle Allen, "Youth, New Media, and the Rise of Participatory Politics," *Youth, New Media and Citizenship*, 2014; and Emily Weinstein, "The Personal Is Political on Social Media: Online Civic Expression Patterns and Pathways among Civically Engaged Youth," *International Journal of Communications* 8 (2014): 210–33.

28. Weinstein, "The Personal Is Political on Social Media: Online Civic Expression Patterns and Pathways among Civically Engaged Youth."

29. Kahne, Middaugh, and Allen, "Youth, New Media, and the Rise of Participatory Politics."

30. Earl and Kimport, "Movement Societies and Digital Protest: Fan Activism and Other Nonpolitical Protest Online," 223–24.

31. Jennifer Earl and Katrina Kimport, *Digitally Enabled Social Change: Activism in the Internet Age* (Cambridge, MA: MIT Press, 2011).

32. Dennis Shirley, *Community Organizing for Urban School Reform* (Austin: University of Texas Press, 1997); Dennis Shirley, *Valley Interfaith and School Reform: Organizing for Power in South Texas* (Austin: University of Texas Press, 2010); Mark R. Warren, "Communities and Schools: A New View of Urban Education Reform," *Harvard Educational Review* 75, no. 2 (2005): 133–73; and Mark R. Warren and Karen L. Mapp, *A Match on Dry Grass: Community Organizing as a Catalyst for School Reform* (Oxford: Oxford University Press, 2011).

33. Eva Gold, Elaine Simon, and Chris Brown, *Successful Community Organizing for School Reform* (Chicago: Cross-City Campaign for Urban School Reform, 2002).

34. Ibid., 12.

35. Susan Stall and Randy Stoecker, "Community Organizing or Organizing Community? Gender and the Crafts of Empowerment," *Gender & Society* 12, no. 6 (1998): 729–56.

36. Weinstein, "The Personal Is Political on Social Media: Online Civic Expression Patterns and Pathways among Civically Engaged Youth."

37. Kira J. Baker-Doyle, *The Networked Teacher: How New Teachers Build Social Networks for Professional Support* (New York: Teachers College Press, 2011); Cochran-Smith and Lytle, "The Teacher Research Movement: A Decade Later"; Darling-Hammond, "Policy and Professionalism"; Lieberman and Miller, *Teachers—Transforming Their World and Their Work*; J. W. Little, "Professional Development in Pursuit of Reform," ed. A. Lieberman and L. Miller, *Teachers Caught in the Action: Professional Development That Matters* (New York: Teachers College Press, 2001), 23–44; and Pounder, "Transformational Classroom Leadership the Fourth Wave of Teacher Leadership?"

38. Henry Giroux, "Teachers as Transformatory Intellectuals," *Symposium on Understanding Quality Education* 24 (2011); Henry Giroux, "Teachers as Transformative Intellectuals," in *Kaleidoscope: Contemporary and Classic Readings in Education*, ed. K. Ryan and J. M. Cooper (Belmont, CA: Wadsworth Cengage Learning, 2009).

39. Giroux, "Teachers as Transformatory Intellectuals," 3.

40. James A. Banks, "The Historical Reconstruction of Knowledge about Race: Implications for Transformative Teaching," *Educational Researcher* 24, no. 2 (1995): 15–25.

41. Ibid., 22.

42. Lieberman and Miller, *Teachers—Transforming Their World and Their Work*.

43. Nicole Mockler, "Trans/forming Teachers: New Professional Learning and Transformative Teacher Professionalism," *Journal of In-Service Education* 31, no. 4 (2005): 733–46.

44. Betty Achinstein and Rodney T. Ogawa, "(In) Fidelity: What the Resistance of New Teachers Reveals about Professional Principles and Prescriptive Educational Policies," *Harvard Educational Review* 76, no. 1 (2006): 30–63; Wayne Au, "High-Stakes Testing and Curricular Control: A Qualitative Metasynthesis," *Educational Researcher* 36, no. 5 (2007): 258–67; Margaret S. Crocco and Arthur T. Costigan, "The Narrowing of Curriculum and Pedagogy in the Age of Accountability Urban Educators Speak out," *Urban Education* 42, no. 6 (2007): 512–35; Brad Olsen and Dena Sexton, "Threat Rigidity, School Reform, and How Teachers View Their Work inside Current Education Policy Contexts," *American Educational Research Journal* 46, no. 1 (2009): 9–44; and

John S. Wills and Judith Haymore Sandholtz, "Constrained Professionalism: Dilemmas of Teaching in the Face of Test-Based Accountability," *Teachers College Record* 111, no. 4 (2009): 1065–1114.

45. Cochran-Smith and Lytle, "The Teacher Research Movement: A Decade Later"; Marian M. Mohr, *Teacher Research for Better Schools* (New York: Teachers College Press, 2004); E. W. Ross, J. W. Cornett, and G. McCutcheon, *Teacher Personal Theorizing: Connecting Curriculum Practice, Theory, and Research* (Albany: SUNY Press, 1992); and F. Schoonmaker, *"Growing Up" Teaching: From Personal Knowledge to Professional Knowledge* (New York: Teachers College Press, 2002).

46. Patricia F. Carini, *Starting Strong: A Different Look at Children, Schools, and Standards* (New York: Teachers College Press, 2001).

47. Baker-Doyle, *The Networked Teacher: How New Teachers Build Social Networks for Professional Support.*

48. M. Cochran-Smith and S. Lytle, *Inside/outside: Teacher Research and Knowledge* (New York: Teachers College Press, 1993); Cochran-Smith and Lytle, "The Teacher Research Movement: A Decade Later"; and A. Lieberman, "Networks As Learning Communities: Shaping the Future of Teacher Development," *Journal of Teacher Education* 51, no. 3 (2000): 221–27.

49. "Teacher Action Group—Philadelphia," http://tagphilly.org/.

50. Carini, *Starting Strong: A Different Look at Children, Schools, and Standards.*

51. A. Burns Thomas, "Supporting New Visions for Social Justice Teaching: The Potential for Professional Development Networks," *Penn GSE Perspectives on Urban Education* 5, no. 1 (2007); L. Y. Strieb, *Inviting Families into the Classroom: Learning from a Life in Teaching* (New York: Teachers College Press, 2010).

52. Handel Kashope Wright, "Nailing Jell-O to the Wall: Pinpointing Aspects of State-of-the-Art Curriculum Theorizing," *Educational Researcher* 29, no. 5 (2000): 4–13.

53. Scott Ritchie, "Incubating and Sustaining How Teacher Networks Enable and Support Social Justice Education," *Journal of Teacher Education* 63, no. 2 (2012): 120–31.

54. Michelle Fine, "Postcards from Metro America: Reflections on Youth Participatory Action Research for Urban Justice," *Urban Review* 41, no. 1 (March 1, 2009): 1–6; Julio Cammarota and Michelle Fine, *Revolutionizing Education: Youth Participatory Action Research in Motion* (Abingdon, UK: Taylor & Francis, 2008); John Meiklejohn et al., "Integrating Mindfulness Training into K-12 Education: Fostering the Resilience of Teachers and Students," *Mindfulness* 3, no. 4 (December 1, 2012): 291–307, doi:10.1007/s12671-012-0094-5; Robert W. Roeser et al., "Mindfulness Training and Teachers' Professional Development: An Emerging Area of Research and Practice," *Child Development Perspectives* 6, no. 2 (June 1, 2012): 167–73; Stephanie Chang et al., "The Maker Ed Open Portfolio Project: Maker Portfolios In School," Open Portfolio Project Research Brief Series (Maker Education Initiative, 2015); John Duhring, "Project-Based-Learning Kickstart Tips: Hackathon Pedagogies as Educational Technology" (Hadley, MA: National Collegiate Inventors and Innovators Alliance, 2014); Edward Garcia Fierros, "Using Performance Ethnography to Confront Issues of Privilege, Race, and Institutional Racism: An Account of an Arts-Based Teacher Education Project," *Multicultural Perspectives* 11, no. 1 (2009): 3–11; Tim Grant and Gail Littlejohn, *Teaching Green—The Elementary Years:*

Hands-on Learning in Grades K-5 (Gabriola Island, NB: New Society Publishers, 2005); and Chris Haas and Greg Ashman, "Kindergarten Children's Introduction to Sustainability through Transformative, Experiential Nature Play," *Australasian Journal of Early Childhood* 39, no. 2 (2014): 21.

55. Based on a Google scholar database search of studies using key terms "maker education" and "makerspace, school."

56. Kristen Purcell et al., "How Teachers Are Using Technology at Home and in Their Classrooms," Pew Research Center: Internet, Science & Tech, February 28, 2013, http://www.pewinternet.org/2013/02/28/how-teachers-are-using-technology-at-home-and-in-their-classrooms/.

57. Marilyn Cochran-Smith and Susan L. Lytle, *Inquiry as Stance: Practitioner Research for the next Generation* (New York: Teachers College Press, 2009).

58. Nancy Fichtman Dana, "The Relevancy and Importance of Practitioner Research in Contemporary Times," *Journal of Practitioner Research* 1, no. 1 (April 21, 2016), http://scholarcommons.usf.edu/jpr/vol1/iss1/1.

59. "Teach to Lead," US Department of Education, http://teachtolead.org/.

60. Manuel Castells, *Networks of Outrage and Hope: Social Movements in the Internet Age* (New York: John Wiley & Sons, 2015); Todd Wolfson, *Digital Rebellion: The Birth of the Cyber Left* (Champaign: University of Illinois Press, 2014); and Sasha Costanza-Chock, *Out of the Shadows, Into the Streets! Transmedia Organizing and the Immigrant Rights Movement* (Cambridge, MA: MIT Press, 2014).

Chapter 3

1. Allen Black and Paul Ammon, "A Developmental-Constructivist Approach to Teacher Education," *Journal of Teacher Education* 43, no. 5 (November 1, 1992): 323–35; Eleanor Drago-Severson, *Helping Educators Grow: Strategies and Practices for Leadership Development* (Cambridge, MA: Harvard Education Press, 2012); D. M. Kagan, "Professional Growth among Pre-service and Beginning Teachers," *Review of Educational Research* 62, no. 2 (1992): 129; and Pamela L. Grossman, "Why Models Matter: An Alternate View on Professional Growth in Teaching," *Review of Educational Research* 62, no. 2 (July 1, 1992): 171–79.

2. Black and Ammon, "A Developmental-Constructivist Approach to Teacher Education"; and Punya Mishra and Matthew Koehler, "Technological Pedagogical Content Knowledge: A Framework for Teacher Knowledge," *Teachers College Record* 108, no. 6 (2006): 1017–54.

3. Sandra Hollingsworth, "Prior Beliefs and Cognitive Change in Learning to Teach," *American Educational Research Journal* 26, no. 2 (1989): 160–89; and Sandra Hollingsworth, Mary Dybdahl, and Leslie Turner Minarik, "By Chart and Chance and Passion: The Importance of Relational Knowing in Learning to Teach," *Curriculum Inquiry* 23, no. 1 (1993).

4. Barnett Berry, Ann Byrd, and Alan Wieder, *Teacherpreneurs: Innovative Teachers Who Lead but Don't Leave* (San Francisco: Jossey Bass, 2013).

5. Mary Chayko, "Techno-Social Life: The Internet, Digital Technology, and Social Connectedness," *Sociology Compass* 8, no. 7 (July 1, 2014): 976–91, doi:10.1111/soc4.12190; and Mary Chayko, *Superconnected: The Internet, Digital Media, and Techno-Social Life* (Thousand Oaks: Sage Publications, 2016).

6. James Gee, "The New Literacy Studies and the 'Social Turn'" (opinion paper, 1999), http://www.schools.ash.org/au/litweb/page300.html.

7. Roderick J. Watts, Nat Chioke Williams, and Robert J. Jagers, "Sociopolitical Development," *American Journal of Community Psychology* 31, no. 1–2 (2003): 185–94.

8. Paulo Freire, *Pedagogy of the Oppressed* (New York: Continuum International Publishing Group, 1970).

9. Watts, Williams, and Jagers, "Sociopolitical Development," 185.

10. José Luis Vilson, *This Is Not A Test: A New Narrative on Race, Class, and Education* (New York: Haymarket Books, 2014).

11. Annie Huynh, "Courageous Conversations about Race: Exploring Counter-Narratives on Black Heritage Day," *Schools: Studies in Education* 10, no. 2 (2013): 274–80; Annie Huynh, "'Hacking' as Critical Literacy: Teaching Tolerance—Diversity, Equity and Justice," *Teaching Tolerance Blog Post*, 2014, http://www.tolerance.org/blog/hacking-critical -literacy; and Alexandra Fenwick, "Eight Questions for Emerging Leader Annie Huynh," *ASCD Inservice*, September 26, 2014, http://inservice.ascd.org/eight-questions-for -emerging-leader-annie-huynh/.

12. Kathleen Melville, "Students Struggle to Fit in Small Classroom," *Teaching Tolerance* blog, March 4, 2013, http://www.tolerance.org/blog/students-struggle-fit-small-classroom.

Chapter 4

1. This is not to discount the value and importance of the professional relationships that teachers build in their school context. It is vital that teachers do so to sustain them through the emotional, social, and mental challenges of the work. Rather, it is to highlight ways in which teachers are finding alternatives spaces in which they have some greater freedom to take risks with their professional learning and express other aspects of their identities.

2. Homi Bhabha, "The Postcolonial and the Postmodern," *The Location of Culture* 172 (1994).

3. Ken Zeichner, "Rethinking the Connections between Campus Courses and Field Experiences in College- and University-Based Teacher Education," *Journal of Teacher Education* 61, no. 1–2 (2010): 89–99; Kris D. Gutiérrez, "Developing a Sociocritical Literacy in the Third Space," *Reading Research Quarterly* 43, no. 2 (2008): 148–64; and Michael J. Muller, "Participatory Design: The Third Space in HCI," *Human-Computer Interaction: Development Process* 4235 (2003): 165–85.

4. Alison Cook-Sather and Bernadette Youens, "Repositioning Students in Initial Teacher Preparation: A Comparative Descriptive Analysis of Learning to Teach for Social Justice in the United States and in England," *Journal of Teacher Education* 58, no. 1 (2007): 62–75.

5. C. J. Cohen and Joseph Kahne, "Participatory Politics: New Media and Youth Political Action," *Youth and Participatory Politics* (MacArthur Research Network on Youth & Participatory Politics, 2011), http://ictlogy.net/bibliography/reports/projects.php?idp=2180&lang =es.

6. Todd Wolfson, *Digital Rebellion: The Birth of the Cyber Left* (Champaign: University of Illinois Press, 2014); Joseph Kahne, Ellen Middaugh, and Danielle Allen, "Youth, New Media, and the Rise of Participatory Politics," *Youth, New Media and Citizenship*, 2014;

Manuel Castells, *Networks of Outrage and Hope: Social Movements in the Internet Age* (New York: John Wiley & Sons, 2015); Sasha Costanza-Chock, *Out of the Shadows, Into the Streets! Transmedia Organizing and the Immigrant Rights Movement* (Cambridge, MA: MIT Press, 2014); Brian D. Loader and Dan Mercea, "Networking Democracy? Social Media Innovations and Participatory Politics," *Information, Communication & Society* 14, no. 6 (2011): 757–69; Donatella Della Porta, "Communication in Movement," *Information, Communication & Society* 14, no. 6 (September 1, 2011): 800–19, doi:10.1080 /1369118X.2011.560954; W. Lance Bennett and Alexandra Segerberg, "Digital Media and the Personalization of Collective Action," *Information, Communication & Society* 14, no. 6 (September 1, 2011): 770–99, doi:10.1080/1369118X.2011.579141; and Jodi H. Cohen and Jennifer M. Raymond, "How the Internet Is Giving Birth (to) a New Social Order," *Information, Communication & Society* 14, no. 6 (September 1, 2011): 937–57, doi:10.1080/1369118X.2011.582132.

7. Loader and Mercea, "Networking Democracy? Social Media Innovations and Participatory Politics," 3.

8. Wolfson, *Digital Rebellion: The Birth of the Cyber Left*.

9. Paulo Freire and Donaldo Macedo, *Literacy: Reading the Word and the World* (New York: Routledge, 2005).

10. Sue Lasky, "A Sociocultural Approach to Understanding Teacher Identity, Agency and Professional Vulnerability in a Context of Secondary School Reform," *Teaching and Teacher Education* 21, no. 8 (November 2005): 899–916.

11. Valerie Strauss, "Arne Duncan asks 'What if,' here's the response," *Washington Post, Answer Sheet Blog*, January 1, 2015, https://www.washingtonpost.com/news/answer-sheet /wp/2015/01/01/arne-duncan-asks-what-if-heres-the-response/.

12. "EduColor—A Movement, Not a Moment," *EduColor*, http://www.educolor.org/.

13. Christopher Rogers, interview with author, November 2015.

14. Simon Rogers, "What Fuels a Tweet's Engagement?," *Twitter Blogs*, March 10, 2014, https://blog.twitter.com/2014/what-fuels-a-tweets-engagement.

15. Gerard Briscoe and Catherine Mulligan, "Digital Innovation: The Hackathon Phenomenon" (working paper, Creativeworks, London, May 2014), http://www.creative workslondon.org.uk/wp-content/uploads/2013/11/Digital-Innovation-The-Hackathon -Phenomenon1.pdf.

16. University of Denver, "Curriculum Hack," *Curriculum Hack*, https://thecurriculum hack.wordpress.com/.

17. Mark Barnes and Jennifer Gonzalez, *Hacking Education: 10 Quick Fixes for Every School*, vol. 1, Hack Learning Series (Cleveland: Hack Learning, 2015); Starr Sackstein, *Hacking Assessment: 10 Ways to Go Gradeless in a Traditional Grades School* (Cleveland: Times 10 Publications, 2015); and Dave Burgess, *Teach Like a Pirate: Increase Student Engagement, Boost Your Creativity and Transform Your Life as an Educator* (San Diego: Dave Burgess Consulting, 2012).

18. Howard Rheingold, *Net Smart: How to Thrive Online* (Cambridge, MA: MIT Press, 2012).

19. Stan Spring, "Teaching for the 21st Century and Beyond with MakerBot," http://www.maker bot.com/blog/2016/01/04/teaching-for-the-21st-century-and-beyond-with-makerbot.

20. Mizuko Ito et al., "Hanging Out, Messing Around, and Geeking Out," *Digital Media*, 2010; Shirin Vossoughi and Bronwyn Bevan, "Making and Tinkering: A Review of the Literature," National Research Council Committee on Out of School Time STEM (Washington, DC: National Research Council, 2014); and Sylvia Libow Martinez and Gary Stager, *Invent to Learn: Making, Tinkering, and Engineering in the Classroom*, (Torrance, CA: Constructing Modern Knowledge Press, 2013).

Chapter 5

1. Pseudonym of research study participant.
2. "FACT SHEET: President Obama to Host First-Ever White House Maker Faire," *Whitehouse.gov*, June 18, 2014, https://www.whitehouse.gov/the-press-office/2014/06/18/fact-sheet-president-obama-host-first-ever-white-house-maker-faire.
3. The White House Maker Faire: "Today's D.I.Y. Is Tomorrow's 'Made in America,'" *Whitehouse.gov*, June 18, 2014, https://www.whitehouse.gov/blog/2014/06/18/president-obama-white-house-maker-faire-today-s-diy-tomorrow-s-made-america.
4. John Tierney, "How Makerspaces Help Local Economies," *The Atlantic*, April 17, 2015, http://www.theatlantic.com/technology/archive/2015/04/makerspaces-are-remaking-local-economies/390807/; Erica Rosenfeld Halverson and Kimberly Sheridan, "The Maker Movement in Education," *Harvard Educational Review* 84, no. 4 (December 1, 2014): 495–504; Kylie A. Peppler, "New Opportunities for Interest-Driven Arts Learning in a Digital Age," (commissioned report, Wallace Foundation, July 2013), http://kpeppler.com/Docs/2013_Peppler_New-Opportunities-for-Interest-Driven-Art.pdf; Joshua G. Tanenbaum et al., "Democratizing Technology: Pleasure, Utility and Expressiveness in DIY and Maker Practice" (proceedings of the SIGCHI Conference on Human Factors in Computing Systems, ACM, 2013), 2603–12; and Red Chidgey, "Developing Communities of Resistance? Maker Pedagogies, Do-It-Yourself Feminism, and DIY Citizenship," in *DIY Citizenship: Critical Making and Social Media*, ed. Matt Ratto and Meg Boler (Cambridge, MA: MIT Press, 2014), 101–13.
5. Kimberly Sheridan et al., "Learning in the Making: A Comparative Case Study of Three Makerspaces," *Harvard Educational Review* 84, no. 4 (2014): 505–31.
6. Halverson and Sheridan, "The Maker Movement in Education"; and Sylvia Libow Martinez and Gary Stager, *Invent to Learn: Making, Tinkering, and Engineering in the Classroom* (Torrence, CA: Constructing Modern Knowledge, 2013).
7. Seymour Papert, *Mindstorms: Children, Computers, and Powerful Ideas* (New York: Basic Books, Inc., 1980).
8. Matt Ratto and Megan Boler, "Introduction," in *DIY Citizenship: Critical Making and Social Media*, ed. Ronald Deibert, Matt Ratto, and Meg Bolar (Cambridge, MA: MIT Press, 2014), 1–22.
9. Ibid.
10. J. Dunn, "O'Reilly Media Founder Finds Fruit in Failures," *North Bay Business Journal*, September 22, 2014, http://www.northbaybusinessjournal.com/csp/mediapool/sites/NBBJ/IndustryNews/story.csp?cid=4185776&sid=778&fid=181.
11. Lee Martin, "The Promise of the Maker Movement for Education," *Journal of Pre-College Engineering Research* 5, no. 1 (2015): 30–39; Maria Montessori and Barbara Barclay

Carter, *The Secret of Childhood* (Calcutta: Orient Longmans, 1936); and L. Katz, "What Can We Learn from Reggio Emilia," *The Hundred Languages of Children: The Reggio Emilia Approach–Advanced Reflections* 2 (1998): 27–45.

12. Paulo Blikstein, "Digital Fabrication and 'making' in Education: The Democratization of Invention," in *FabLabs: Of Machines, Makers and Inventors*, eds. Julia Walter-Hermann and Corinne Büching (Bielefeld: Transcript Verlag, 2013).

13. Halverson and Sheridan, "The Maker Movement in Education."

14. Blikstein, "Digital Fabrication and 'making' in Education: The Democratization of Invention"; Ratto and Boler, "Introduction"; Sheridan et al., "Learning in the Making: A Comparative Case Study of Three Makerspaces"; Shirin Vossoughi and Bronwyn Bevan, "Making and Tinkering: A Review of the Literature," National Research Council Committee on Out of School Time STEM (Washington, DC: National Research Council, 2014); Alexandra Bal, Jason Nolan, and Yukari Seko, "Mélange of Making: Bringing Children's Informal Learning Cultures to the Classroom," in *DIY Citizenship: Critical Making and Social Media*, ed. Matt Ratto and Meg Boler (Cambridge, MA: MIT Press, 2014), 157–68; Kylie A. Peppler et al., "The Maker Ed Open Portfolio Project Survey of Maker Spaces, Part 2," Open Portfolio Project Research Brief Series (Maker Education Initiative, 2015); Halverson and Sheridan, "The Maker Movement in Education"; Martin, "The Promise of the Maker Movement for Education"; and Martinez and Stager, *Invent to Learn: Making, Tinkering, and Engineering in the Classroom*.

15. Halverson and Sheridan, "The Maker Movement in Education."

16. Tim Brown, *Change By Design: How Design Thinking Transforms Organizations and Inspires Innovation* (New York: Harper Collins, 2009).

17. Michail Giannakos et al., "Proceedings of the Workshop of Making as a Pathway to Foster Joyful Engagement and Creativity in Learning" (Make2Learn 2015, Ceur Workshop Proceedings, Trondheim, Norway, 2015), 4.

18. Blikstein, "Digital Fabrication and 'making' in Education: The Democratization of Invention"; Peppler et al., "The Maker Ed Open Portfolio Project Survey of Maker Spaces, Part 2"; Martin, "The Promise of the Maker Movement for Education"; Vossoughi and Bevan, "Making and Tinkering: A Review of the Literature."

19. Ratto and Boler, "Introduction."

20. Vossoughi and Bevan, "Making and Tinkering: A Review of the Literature."

21. *Toward Building Makerspaces for All: New Theories and Practices to Design Inclusive Makerspaces* (American Educational Research Association Annual Conference, Washington, DC, April 11, 2016).

22. Ibid.; Kevin Crowley, Lisa Brahms, and Peter Wardrip, "Making as Learning: The Case of Families With Young Children," *Toward Building Makerspaces for All*; Faith Brown Freeman and Edna Tan, "Exploring How a 'Judgment-Free' Makerspace Supports African American Girls' Identity Work as Community Makers and Engineers," *Toward Building Makerspaces for All*; Paula K. Hooper, Shirin Vossoughi, and Meg Elena Escude, "Making Equity Explicit: On the Pedagogical and Sociopolitical Dimensions of Learning Within Making," *Toward Building Makerspaces for All*; Kristin Searle, "Making Activities With Electronic Textiles in an American Indian Community School," *Toward Building Makerspaces for All*; Myunghwan Shin et al., "Youth Engagement and

Mobilities of Learning During Making in an Equity-Oriented Makerspace," *Toward Building Makerspaces for All*; Breanne Litts, "Strategies for Broadening Participation in Makerspaces: A Comparative Case Study of Three Youth Makerspaces," *Toward Building Makerspaces for All*; Alexandra Lakind, Erica Rosenfeld Halverson, and Rebekah Willett, "Making Across Spaces: Madison Public Library's System-Wide Approach," *Toward Building Makerspaces for All*; and Kimberly Sheridan et al., "Resourceful and Inclusive: Toward Design Principles for Makerspaces," *Toward Building Makerspaces for All*.

23. Hooper, Vossoughi, and Escude, "Making Equity Explicit: On the Pedagogical and Sociopolitical Dimensions of Learning Within Making."

24. Blikstein, "Digital Fabrication and 'making' in Education: The Democratization of Invention"; Stephanie Chang et al., "The Maker Ed Open Portfolio Project: Maker Portfolios In School," Open Portfolio Project Research Brief Series (Maker Education Initiative, 2015), http://makered.org/wp-content/uploads/2015/03/Open-Portfolio-Project-Research-Brief-Series_FULL_final-small.pdf; and Halverson and Sheridan, "The Maker Movement in Education."

25. Peppler et al., "The Maker Ed Open Portfolio Project Survey of Maker Spaces, Part 2"; Peppler, "New Opportunities for Interest-Driven Arts Learning in a Digital Age."

26. Mia Zamora, "Paper Circuitry & Writing as Making," *Hypperhiz: New Media Cultures* 14 (2016).

27. Halverson and Sheridan, "The Maker Movement in Education"; Blikstein, "Digital Fabrication and 'making' in Education: The Democratization of Invention"; Peppler et al., "The Maker Ed Open Portfolio Project Survey of Maker Spaces, Part 2."

28. Halverson and Sheridan, "The Maker Movement in Education."

29. J. Lave and E. Wenger, *Situated Learning. Legitimate Peripheral Participation* (Cambridge: University of Cambridge Press, 1991).

30. R. D. Putnam, "Bowling Alone: America's Declining Social Capital," *Journal of Democracy* 6 (1995): 65–78; and David O'Donnell et al., "Creating Intellectual Capital: A Habermasian Community of Practice (CoP) Introduction," *Journal of European Industrial Training* 27, no. 2/3/4 (2003): 80–87.

31. Ratto and Boler, "Introduction."

32. Ibid., 2.

33. Vossoughi and Bevan, "Making and Tinkering: A Review of the Literature"; Brian D. Loader and Dan Mercea, "Networking Democracy? Social Media Innovations and Participatory Politics," *Information, Communication & Society* 14, no. 6 (2011): 757–69; and Halverson and Sheridan, "The Maker Movement in Education."

34. Halverson and Sheridan, "The Maker Movement in Education."

35. Yasmin Kafai, Deborah Fields, and Kristin Searle, "Electronic Textiles as Disruptive Designs: Supporting and Challenging Maker Activities in Schools," *Harvard Educational Review* 84, no. 4 (2014): 532–56; Leah Buechley et al., *Textile Messages: Dispatches from the World of E-Textiles and Education* (New York: Peter Lang Publishing Incorporated, 2013); Peppler, "New Opportunities for Interest-Driven Arts Learning in a Digital Age"; and Peppler et al., "The Maker Ed Open Portfolio Project Survey of Maker Spaces, Part 2."

36. Twenty percent time is also known as "genius hour." It refers to a workplace policy popularized by Google that allots 20 percent of employee time to personal inquiries and

explorations. John Spencer and A. J. Juliani, *Launch: Using Design Thinking to Boost Creativity and Bring Out the Maker in Every Student* (San Diego, CA: Dave Burgess Consulting, 2016).

37. Blikstein, "Digital Fabrication and 'making' in Education: The Democratization of Invention"; Vossoughi and Bevan, "Making and Tinkering: A Review of the Literature"; Chang et al., "The Maker Ed Open Portfolio Project: Maker Portfolios In School"; Halverson and Sheridan, "The Maker Movement in Education"; and Martin, "The Promise of the Maker Movement for Education."

38. David Acevedo et al., "Not Playing School: How Can Asynchronous Learning Empower Students in Their Own Education?" (Penn GSE Ethnography in Education Forum, Philadelphia, 2016).

39. Jon Kolko, *Wicked Problems Worth Solving: A Handbook & a Call to Action* (Austen, TX: Austen Center for Design, 2012).

40. Patricia F. Carini, *Starting Strong: A Different Look at Children, Schools, and Standards.* (New York: Teachers College Press, 2001).

41. Yasmin B. Kafai and Kylie A. Peppler, "Youth, Technology, and DIY Developing Participatory Competencies in Creative Media Production," *Review of Research in Education* 35, no. 1 (2011): 2.

42. Matt Ratto and Megan Boler, *DIY Citizenship: Critical Making and Social Media* (Cambridge, MA: MIT Press, 2014).

43. Halverson and Sheridan, "The Maker Movement in Education"; Blikstein, "Digital Fabrication and 'making' in Education: The Democratization of Invention"; and Peppler, "New Opportunities for Interest-Driven Arts Learning in a Digital Age."

44. Becky Herr-Stephenson, Meryl Alper, Erin Reilly, and Henry Jenkins, "T is for transmedia: Learning through transmedia play," vol. 10 (Los Angeles and New York: USC Annenberg Innovation Lab and the Joan Ganz Cooney Center at Sesame Workshop, 2015, 2013).

45. Paulo Freire, *Pedagogy of the Oppressed* (New York: Continuum International Publishing Group, 1970).

46. Blikstein, "Digital Fabrication and 'making' in Education: The Democratization of Invention"; Tanenbaum et al., "Democratizing Technology: Pleasure, Utility and Expressiveness in DIY and Maker Practice"; and Chidgey, "Developing Communities of Resistance? Maker Pedagogies, Do-It-Yourself Feminism, and DIY Citizenship."

47. Martin, "The Promise of the Maker Movement for Education"; and Vossoughi and Bevan, "Making and Tinkering: A Review of the Literature."

48. Chang et al., "The Maker Ed Open Portfolio Project: Maker Portfolios In School"; and Peppler et al., "The Maker Ed Open Portfolio Project Survey of Maker Spaces, Part 2."

49. Kafai and Peppler, "Youth, Technology, and DIY Developing Participatory Competencies in Creative Media Production."

50. Vossoughi and Bevan, "Making and Tinkering: A Review of the Literature."

51. Ibid., 410.

52. Latricia Whitfield, Katie Miller, and Kira J. Baker-Doyle, "Fostering Social Capital through Connected Learning: Five Case Studies in Teacher Education" (Penn GSE Ethnography in Education Research Forum, Philadelphia, 2016).

53. Vossoughi and Bevan, "Making and Tinkering: A Review of the Literature"; and L. Darling-Hammond, "Keeping Good Teachers: Why It Matters . . . What Leaders Can Do," *Educational Leadership* 60, no. 8 (2003): 6–13.

Chapter 6

1. Diane Laufenberg, "EduCon 2.8 Conversation—Silver Bullets, Panaceas and Elixirs: The False Prophets of Educational Reform," *Living the Dream*, February 9, 2016, https://laufenberg.wordpress.com/2016/02/08/educon-2-8-conversation-silver-bullets-panaceas-and-elixirs-the-false-prophets-of-educational-reform/.

2. Sasha Costanza-Chock, *Out of the Shadows, Into the Streets! Transmedia Organizing and the Immigrant Rights Movement* (Cambridge, MA: MIT Press, 2014).

3. Emma Eisenberg, "'11,000 Smart, Committed Teachers Can Change the World': A Group of Working Philadelphia Teachers Is Looking to Upset the Status Quo of the Teachers Union," *Salon*, http://www.salon.com/2016/01/24/11000_smart_committed_teachers_can_change_the_world_a_group_of_working_philadelphia_teachers_is_looking_to_upset_the_status_quo_of_the_teachers_union/.

4. Gerard Briscoe and Catherine Mulligan, "Digital Innovation: The Hackathon Phenomenon" (working paper, Creativeworks, London, May 2014), http://www.creativeworkslondon.org.uk/wp-content/uploads/2013/11/Digital-Innovation-The-Hackathon-Phenomenon1.pdf; Tyson E. Lewis and Daniel Friedrich, "Educational States of Suspension," *Educational Philosophy and Theory* 48, no. 3 (February 23, 2016): 237–50, doi:10.1080/00131857.2015.1004153; Mark Barnes and Jennifer Gonzalez, *Hacking Education: 10 Quick Fixes for Every School*, vol. 1, Hack Learning Series (Cleveland: Hack Learning, 2015); and Steve Mann, "Maktivism: Authentic Making for Technology in the Service of Humanity," in *DIY Citizenship: Critical Making and Social Media*, ed. Matt Ratto and Meg Boler (Cambridge, MA: MIT Press, 2014), 29–51.

5. E. Gabriella Coleman, *Coding Freedom: The Ethics and Aesthetics of Hacking* (Princeton, NJ: Princeton University Press, 2013); Douglas Thomas, *Hacker Culture* (Minneapolis: University of Minnesota Press, 2002); and Pekka Himanen, *The Hacker Ethic* (New York: Random House, 2001).

6. Coleman, *Coding Freedom: The Ethics and Aesthetics of Hacking*; and Thomas, *Hacker Culture*.

7. Coleman, *Coding Freedom: The Ethics and Aesthetics of Hacking*; Briscoe and Mulligan, "Digital Innovation: The Hackathon Phenomenon"; Himanen, *The Hacker Ethic*; Thomas, *Hacker Culture*; Sergey Bratus, "What Hackers Learn That the Rest of Us Don't" (white paper, 2008), http://cs.dartmouth.edu/~sergey/hacker-methodology.pdf; and Mann, "Maktivism: Authentic Making for Technology in the Service of Humanity."

8. Himanen, *The Hacker Ethic*.

9. Sebastian Anthony, "International Space Station Switches from Windows to Linux, for Improved Reliability," *ExtremeTech*, May 9, 2013, http://www.extremetech.com/extreme/155392-international-space-station-switches-from-windows-to-linux-for-improved-reliability; and Chris Hoffman, "Android Is Based on Linux, But What Does That Mean?," *How-To Geek*, May 12, 2014, http://www.howtogeek.com/189036/android-is-based-on-linux-but-what-does-that-mean/.

10. Coleman, *Coding Freedom: The Ethics and Aesthetics of Hacking*; and Briscoe and Mulligan, "Digital Innovation: The Hackathon Phenomenon."

11. Briscoe and Mulligan, "Digital Innovation: The Hackathon Phenomenon."

12. Ibid., 2.

13. Rafi Santo, "Hacker Literacies: Synthesizing Critical and Participatory Media Literacy Frameworks," *International Journal of Learning and Media* 3, no. 3 (July 1, 2011): 1–5; and Rafi Santo, "Towards Hacker Literacies: What Facebook's Privacy Snafus Can Teach Us about Empowered Technological Practices," *Digital Culture and Education* 5, no. 1 (2013): 18–33.

14. Coleman, *Coding Freedom: The Ethics and Aesthetics of Hacking*; and Himanen, *The Hacker Ethic*.

15. Briscoe and Mulligan, "Digital Innovation: The Hackathon Phenomenon."

16. Coleman, *Coding Freedom: The Ethics and Aesthetics of Hacking*; Sue Lasky, "A Sociocultural Approach to Understanding Teacher Identity, Agency and Professional Vulnerability in a Context of Secondary School Reform," *Teaching and Teacher Education* 21, no. 8 (November 2005): 899–916, doi:10.1016/j.tate.2005.06.003; Kira J. Baker-Doyle and Leif Gustavson, "Permission-Seeking as an Agentive Tool for Transgressive Teaching: An Ethnographic Study of Teachers Organizing for Curricular Change," *Journal of Educational Change* 17, no. 1 (July 2015): 51–84; and James V. Wertsch, Peter Tulviste, and Fran Hagstrom, "A Sociocultural Approach to Agency," *Contexts for Learning: Sociocultural Dynamics in Children's Development* 23 (1993): 336–56.

17. Ben Yagoda, "A Short History of 'Hack,'" *New Yorker*, March 6, 2014, http://www.newyorker.com/tech/elements/a-short-history-of-hack.

18. Zapico Lamela et al., "Hacking Sustainability : Broadening Participation through Green Hackathons" (Fourth International Symposium on End-User Development, IT University of Copenhagen, Denmark, 2013), 1–9; and Mann, "Maktivism: Authentic Making for Technology in the Service of Humanity."

19. Manuel Castells, *Networks of Outrage and Hope: Social Movements in the Internet Age* (New York: John Wiley & Sons, 2015); and Kate Milberry, "(Re) Making the Internet: Free Software and the Social Factory Hack," in *DIY Citizenship: Critical Making and Social Media*, ed. Matt Ratto and Meg Boler (Cambridge, MA: MIT Press, 2014), 53–65.

20. Castells, *Networks of Outrage and Hope*, 231.

21. Marla Kilfoyle and Melissa Tomlinson, "Badass Teachers: Fighting for Education in the Age of Corporate Reform," in *Resisting Reform*, ed. Kjersti VanSlyke-Briggs, Elizabeth Bloom, and Danielle Boudet (Charlotte, NC: Information Age Publishing, 2015), 287.

22. James Gee, "The New Literacy Studies and the 'Social Turn'" (opinion paper, 1999), http://www.schools.ash.org/au/litweb/page300.html; The New London Group, "A Pedagogy of Multiliteracies: Designing Social Futures," *Harvard Educational Review* 66, no. 1 (1996): 60–93; and Donna E. Alvermann, Jennifer S. Moon, and Margaret C. Hagood, *Popular Culture in the Classroom: Teaching and Researching Critical Media Literacy*, Literacy Studies Series (New York: Routledge, 1999).

23. J. Gee, in Glynda A. Hull and Katherine Schultz, *School's Out: Bridging Out-of-School Literacies with Classroom Practice* (New York: Teachers College Press, 2002), viii.

24. Gee, "The New Literacy Studies and the 'Social Turn.'"

25. Allan Luke, "When Literacy Might (Not) Make a Difference: Textual Practice and Capital" (paper presented at the annual meeting of the American Educational Research Association, San Francisco, April 18–22, 1995), http://files.eric.ed.gov/fulltext/ED384001.pdf.

26. P. A. Dhillon and P. Standish, *Lyotard: Just Education* (London: Routledge, 2000).

27. Wertsch, Tulviste, and Hagstrom, "A Sociocultural Approach to Agency."

28. Bill Cope and Mary Kalantzis, "'Multiliteracies': New Literacies, New Learning," *Pedagogies: An International Journal* 4, no. 3 (2009): 164–95.

29. Kira J. Baker-Doyle, Katie Miller, and Latricia Whitfield, "Teacher/Maker/Re-Mixer/Connector: Connected Learning in Teacher Education" (American Educational Research Association Annual Conference, Dallas, TX, under review).

30. Luke, "When Literacy Might (Not) Make a Difference: Textual Practice and Capital"; Gee, "The New Literacy Studies and the 'Social Turn'"; Kris D. Gutiérrez, "Developing a Sociocritical Literacy in the Third Space," *Reading Research Quarterly* 43, no. 2 (2008): 148–64; and Alison Cook-Sather, "Re (in) Forming the Conversations: Student Position, Power, and Voice in Teacher Education," *Radical Teacher*, no. 64 (2002): 21–28.

31. Castells, *Networks of Outrage and Hope*, 9.

32. Costanza-Chock, *Out of the Shadows, Into the Streets! Transmedia Organizing and the Immigrant Rights Movement*, 50.

33. Michalinos Zembylas and Heidi Bulmahn Barker, "Teachers' Spaces for Coping with Change in the Context of a Reform Effort," *Journal of Educational Change* 8, no. 3 (August 1, 2007): 235–56, doi:10.1007/s10833-007-9025-y; and Andy Hargreaves, "The Emotional Politics of Teaching and Teacher Development: With Implications for Educational Leadership," *International Journal of Leadership in Education* 1, no. 4 (1998): 315–36.

34. Dan Geringer, "Palumbo H.S. Students Loudly Say 'No!' to Islamophobia—Philly Archives," *Philadelphia Inquirer*, January 14, 2016, http://articles.philly.com/2016-01-14/news/69738717_1_islamophobia-muslims-friend.

35. Tyson E. Lewis and Daniel Friedrich, "Educational States of Suspension," *Educational Philosophy and Theory* 48, no. 3 (2016): 237–250.

36. Antero Garcia and Cindy O'Donnell-Allen, *Pose, Wobble, Flow: A Culturally Proactive Approach to Literary Instruction* (New York: Teachers College Press, 2015).

37. Sarah Brown Wessling, Danielle Lillge, and Crystal VanKooten, *Supporting Students in a Time of Core Standards: English Language Arts, Grades 9-12* (Urbana, IL: National Council of Teachers of English, 2011).

38. Garcia and O'Donnell-Allen, *Pose, Wobble, Flow*.

39. Sarabeth Berk and Jim Stephens, "Curriculum Hack Participant Guide," University of Denver, 2013, 4, https://thecurriculumhack.files.wordpress.com/2013/10/final-handout-curric-hack-guide-for-participants.pdf.

40. Knowledge Works Foundation, "Knowledge 2020," 2008, www.knowledgeworks.org.

41. Briscoe and Mulligan, "Digital Innovation: The Hackathon Phenomenon."

42. Scott Doorley and Scott Witthoft, *Make Space: How to Set the Stage for Creative Collaboration* (Hoboken, NJ: John Wiley & Sons, 2011).

43. Ibid., 5.

44. Garcia and O'Donnell-Allen, *Pose, Wobble, Flow*.

45. Ibid., 111.
46. Kjersti VanSlyke-Briggs, "Harnessing the Smart Mob: Using Social Media to Enact Change," in *Resisting Reform*, ed. Kjersti VanSlyke-Briggs, Elizabeth Bloom, and Danielle Boudet (Charlotte, NC: Information Age Publishing, 2015), 285–99.
47. Ibid.
48. Ibid.
49. Kilfoyle and Tomlinson, "Badass Teachers: Fighting for Education in the Age of Corporate Reform," 258.
50. Castells, *Networks of Outrage and Hope*; and Todd Wolfson, *Digital Rebellion: The Birth of the Cyber Left* (Chicago: University of Illinois Press, 2014).
51. Milberry, "(Re) Making the Internet: Free Software and the Social Factory Hack," 56.
52. Garcia and O'Donnell-Allen, *Pose, Wobble, Flow*, 34.
53. G. Kelchtermans and K. Ballet, "The Micropolitics of Teacher Induction: A Narrative—Biographical Study on Teacher Socialization," *Teaching and Teacher Education* 18 (2002): 105–20.
54. Baker-Doyle and Gustavson, "Permission-Seeking as an Agentive Tool for Transgressive Teaching."
55. Coleman, *Coding Freedom: The Ethics and Aesthetics of Hacking*, 11.
56. bell hooks, *Teaching to Transgress: Education as the Practice of Freedom* (New York: Routledge, 1994), 207.
57. Garcia and O'Donnell-Allen, *Pose, Wobble, Flow*, 33.

Chapter 7

1. Brené Brown, *Daring Greatly: How the Courage to Be Vulnerable Transforms the Way We Live, Love, Parent, and Lead* (New York: Penguin, 2012).
2. Peter F. Drucker, "Knowledge-Worker Productivity: The Biggest Challenge," *California Management Review* 41, no. 2 (1999): 79–94; and Daniel Lee Kleinman and Steven P. Vallas, "Science, Capitalism, and the Rise of the 'Knowledge Worker': The Changing Structure of Knowledge Production in the United States," *Theory and Society* 30, no. 4 (2001): 451–92.
3. Carrie James, *Disconnected: Youth, New Media, and the Ethics Gap* (Cambridge, MA: MIT Press, 2014), 17.
4. Sherry Turkle, *Alone Together: Why We Expect More from Technology and Less from Each Other* (New York: Basic Books, 2012).
5. Rafi Santo, "Hacker Literacies: Synthesizing Critical and Participatory Media Literacy Frameworks," *International Journal of Learning and Media* 3, no. 3 (July 1, 2011): 1–5; and Howard Rheingold, *Net Smart: How to Thrive Online* (Cambridge, MA: MIT Press, 2012).
6. D. Tyack and L. Cuban, *Tinkering Toward Utopia: A Century of Public School Reform* (Cambridge, MA: Harvard University Press, 1995); and S. Saronson, *The Culture of School and the Problem of Change* (Boston: Allyn & Bacon, 1971).
7. K. Rousmaniere, *City Teachers: Teaching and School Reform in Historical Perspective* (New York: Teachers College Press, 1997); M. Fullan, *Change Forces: Probing the Depths of Educational Reform* (London: Falmer Press, 1993); J. W. Little, "Professional Development

in Pursuit of Reform," ed. A. Lieberman and L. Miller, *Teachers Caught in the Action: Professional Development That Matters* (New York: Teachers College Press, 2001), 23–44; L. Darling-Hammond and M. W. McLaughlin, "Policies That Support Professional Development in an Era of Reform," *Phi Delta Kappan*, April 1995; William Lowe Boyd, "The 'R's' of School Reform and the Politics of Reforming or Replacing Public Schools," *Journal of Educational Change* 1, no. 3 (2000): 225–52; and Frederick M. Hess, *Spinning Wheels: The Politics of Urban School Reform* (Washington, DC: Brookings Institution Press, 2011).

8. Manuel Castells, *Networks of Outrage and Hope: Social Movements in the Internet Age* (Hoboken, NJ: John Wiley & Sons, 2015).

9. M. W. Apple, "Curricular Form and the Logic of Technical Control," ed. M. W. Apple and L. Wies, *Ideology and the Practice of Schooling* (Philadelphia: Temple University Press, 1983), 143–65; and M. W. Apple, "Controlling the Work of Teachers," ed. D. J. Flinders and S. J. Thornton, *The Curriculum Studies Reader* (New York: Routledge Falmer, 2004).

10. L. Darling-Hammond, "Policy and Professionalism," ed. A. Lieberman, *Building a Professional Culture in Schools* (New York: Teachers College Press, 1988), 55–77; D. Kirk and D. MacDonald, "Teacher Voice and Ownership of Curriculum Change," *Journal of Curriculum Studies* 33, no. 5 (2001): 551–67; A. Lieberman, "Networks As Learning Communities: Shaping the Future of Teacher Development," *Journal of Teacher Education* 51, no. 3 (2000): 221–27; and E. W. Ross, J. W. Cornett, and G. McCutcheon, *Teacher Personal Theorizing: Connecting Curriculum Practice, Theory, and Research* (Albany: SUNY Press, 1992).

11. Ann Lieberman and Lynne Miller, *Teachers—Transforming Their World and Their Work* (New York: Teachers College Press, 1999); and Darling-Hammond and McLaughlin, "Policies That Support Professional Development in an Era of Reform."

12. J. W. Little, "The Mentor Phenomenon and the Social Organization of Teaching," *Review of Research in Education* 16 (1990): 297–351; James S. Pounder, "Transformational Classroom Leadership: The Fourth Wave of Teacher Leadership?," *Educational Management Administration & Leadership* 34, no. 4 (2006): 533–45; and Jennifer York-Barr and Karen Duke, "What Do We Know about Teacher Leadership? Findings from Two Decades of Scholarship," *Review of Educational Research* 74, no. 3 (2004): 255–316.

13. Lieberman, "Networks as Learning Communities: Shaping the Future of Teacher Development."

14. Amanda Datnow, "Collaboration and Contrived Collegiality: Revisiting Hargreaves in the Age of Accountability," *Journal of Educational Change* 12, no. 2 (February 22, 2011); Kevin M. Leander and Margery D. Osborne, "Complex Positioning: Teachers as Agents of Curricular and Pedagogical Reform," *Journal of Curriculum Studies* 40, no. 1 (February 1, 2008): 23–46; M. A. Smylie, "From Bureaucratic Control to Building Human Capital: The Importance of Teacher Learning in Education Reform," *Educational Researcher* 25, no. 9 (December 1996): 9–11; Diann Musial, "Schools as Social-Capital Networks: A New Vision for Reform," *Educational Forum* 63 (Winter 1999): 113–20; Amanda Datnow, "The Sustainability of Comprehensive School Reform Models in Changing District and State Contexts," *Educational Administration Quarterly* 41,

no. 1 (February 1, 2005): 121–53, doi:10.1177/0013161X04269578; and Brad Olsen and Dena Sexton, "Threat Rigidity, School Reform, and How Teachers View Their Work Inside Current Education Policy Contexts," *American Educational Research Journal* 46, no. 1 (2009): 9–44.

15. J. P. Spillane, R. Halverson, and J. B. Diamond, "Towards a Theory of Leadership Practice: A Distributed Perspective," *Journal of Curriculum Studies* 36, no. 1 (2004): 3–34; and J. P. Spillane, "External Reform Initiatives and Teachers' Efforts to Reconstruct Their Practice: The Mediating Role of Teachers' Zones of Enactment," *Journal of Curriculum Studies* 31, no. 2 (1999): 143–75.

16. Dorothy Andrews and Frank Crowther, "Parallel Leadership: A Clue to the Contents of the 'Black Box' of School Reform," *International Journal of Educational Management* 16, no. 4 (2002): 152–59.

17. Ann Lieberman and Lynne Miller, *Teacher Leadership* (Hoboken, NJ: John Wiley & Sons, 2011); Ann Lieberman and Desiree Pointer-Mace, "Making Practice Public: Teacher Learning in the 21st Century," *Journal of Teacher Education*, October 7, 2009; and Daniel Muijs and Alma Harris, "Teacher Leadership—Improvement through Empowerment? An Overview of the Literature," *Educational Management & Administration* 31, no. 4 (2003): 437–48.

18. Barnett Berry, "Teacherpreneurs: A Bold Brand of Teacher Leadership for 21st-Century Teaching and Learning," *Science* 340, no. 6130 (2013): 309–10.

19. Pounder, "Transformational Classroom Leadership: The Fourth Wave of Teacher Leadership?"

20. Andy Hargreaves and Michael Fullan, *Professional Capital: Transforming Teaching in Every School* (New York: Teachers College Press, 2012).

21. Nienke M. Moolenaar, Peter J. C. Sleegers, and Alan J. Daly, "Teaming Up: Linking Collaboration Networks, Collective Efficacy, and Student Achievement," *Teaching and Teacher Education* 28, no. 2 (2012): 251–62; Frits K. Pil and Carrie Leana, "Applying Organizational Research to Public School Reform: The Effects of Teacher Human and Social Capital on Student Performance," *Academy of Management Journal* 52, no. 6 (December 1, 2009): 1101–24; Megan Tschannen-Moran and Marilyn Barr, "Fostering Student Learning: The Relationship of Collective Teacher Efficacy and Student Achievement," *Leadership and Policy in Schools* 3, no. 3 (2004): 189–209; and R. D. Goddard, "Relational Networks, Social Trust, and Norms: A Social Capital Perspective on Students' Chances of Academic Success," *Educational Evaluation and Policy Analysis* 25, no. 1 (2003): 59–74.

22. P. Lather, *Getting Smart: Feminist Research and Pedagogy With/In the Postmodern* (New York: Routledge, 1991); Andy Hargreaves and Ruth Dawe, "Paths of Professional Development: Contrived Collegiality, Collaborative Culture, and the Case of Peer Coaching," *Teaching and Teacher Education* 6, no. 3 (1990): 227–41; and B. Achinstein and R. T. Ogawa, "(In)Fidelity: What the Resistance of New Teachers Reveals about Professional Principles and Prescriptive Educational Policies," *Harvard Educational Review* 76, no. 1 (2006): 28.

23. Roger D. Goddard, Wayne K. Hoy, and Anita Woolfolk Hoy, "Collective Teacher Efficacy: Its Meaning, Measure, and Impact on Student Achievement," *American Educational Research Journal* 37, no. 2 (2000): 479–507; Cheri Ostroff, "The Relationship

between Satisfaction, Attitudes, and Performance: An Organizational Level Analysis," *Journal of Applied Psychology* 77, no. 6 (1992): 963; and Gian Vittorio Caprara et al., "Teachers' Self-Efficacy Beliefs as Determinants of Job Satisfaction and Students' Academic Achievement: A Study at the School Level," *Journal of School Psychology* 44, no. 6 (December 2006): 473–90.

24. Moolenaar, Sleegers, and Daly, "Teaming up: Linking Collaboration Networks, Collective Efficacy, and Student Achievement"; Kira J. Baker-Doyle and Leif Gustavson, "Permission-Seeking as an Agentive Tool for Transgressive Teaching: An Ethnographic Study of Teachers Organizing for Curricular Change," *Journal of Educational Change*, July 1, 2015, 1–34; W. R. Penuel et al., "Analyzing Teachers' Professional Interactions in a School as Social Capital: A Social Network Approach," *Teachers College Record* 111, no. 1 (2009): 124–63; and Milbrey Wallin McLaughlin and Joan E. Talbert, *Building School-Based Teacher Learning Communities: Professional Strategies to Improve Student Achievement* (New York: Teachers College Press, 2006).

25. D. Boyd et al., "The Draw of Home: How Teachers' Preferences for Proximity Disadvantage Urban Schools" (Cambridge, MA: National Bureau of Economic Research, 2003); and A. Thomas, "Teacher Attrition, Social Capital, and Career Advancement: An Unwelcome Message," *Research and Practice in Social Sciences* 3, no. 1 (2007): 19–47.

26. K. A. Frank, Y. Zhao, and K. Borman, "Social Capital and the Diffusion of Innovations Within Organizations: The Case of Computer Technology in Schools," *Sociology of Education* 77, no. April (2004): 148–71; K. J. Baker-Doyle, "First-year teachers' support networks: Intentional professional networks and diverse professional allies," *The New Educator* 8, no. 1 (2012): 65–85; and Nienke M. Moolenaar and P. J. Sleegers, "Social Networks, Trust, and Innovation: The Role of Relationships in Supporting an Innovative Climate in Dutch Schools," in *Social Network Theory and Educational Change* (Cambridge, MA: Harvard Education Press, 2010).

27. Baker-Doyle, " First-year teachers' support networks: Intentional professional networks and diverse professional allies"; and Kira J. Baker-Doyle, *The Networked Teacher: How New Teachers Build Social Networks for Professional Support* (New York: Teachers College Press, 2011).

28. Spillane, "External Reform Initiatives and Teachers' Efforts to Reconstruct Their Practice: The Mediating Role of Teachers' Zones of Enactment."

29. Lieberman, "Networks as Learning Communities: Shaping the Future of Teacher Development"; Lieberman and Miller, *Teacher Leadership*; and A. Lieberman and D. R. Wood, *Inside the National Writing Project: Connecting Network Learning and Classroom Teaching* (New York: Teachers College Press, 2003).

30. Kira J. Baker-Doyle, "No Teacher Is an Island: How Social Networks Shape Teacher Quality," in *Promoting and Sustaining a Quality Teacher Workforce*, vol. 27, *International Perspectives on Education and Society* 27 (Somerville, MA: Emerald Group Publishing Limited, 2015), 367–83.

31. Lauren Anderson, "Embedded, Emboldened, and (Net)Working for Change: Support-Seeking and Teacher Agency in Urban, High-Needs Schools," *Harvard Educational Review* 80, no. 4 (December 1, 2010): 541–73.

32. Drucker, "Knowledge-Worker Productivity: The Biggest Challenge."

33. R. Ingersoll, *Who Controls Teachers' Work? Power and Accountability in America's Schools* (Cambridge, MA: Harvard University Press, 2003); C. Bidwell, K. A. Frank, and P. A. Quiroz, "Teacher Types, Workplace Controls, and the Organization of Schools," *Sociology of Education* 70, no. 4 (October 1997): 285–307; B. Rowan, "Commitment and Control: Alternative Strategies for the Organization and Design of Schools," *Review of Research in Education* 16 (1990): 353–89.

34. José Vilson, *This Is Not a Test: A New Narrative on Race, Class, and Education* (New York: Haymarket Books, 2014).

35. James, *Disconnected*.

36. Ashley Lee, "John Legend on the Startling High School 'Revelation' That Sparked His Music Career," *Hollywood Reporter*, August 14, 2014, http://www.hollywoodreporter.com/news/john-legend-startling-high-school-725407.

37. Brown, *Daring Greatly: How the Courage to Be Vulnerable Transforms the Way We Live, Love, Parent, and Lead.*

38. Todd Wolfson, *Digital Rebellion: The Birth of the Cyber Left* (Champaign: University of Illinois Press, 2014); Sasha Costanza-Chock, *Out of the Shadows, Into the Streets! Transmedia Organizing and the Immigrant Rights Movement* (Cambridge, MA: MIT Press, 2014); Castells, *Networks of Outrage and Hope*; E. Gabriella Coleman, *Coding Freedom: The Ethics and Aesthetics of Hacking* (Princeton, NJ: Princeton University Press, 2013); Stephanie Chang et al., "The Maker Ed Open Portfolio Project: Maker Portfolios In School," Open Portfolio Project Research Brief Series (Maker Education Initiative, 2015); Lee Martin, "The Promise of the Maker Movement for Education," *Journal of Pre-College Engineering Research* 5, no. 1 (2015): 30–39; and Henry Jenkins, *Fans, Bloggers, and Gamers: Exploring Participatory Culture* (New York: NYU Press, 2006).

39. Benjamin Herold, "'EduCon,' an Ed-Tech Conference Without Vendors, Set to Begin," *Philadelphia Public School Notebook*, January 23, 2015, http://thenotebook.org/articles/2015/01/23/educon-an-ed-tech-conference-without-vendors-set-to-begin.

40. "PRAXIS Professional Development," http://www.razaeducators.org/praxis-professional-development.html.

41. J. Lave and E. Wenger, *Situated Learning. Legitimate Peripheral Participation* (Cambridge: University of Cambridge Press, 1991); and E. Wenger, "Communities of Practice: Learning as a Social System," *Systems Thinker* 5, no. 9 (1998).

42. J. Corneli et al., "The Peeragogy Handbook" (Chicago/Somerville, MA: PomDomEd/Pierce Press, 2016), http://peeragogy.org.

43. Michael D. Siciliano, "It's the Quality Not the Quantity of Ties That Matters: Social Networks and Self-Efficacy Beliefs," *American Educational Research Journal* 53, no. 2 (2016): 227–62.

44. P. S. Adler and S-W. Kwon, "Social Capital: Prospects for a New Concept," *Academy of Management Journal* 27, no. 1 (2002): 17–40; and K. Baker-Doyle and S. A. Yoon, "In Search of Practitioner-Based Social Capital: A Social Network Analysis Tool for Understanding and Facilitating Teacher Collaboration in a Professional Development Program," *Professional Development in Education* 37, no. 1 (2010): 75–93.

45. M. Granovetter, "The Strength of Weak Ties," ed. R. Cross, A. Parker, and L. Sasson, *Networks in the Knowledge Economy* (New York: Oxford University Press, 2003), 109–29.

46. Baker-Doyle, " First-year teachers' support networks: Intentional professional networks and diverse professional allies."

47. Turkle, *Alone Together: Why We Expect More from Technology and Less from Each Other*, 13.

48. D. Krackhardt, "Assessing the Political Landscape: Structure, Cognition, and Power in Organizations," *Administration Science Quarterly* 35, no. 2 (1990): 342–69.

49. Kira J. Baker-Doyle and Emery Petchauer, "Rumor Has It: Investigating Teacher Licensure Exam Advice Networks," *Teacher Education Quarterly* 42, no. 3 (2015): 3.

50. Miller McPherson, Lynn Smith-Lovin, and James M. Cook, "Birds of a Feather: Homophily in Social Networks," *Annual Review of Sociology* 27 (January 1, 2001): 415–44.

51. Baker-Doyle and Gustavson, "Permission-Seeking as an Agentive Tool for Transgressive Teaching"; and Baker-Doyle, "No Teacher Is an Island."

52. Mizuko Ito et al., *Connected Learning: An Agenda for Research and Design* (Irvine, CA: Digital Media and Learning Research Hub, 2013).

53. Ibid.

54. Antero Garcia et al., *Teaching in the Connected Learning Classroom* (Irvine, CA: Digital Media and Learning Research Hub, 2014).

55. Ibid., 76.

56. Lalitha Vasudevan, "Making Known Differently: Engaging Visual Modalities as Spaces to Author New Selves," *E-Learning and Digital Media* 3, no. 2 (2006): 207–16; Donna E. Alvermann, Jennifer S. Moon, and Margaret C. Hagood, *Popular Culture in the Classroom: Teaching and Researching Critical Media Literacy*, Literacy Studies Series (Newark, DE: International Reading Association, 1999); and Mizuko Ito et al., "Living and Learning with New Media: Summary of Findings from the Digital Youth Project," John D. and Catherine T. MacArthur Foundation, 2008.

57. Danielle Filipiak and Isaac Miller, "Me and the D:(Re) Imagining Literacy and Detroit's Future," *English Journal* 103, no. 5 (2014): 59.

58. Latricia Whitfield, Katie Miller, and Kira J. Baker-Doyle, "Fostering Social Capital Through Connected Learning: Five Case Studies in Teacher Education" (Penn GSE Ethnography in Education Research Forum, Philadelphia, 2016).

59. Ito et al., *Connected Learning: An Agenda for Research and Design*.

Chapter 8

1. Cindy Rottmann et al., "Remembering, Reimagining, and Reviving Social Justice Teacher Unionism," *Teacher Unions in Public Education: Politics, History, and the Future*, 2015, ed. Nina Bascia (New York: Palgrave Macmillan, 2015), 53–70.

2. Ibid.

3. Bob Peterson, "A New Teacher Union Movement Is Rising | Common Dreams | Breaking News & Views for the Progressive Community," *Common Dreams*, May 25, 2014, http://www.commondreams.org/views/2014/05/23/new-teacher-union-movement-rising.

4. Kathleen Riley, "Reading for Change: Social Justice Unionism Book Groups as an Organizing Tool," *Perspectives on Urban Education* 12, no. 1 (2015).

5. Rottmann et al., "Remembering, Reimagining, and Reviving Social Justice Teacher Unionism," 54.

6. "Maker Faire: Find a Faire Near You," *Maker Faire*, 2016, http://makerfaire.com/map/.

7. Kylie A. Peppler et al., "The Maker Ed Open Portfolio Project Survey of Maker Spaces, Part 1," Open Portfolio Project Research Brief Series (Maker Education Initiative, 2015).

8. "Member Blogs—Resources for K-12 Fab Labs and Makerspaces," https://sites.google .com/site/k12makers/member-blogs.

9. Marlene Berg, Emil Coman, and Jean J. Schensul, "Youth Action Research for Prevention: A Multi-Level Intervention Designed to Increase Efficacy and Empowerment Among Urban Youth," *American Journal of Community Psychology* 43, no. 3–4 (April 2009): 345–59; Emily J. Ozer and Dana Wright, "Beyond School Spirit: The Effects of Youth-Led Participatory Action Research in Two Urban High Schools," *Journal of Research on Adolescence* 22, no. 2 (June 2012): 267–83; and Julio Cammarota and Michelle Fine, *Revolutionizing Education: Youth Participatory Action Research in Motion* (Oxfordshire, UK: Taylor & Francis, 2008).

10. For example, see the list of books by teacher writers in chapter 5's section on transformative teachers designing with a maker mind-set.

11. Emanuella Grinberg, "'Genius Hour': Students, What Would You like to Learn Today?," CNN News, CNN.com, March 10, 2014, http://www.cnn.com/2014/03/09/living /genius-hour-education-schools/.

12. Denise Krebs, "#GeniusHour Blog Post Index | Dare to Care," December 2, 2011, http:// mrsdkrebs.edublogs.org/2011/12/02/geniushour-blog-post-index/.

13. "Genius Hour Wiki," 2016, http://geniushour.wikispaces.com/.

14. Kristen Purcell et al., "How Teachers Are Using Technology at Home and in Their Classrooms," Pew Research Center: Internet, Science & Tech, February 28, 2013, http://www .pewinternet.org/2013/02/28/how-teachers-are-using-technology-at-home-and-in -their-classrooms/.

15. Celine Provini, "Education World: Use Crowdfunding to Raise Money: Top 9 Tips," *Education World*, 2014, http://www.educationworld.com/a_admin/crowdfunding-fund raising-schools-tips-best-practices.shtml.

16. EdCamp, "Complete EdCamp Calendar," EdCamp Wiki, n.d., http://edcamp.wiki spaces .com/complete+edcamp+calendar; and "TeachMeet: Teachers Sharing Ideas with Teachers Wiki," 2016, http://teachmeet.pbworks.com/w/page/19975349/FrontPage.

17. "Session on Doing Research on EdCamp" (EdCamp Organizers Summit, Philadelphia, April 30, 2016).

18. MetLife Foundation, "The MetLife Survey of the American Teacher: Collaborating for Student Success," Survey of the American Teacher (New York: MetLife Foundation, 2010), http://files.eric.ed.gov/fulltext/ED509650.pdf.

19. MetLife Foundation, "The MetLife Survey of the American Teacher: Challenges for School Leadership," Survey of the American Teacher (New York: MetLife Foundation, 2013), http://files.eric.ed.gov/fulltext/ED542202.pdf.

20. Marilyn Cochran-Smith and Susan L. Lytle, *Inquiry as Stance: Practitioner Research for the next Generation* (New York: Teachers College Press, 2009).

21. Ibid., 16.

22. Jerusha Osberg Conner and Sonia M. Rosen, "Zombies, Truants, and Flash Mobs: How Youth Organizers Respond to and Shape Youth Policy," *Teachers College Record* 117, no. 13 (2015): 203–20.

Chapter 9

1. Carol Dweck, *Mindset: The New Psychology of Success* (New York: Random House, 2006); and Brent Davis and Dennis Sumara, "Fitting Teacher Education In/to/for an Increasingly Complex World," *Complicity* 9, no. 1 (2012): 30.

2. Mark Priestley et al., "Teacher Agency in Curriculum Making: Agents of Change and Spaces for Manoeuvre," *Curriculum Inquiry* 42, no. 2 (March 1, 2012): 191–214; Kira J. Baker-Doyle and Leif Gustavson, "Permission-Seeking as an Agentive Tool for Transgressive Teaching: An Ethnographic Study of Teachers Organizing for Curricular Change," *Journal of Educational Change*, July 1, 2015, 1–34; C. L. Paris, *Teacher Agency and Curriculum Making in Classrooms* (New York: Teachers College Press, 1993); and B. Fecho, "Developing a Critical Mass: Teacher Education and Critical Inquiry Pedagogy," *Journal of Teacher Education* 51, no. 3 (2000): 194–99.

3. Matthew Koehler and Punya Mishra, "What Is Technological Pedagogical Content Knowledge (TPACK)?," *Contemporary Issues in Technology and Teacher Education* 9, no. 1 (2009): 60–70; Punya Mishra and Matthew Koehler, "Technological Pedagogical Content Knowledge: A Framework for Teacher Knowledge," *Teachers College Record* 108, no. 6 (2006): 1017–54; Joan E. Hughes and Ann Ooms, "Content-Focused Technology Inquiry Groups: Preparing Urban Teachers to Integrate Technology to Transform Student Learning," *Journal of Research on Technology in Education* 36, no. 4 (2004): 397–411; Peggy A. Ertmer and Anne T. Ottenbreit-Leftwich, "Teacher Technology Change: How Knowledge, Confidence, Beliefs, and Culture Intersect," *Journal of Research on Technology in Education* 42, no. 3 (2010): 255–84.

4. Andrea Forte, Melissa Humphreys, and Thomas H. Park, "Grassroots Professional Development: How Teachers Use Twitter" (paper presented at the International Association for the Advancement of Artificial Intelligence on Web and Social Media, Dublin, Ireland, June 4–8, 2012).

5. Latricia Whitfield, Katie Miller, and Kira J. Baker-Doyle, "Fostering Social Capital through Connected Learning: Five Case Studies in Teacher Education" (Penn GSE Ethnography in Education Research Forum, Philadelphia, 2016).

6. Susanna Tesconi and Lucía Arias, "The Transformative Potential of Making in Teacher Education: A Case Study on Teacher Training Through Making and Prototyping," in *Distributed, Ambient, and Pervasive Interactions* (New York: Springer, 2015), 119–28.

7. Sean Justice and Sandra Markus, "Educators, Gender Equity and Making: Opportunities and Obstacles." Presented at FabLearn '15, Stanford University, Palo Alto, CA, September 2015.

8. George Belliveau, "Engaging in Drama: Using Arts-Based Research to Explore a Social Justice Project in Teacher Education," *International Journal of Education & the Arts* 7, no. 5 (2006): 1–15; and Mary Dixon and Kim Senior, "Traversing Theory and Transgressing Academic Discourses: Arts-Based Research in Teacher Education," *International Journal of Education & the Arts* 10, no. 24 (2009): 1–22.

9. Marlo Steed, "3D Printing and Maker Spaces: Design as Storytelling" (paper presented at EdMedia: World Conference on Educational Media and Technology, Montreal, Quebec, June 22, 2015).

10. Désirée H. Pointer-Mace, *Teacher Practice Online: Sharing Wisdom, Opening Doors* (New York: Teachers College Press, 2009).

11. Ann Lieberman and Désirée Pointer-Mace, "Making Practice Public: Teacher Learning in the 21st Century," *Journal of Teacher Education* 61, no. 1–2 (2010): 77–88.

12. Elinor L. Brown, "What Precipitates Change in Cultural Diversity Awareness during a Multicultural Course: The Message or the Method?," *Journal of Teacher Education* 55, no. 4 (2004): 325–40; and Heidi J. Nast, "'Sex', 'Race' and Multiculturalism: Critical Consumption and the Politics of Course Evaluations," *Journal of Geography in Higher Education* 23, no. 1 (1999): 102–15.

13. Matthew N. Sanger, "What We Need to Prepare Teachers for the Moral Nature of Their Work," *Journal of Curriculum Studies* 40, no. 2 (2008): 169–85; and Geert Kelchtermans, "Teachers' Emotions in Educational Reforms: Self-Understanding, Vulnerable Commitment and Micropolitical Literacy," *Teaching and Teacher Education* 21, no. 8 (2005): 995–1006.

14. Matthew Sanger, "The Schizophrenia of Contemporary Education and the Moral Work of Teaching," *Curriculum Inquiry* 42, no. 2 (2012): 285–307.

15. W. R. Penuel and M. Riel, "The 'New' Science of Networks and the Challenge of School Change," *Phi Delta Kappan* (April 2007): 611–15; Alan J. Daly et al., "Relationships in Reform: The Role of Teachers' Social Networks," *Journal of Educational Administration* 48, no. 3 (November 5, 2010); Kira J. Baker-Doyle, "First-Year Teachers' Support Networks: Intentional Professional Networks and Diverse Professional Allies," *New Educator* 8, no. 1 (January 1, 2012): 65–85; Frits K. Pil and Carrie Leana, "Applying Organizational Research to Public School Reform: The Effects of Teacher Human and Social Capital on Student Performance," *Academy of Management Journal* 52, no. 6 (December 1, 2009): 1101–24; K. A. Frank, Y. Zhao, and K. Borman, "Social Capital and the Diffusion of Innovations Within Organizations: The Case of Computer Technology in Schools," *Sociology of Education* 77, no. 2 (April 2004): 148–71; Cynthia E. Coburn, "Collective Sensemaking about Reading: How Teachers Mediate Reading Policy in Their Professional Communities," *Educational Evaluation and Policy Analysis* 23, no. 2 (2001): 145–70; J. P. Spillane, "External Reform Initiatives and Teachers' Efforts to Reconstruct Their Practice: The Mediating Role of Teachers' Zones of Enactment," *Journal of Curriculum Studies* 31, no. 2 (1999): 143–75; R. D. Goddard, "Relational Networks, Social Trust, and Norms: A Social Capital Perspective on Students' Chances of Academic Success," *Educational Evaluation and Policy Analysis* 25, no. 1 (2003): 59–74; E. M. Horvat, E. B. Weininger, and A. Lareau, "From Social Ties to Social Capital: Class Differences in the Relations Between Schools and Parent Networks," *American Educational Research Journal* 40, no. 2 (2003): 319–51; K. Baker-Doyle and S. A. Yoon, "In Search of Practitioner-Based Social Capital: A Social Network Analysis Tool for Understanding and Facilitating Teacher Collaboration in a Professional Development Program," *Professional Development in Education* 37, no. 1 (2010): 75–93; Ricardo D. Stanton-Salazar, "A Social Capital Framework for the Study of Institutional Agents and Their Role in the Empowerment of Low-Status Students and Youth," *Youth & Society*, October 11, 2010; Lauren Anderson, "Embedded, Emboldened, and (Net)Working for Change: Support-Seeking

and Teacher Agency in Urban, High-Needs Schools," *Harvard Educational Review* 80, no. 4 (December 1, 2010): 541–73; and C. R. Stone and G. G. Wehlage, "Social Capital, Community Collaboration and the Restructuring of Schools," ed. F. Rivera-Batiz, *Reinventing Urban Education: Multiculturalism and the Social Context of Schooling* (Ephrata, PA: Science Press, 1994).

16. Pil and Leana, "Applying Organizational Research to Public School Reform"; Nienke M. Moolenaar, Peter J. C. Sleegers, and Alan J. Daly, "Teaming up: Linking Collaboration Networks, Collective Efficacy, and Student Achievement," *Teaching and Teacher Education* 28, no. 2 (2012): 251–62; Baker-Doyle, "First-Year Teachers' Support Networks"; and James P. Spillane, Kaleen Healey, and Chong Min Kim, "Leading and Managing Instruction: Formal and Informal Aspects of the Elementary School Organization," in *Social Network Theory and Educational Change* (Cambridge, MA: Harvard Education Press, 2010).

17. Sara Van Waes et al., "Know-Who? Linking Faculty's Networks to Stages of Instructional Development," *Higher Education* 70, no. 5 (2015): 807–26.

18. Andy Hargreaves and Michael Fullan, *Professional Capital: Transforming Teaching in Every School* (New York: Teachers College Press, 2012).

19. L. Darling-Hammond and M. W. McLaughlin, "Policies That Support Professional Development in an Era of Reform," *Phi Delta Kappan* (April 1995); J. W. Little, "Professional Development in Pursuit of School Reform," ed. A. Lieberman and L. Miller, *Teachers Caught in the Action: Professional Development That Matters* (New York: Teachers College Press, 2001), 23–44; Ann Lieberman and Lynne Miller, *Teachers Caught in the Action: Professional Development That Matters*, vol. 31 (New York: Teachers College Press, 2001); Marilyn Cochran-Smith and Susan L. Lytle, *Inquiry as Stance: Practitioner Research for the next Generation* (New York: Teachers College Press, 2009); Michael S. Garet et al., "What Makes Professional Development Effective? Results From a National Sample of Teachers," *American Educational Research Journal* 38, no. 4 (January 1, 2001): 915–45; Betty Lou Whitford and Diane R. Wood, "Professional Learning Communities for Collaborative Professional Development," in *Teachers Learning in Community: Realities and Possibilities*, ed. Betty Lou Whitford and Diane R. Wood (Albany: State University of New York Press, 2010), 1–20; Milbrey Wallin McLaughlin and Joan E. Talbert, *Building School-Based Teacher Learning Communities: Professional Strategies to Improve Student Achievement* (New York: Teachers College Press, 2006); Shirley M. Hord, "Professional Learning Communities: Communities of Continuous Inquiry and Improvement" (Southwest Educational Development Laboratory, Austin, TX, 1997), http://www.eric.ed.gov/ERIC WebPortal/contentdelivery/servlet/ERICServlet?accno=ED410659; and Louise Stoll et al., "Professional Learning Communities: A Review of the Literature," *Journal of Educational Change* 7 (2006): 221–58.

20. Ken Zeichner, "Rethinking the Connections between Campus Courses and Field Experiences in College- and University-Based Teacher Education," *Journal of Teacher Education* 61, no. 1–2 (2010): 89–99; Kris D. Gutiérrez, "Developing a Sociocritical Literacy in the Third Space," *Reading Research Quarterly* 43, no. 2 (2008): 148–64; Michael J. Muller, "Participatory Design: The Third Space in HCI," *Human-Computer Interaction: Development Process* 4235 (2003): 165–85; Susan D. Martin, Jennifer L. Snow, and Cheryl A. Franklin Torrez, "Navigating the Terrain of Third Space: Tensions With/in

Relationships in School-University Partnerships," *Journal of Teacher Education* 62, no. 3 (2011): 299–311; Alexander Cuenca et al., "Creating a 'Third Space' in Student Teaching: Implications for the University Supervisor's Status as Outsider," *Teaching and Teacher Education* 27, no. 7 (2011): 1068–77; and Ken Zeichner, Katherina Payne, and Kate Brayko, "Democratizing Knowledge in University Teacher Education through Practice-Based Methods Teaching and Mediated Field Experience in Schools and Communities," (issue paper, University of Washington-Seattle Center for the Study of Teacher Learning in Practice, January 2012), http://www.ccte.org/wp-content/pdfs-conferences/ccte-conf -2012-fall-zeichner-democratizing-knowledge.pdf.

21. Zeichner, "Rethinking the Connections between Campus Courses and Field Experiences in College- and University-Based Teacher Education."

22. Luis C. Moll et al., "Funds of Knowledge for Teaching: Using a Qualitative Approach to Connect Homes and Classrooms," *Theory into Practice* 31, no. 2 (April 1, 1992): 132–41.

23. "Edcamp Wiki," 2016, https://edcamp.wikispaces.com/.

24. Glenn Robbins, "Student Led EdCamp Period Takes NCMS To New Heights—NCMS Innovates," *NCMS Innovates*, January 24, 2016, http://blogs.ncs-nj.org/grobbins/2016 /01/24/student-led-edcamp-period-takes-ncms-to-new-heights/.

25. Mizuko Ito et al., *Connected Learning: An Agenda for Research and Design* (Cambridge, MA: Digital Media and Learning Research Hub, 2013), 8.

26. Anna Smith et al., "Remix as Professional Learning: Educators' Iterative Literacy Practice in CLMOOC," *Education Sciences* 6, no. 1 (March 18, 2016): 12.

27. Kira J. Baker-Doyle, Katie Miller, and Latricia Whitfield, "Teacher/Maker/Re-Mixer /Connector: Connected Learning in Teacher Education" (American Educational Research Association Annual Conference, Dallas, TX: AERA, under review).

28. Joseph Kahne, Erica Hodgin, and Elyse Eidman-Aadahl, "Redesigning Civic Education for the Digital Age: Participatory Politics and the Pursuit of Democratic Engagement," *Theory & Research in Social Education* 44, no. 1 (January 2, 2016): 1–35.

29. Daniel Schiff et al., "Teacher Networks in Philadelphia: Landscape, Engagement, and Value," *Penn GSE Perspectives on Urban Education* 12, no. 1 (2015): n1.

30. Alison Cook-Sather, "Re (in) Forming the Conversations: Student Position, Power, and Voice in Teacher Education," *Radical Teacher*, no. 64 (2002): 21–8; and Alison Cook-Sather and Bernadette Youens, "Repositioning Students in Initial Teacher Preparation A Comparative Descriptive Analysis of Learning to Teach for Social Justice in the United States and in England," *Journal of Teacher Education* 58, no. 1 (2007): 62–75.

31. Moll et al., "Funds of Knowledge for Teaching."

32. I use the term "affinity group" instead of "affinity space" to differentiate between James Gee's term "affinity space" and this concept, which relates more closely to Beverly Tatum's "affinity group" concept. Stephen John Quaye and Shaun R Harper, "Student Organizations as Venues for Black Identity Expression and Development among African American Male Student Leaders," *Journal of College Student Development* 48, no. 2 (2007): 127–44; Brian O. Culp, Jepkorir Rose Chepyator-Thomson, and Shan-Hui Hsu, "Pre-Service Teachers' Experiential Perspectives Based on a Multicultural Learning Service Practicum," *Physical Educator* 66, no. 1 (2009): 23; and Beverly Tatum, *Why Are All the Black Kids Sitting Together in the Cafeteria?* rev. ed. (New York: Basic Books, 2003).

33. Jesse J. Tauriac et al., "Utilizing Affinity Groups to Enhance Intergroup Dialogue Workshops for Racially and Ethnically Diverse Students," *Journal for Specialists in Group Work* 38, no. 3 (2013): 241–60.

34. Quaye and Harper, "Student Organizations as Venues for Black Identity Expression and Development among African American Male Student Leaders."

35. Ali Michael, *Raising Race Questions: Whiteness and Inquiry in Education* (New York: Teachers College Press, 2014); and Ali Michael and Mary C. Conger, "Becoming an Anti-Racist White Ally: How a White Affinity Group Can Help," *Perspectives on Urban Education* 6, no. 1 (2009): 56–60.

36. Eleanor Drago-Severson, *Helping Educators Grow: Strategies and Practices for Leadership Development* (Cambridge, MA: Harvard Education Press, 2012).

37. Kelchtermans, "Teachers' Emotions in Educational Reforms: Self-Understanding, Vulnerable Commitment and Micropolitical Literacy."

38. Kira J. Baker-Doyle, "There Was This Moment When I Realized . . ." A Framework for Examining Mindful Moments in Teaching," in *Impacting Teaching and Learning: Contemplative Practices, Pedagogy, and Research in Teacher Education*, ed. K. Brynes, J. Dalton, and E. Dorman (Princeton, NJ: Rowman & Littlefield, in press).

Chapter 10

1. Parker J. Palmer, *To Know as We Are Known: Education as a Spiritual Journey* (San Francisco: HarperOne, 1993).

Appendix

1. Howard Rheingold, *NetSmart: How To Thrive Online* (Cambridge, MA: MIT Press, 2012).

2. Mark Naison, *Badass Teachers Unite: Reflections on Education, History, and Youth Activism* (Chicago: Haymarket Books, 2014), 187.

3. Kira J. Baker-Doyle, "First-Year Teachers' Support Networks: Intentional Professional Networks and Diverse Professional Allies," *The New Educator* 8, no. 1 (2012): 65–85; and Kira J. Baker-Doyle, *The Networked Teacher: How New Teachers Build Social Networks for Professional Support* (New York: Teachers College Press, 2011).

4. Mark S. Granovetter, "The Strength of Weak Ties," *American Journal of Sociology* 78, no. 6 (1973): 1360–80; and D. J. Brass, "Being in the Right Place: A Structural Analysis of Individual Influence in an Organization," *Administration Science Quarterly* 29, no. 4 (1984): 518–39.

5. Jerry Blumgarten, "Cybrary man's Educational Websites," http://www.cybraryman.com.

6. Chrissy Romano-Arrabito, "EdJusticeLeague Rocks!," *The Connected Educator Blog*, June 17, 2015, http://theconnectededucator.com/edjusticeleague-rocks.

Acknowledgments

Writing this book was a labor of love . . . of teachers and teaching. I was motivated to write it from a deep desire to give voice and pay homage to the thousands of creative, passionate, caring, and knowledgeable teachers that I have encountered through my work as a teacher educator and researcher. I am eternally grateful to the fifteen teachers who were willing to share their personal stories and lives as examples of transformative teaching in this book: Joshua Block, Kelley Collings, Allison Frick, Annie Huynh, Tara Linney, John McCrann, Kathleen Melville, Noga Newberg, Meenoo Rami, Samuel Reed, Christopher Rogers, Scott Storm, José Luis Vilson, Anissa Weinraub, and Bevan Weissman. Their courage and dedication to fostering social justice through their craft continually inspires me to do the same. I am also indebted to the leaders of several education advocacy organizations who have been incredibly gracious in inviting me to learn about the ways in which they support the work of transformative teachers, including Hadley Ferguson at the EdCamp Foundation, the staff of the Philadelphia Education Fund (with special thanks to Ami Patel Hopkins, Daniel Schiff, and Marina Fradera), Elyse Eidman-Aadahl and Christina Cantrill at the National Writing Project and the Connected Learning Alliance, Robert Friedman and Sam Dyson at Hive Chicago, Chris Lehmann at Science Leadership Academy and Inquiry Schools, Sarah Langer at Boston Teacher Residency, and Gamal Sherif. Further, I am thankful for the following education advocates and thought leaders who were willing to share their insights and experiences with me, which helped me to offer a big-picture understanding of transformative teaching in the digital era: Mimi Ito, Howard Rheingold, Mia Zamora, Jonathan Worth, Antero Garcia, and Audrey Watters.

Writing this book was not a solo project, but a series of conversations of encouragement, exchange of ideas, critical feedback, and inspiration with many close friends and colleagues. To my Writing Tribe—Sonia Rosen, Lynnette Mawhinney, Tabitha Dell'Angelo, and Emery Petchauer—who always have my back and pick me up every time I am down: I feel blessed to have you in my life. To my mentors, Ann Lieberman, Susan Yoon, Lynne Strieb, Lisa Boullion Diaz, Susan Lytle, and Kathy Shultz: thank you for your faith in me, for your encouragement to grow, and always being there when I am in need of advice. I thank my editor, Nancy Walser, for her faith in me as well, and for her support in crafting the book. To my friends, Meredith Broussard, David Grazian, Jessica Falcone, Sanam Roder, Jane and Ivan Dmochowski, Catriona MacLeod, Neil Garrioch, Samer Abboud, Amy Widestrom, Liz Theoharis, Chris Caruso, Christina Puntel, Anne Burns Thomas, Ed Brockenbrough, Cheryl Jones Walker, Traci English Clarke, Anita Chikkatur, Chonika King, Lauren Anderson, Luba Feigenberg, Camika Royal, Lalitha Vasudevan, Marc Lamont Hill, and Jerusha Conner: you all amaze me and inspire me every day to be a better person.

My communities of practice have broadened my horizons and kindled the flames of my curiosity and learning. In my academic community of practice, I am grateful to: Nienke Moolenaar, Alan Daly, Bill Penuel, Barry Fishman, Sara Van Waes, Rafi Santo, Kylie Peppler, Yasmin Kafai, Kim Peck Jaxon, Nicole Mirra, and Lauren Anderson. At Arcadia, I am particularly thankful for the support of my past deans, Leif Gustavson and Graciela Sleslaransky-Poe, to the faculty members in the School of Education, and to all of my students. Also, two former Arcadia students and research assistants, Latricia Whitfield and Katie Miller, have helped me immeasurably with much of my research. Thanks to the crew at John & Kira's for your joy, energy, and spirit in making the world a better place through chocolate and for enduring my last-minute requests to send out thank-you boxes. My spiritual community at the Unitarian Society of Germantown has been a source of much inner strength. Thank you especially to Jessica Slivak, Jenn Leiby, and Daniel Gregoire, who taught me a great deal about children's spiritual development, and to Lee Carpenter, for reminding us all to laugh. Lastly, every writer has a "spot" or a place in which they can both be surrounded by people and friends and also write. My spot has been the High Point Café and the surrounding "Mt. Airy Village" community. Thanks to café owner Meg Hagele, who nourished me daily with home-baked goods and half-caf Americanos, and to Sheila Avelin, the owner of the Big Blue Marble Bookstore, for creating a welcoming space for book lovers like me.

Finally, my most important community of support was my family. I am grateful to my mother and father, Judith Bernstein-Baker and Karl Baker, for always being there for anything I needed, be it babysitting, fixing a broken refrigerator, or advice on writing. They are my role models and life mentors. If I could aspire to be half as amazing at working for social justice as they are, that would be enough. To my brother, Akil Dasan Baker; his wife, Catherine; and their daughters, Aya and Aria, I am in gratitude for the joy they bring to all of us, through music, laughter, playfulness, and creativity. Thank you to my aunt and uncle, Paula Rabinowitz and David Bernstein, and their sons, Jacob and Raphael, for being my exemplars of true intellectual passion. To my mother-in-law, Eleanor Lindbergh; sister- and brother-in-law, Beth and Justin Barsanti; and their children, Nate and Sam, I couldn't have asked for a more supportive and loving extended family. As a family of educators, they have always been interested and intrigued by my work, and I feel so lucky that I can share it with them. Last, but certainly not least, I thank, with all of my heart, my husband, John Doyle, and my son, Jules. It is for Jules, and future generations of learners, that I do this work, and this work only happened because of John's constant encouragement and support. The joy, love, and peace that both of them bring to my heart each day is incalculable.

About the Author

Kira J. Baker-Doyle is an Associate Professor of Education and the Director of Master's Degree and Certificate Programs at Arcadia University School of Education in Glenside, Pennsylvania. Her research has centered on teacher professional development, social network theory, and community engagement, especially in urban schools and communities. She is known in her field for her work in translating the principles of social network theory into practices that foster teacher learning and professional development. She is the author of *The Networked Teacher: How New Teachers Build Social Networks for Professional Support* (2011), and the co-editor of the forthcoming book, *Networked by Design: Interventions for Teachers to Develop Social Capital*. She cofounded the Connected Learning Certificate program at Arcadia, a hybrid graduate program designed to cultivate K–16+ educators' leadership, networking, and engagement in connected learning. At Arcadia University, Baker-Doyle teaches education courses about writing and literacies, with an emphasis on digital media and connected technologies.

Index